The story of Cabeza de Vaca is one of the world's great epics. Son of one of the proudest families of Spain, he was a conquistador with a difference—a leader too just, too honest, too great for his time. This brilliant account of his life presents one of the finest adventure narratives of history (now told completely for the first time), traces the perilous course of the first group of white men who crossed the North American continent form coast to coast, evokes one of the noblest personalities of an age of heroes, and sets forth one man's valorous attempt to establish throughout a fourth of South America a model realm founded on justice tempered by mercy.

Landing on the coast of Florida, one of a group of conquistadors seeking gold and women, this tall son of a long line of conquerors was himself conquered by the Indians of the Texas coast, endured years of degrading slavery, rose on wings of faith and humility to a position of godhood among the brown tribes of the Southwest and Mexico and, after a passion in the wilderness, conceived his flaming vision of a Spanish dominion of the Americas administered by men gentle, able, brave, and honest. He devoted the rest of his life to his vision. It was too high for white men out of Spain. Cabeza de Vaca was a heroic failure, his life a splendid adventure and a magnificent tragedy.

It is by way of poetic justice that after all these years of obscurity Cabeza de Vaca has found his present biographer.

RECEPTION OF HERNANDO DE RIBERA BY THE KING OF THE XARAYES

"The musicians must play whenever it is his pleasure. Then the men and the most beautiful women must dance before him, and such a dance is to us Christians quite wonderful, so much so that looking upon them one could think of nothing else." (See p. 237.)

The ODYSSEY of CABEZA DE VACA

By Morris Bishop

Illustrated with Photographs and Maps

THE CENTURY CO.
New York & London

ACKNOWLEDGMENTS

I wish to express my particular indebtedness to the work of Buckingham Smith (whose manuscript remains hint that he too proposed a life of Cabeza de Vaca); and to Messrs. Harbert Davenport and Joseph K. Wells, whose reconstruction of the North American journey of Cabeza de Vaca may serve as a model of shrewd and thorough study of historical problems.

In the second part of my chronicle, I have been immeasurably aided by the five precious volumes of Enrique de Gandía. I wish also to record my gratitude to Angel Flores and Arthur P. Whitaker of Cornell University; to the officials of the Archives of the Indies, custodians very generous of their treasures; to Don José Torre Revello, most amiable mentor; and to certain citizens of Jerez, courtly upholders of their great tradition; especially Don Adolfo Estevez y Guerrero, Don Alfonso Patrón y Cibo de Sopranis, Don Rafael Barris Muñoz, and Don Diego Manuel de Zurita, Marqués de Campo Real. See Bibliography, p. 293.

CONTENTS

Part I

NORTH AMERICA

Part II

SOUTH AMERICA

ILLUSTRATIONS

MAPS

PART I

NORTH AMERICA

CONTENTS

PART I

CHAPTER I

YOUTH

Jerez de la Frontera lies in southern Spain, some eight miles distant from the sea and a dozen from the port of Cadiz. Its soil is filled with virtue, suckling the vines that yield us our sherry. Its citizens are courteous and bold, with a natural gentility of manner which is ascribed to the Moor, and an enterprise which brought their great wine, the sherris-sack of Falstaff, to all the world before the middle ages were done. To-day the town is one of the richest in Spain, and its trim streets and shining white houses with their sculptured portals speak of prosperity and the satisfactions of active and orderly men. Palm, fig, cactus, oak, and pine meet here and flourish in amity. Storks and swallows inhabit the sky; church bells make constant loud announcements, rather to heaven than to the citizens. By day the sun lingers interminably at the stations of its devotion, and beats down cruelly through the quivering air; but the cool evenings are filled with peace and sober southern gaiety.

In this city Alvar Núñez Cabeza de Vaca was born, as the fifteenth century drew to its close. On father's and mother's side he came of illustrious stock, famed in the annals of the country. His father was Francisco de Vera, veinticuatro, or alderman, of Jerez. His father's father was Pedro de Vera Mendoza, conqueror of the Grand Canary. Going back through nine generations of the Veras, we find a regidor of the Thirteen of the city of Jerez, an alcaide of the Alcázar of Jerez, a first lord of Cadiz, and a caballero of the Golden Scarf. The boy's mother was Doña Teresa Cabeza de Vaca; her proud lineage included the chief builder of the Jerez wall, a captain of the city's fleet, an alférez mayor of Navarre, and a grand master of the Order of Santiago.[1] You may still see the family's emblem, a cow's head, "cabeza de vaca,"

---

[1] Barris Muñoz, in Boletín del Real Centro de Estudios Históricos de Andalucía, I, 42.

carved on the pillars' capitals in the broad patio of the Marqués de Campo Real.

The favorite of the family legends dealt with the origin of their somewhat gross and ludicrous name. During the Reconquest, the Christian host, thrusting the Moor slowly southward, reached the Sierra Morena, north of Seville. The Christians, finding the mountain passes held in strength, were about to retire discouraged, when a shepherd named Martín Alhaja offered to show the king a pass by which to cross the mountains unmolested and take the unbeliever in the rear. He had marked the entrance with a cow's skull. By following this route the Spaniards gained the great battle of Las Navas de Tolosa, on July 12, 1212, and humbled at last the Mohammedan power. King Sancho of Navarre rewarded the shepherd by ennobling him and his descendants, and by changing his name from the lowly Alhaja, jewel, to the glorious Cowhead.

The greatest of these forefathers of the young Cabeza de Vaca, and the one whose example penetrated his life, was his paternal grandfather, Pedro de Vera. Cabeza de Vaca identified himself, in the narrative of his fortunes, as "the grandson of Pedro de Vera, who conquered the Grand Canary." This reference was prompted, probably, not by pride of blood alone, but by the sense that his own achievement might worthily match the stories he had heard in boyhood from his grandfather's lips. They are fine tales indeed, of a sort to turn all a boy's mind to adventure.

Pedro de Vera was one of those fierce and turbulent spirits that the soil of Christian Spain produced for its own instinctive purposes, as antibodies against the Moor. As a courtier in the suite of Henry IV, he heard a cavalier murmuring against his king. Promptly he challenged and killed the murmurer; then, ungauntleting his hand, tore out the offending tongue and threw it among the noble spectators as a pretty demonstration of loyalty.[2]

Under Ferdinand and Isabella, he fought to confine the Moslem within his kingdom of Granada, and when the Moslem sulked, he slew his Christian neighbors. He represented to his monarchs that brawling gentility from which their realm chiefly suffered. To turn

[2] Parada y Barreto, "Hombres ilustres de Jerez," 453.

his powers to the service of the country, they proposed that he subdue the Canary Islands, paying the cost from his own pocket.

Pedro de Vera joyfully accepted the opportunity for lawful and profitable bloodshed. He set sail from Seville in 1480, and headed for the incredible peak of Teneriffe, that rises like a tower twelve thousand feet from the sea. He landed on the Grand Canary, to begin his long battle upward from the shore. He found the island inhabited by the Guanches, descendants of Carthaginians or Numidians, who had lost touch with the mainland at least a thousand years before. They were tall, handsome, and active men, and very strong; they wore only little trousers of palm leaves or of skin. They plowed the earth with goats' horns; they worshiped a wooden image of a naked woman, carved with shocking fidelity, and another sculpture of a she-goat ready to farrow, with a goat-buck rampant. They were a simple and honest race of savages, who had forgotten the rudiments of culture their ancestors had brought with them from Africa.

I must not tell here the splendid tale of that difficult conquest. How Don Pedro slew the native chief Doramas, converting him to Christianity as he died, and standing, with dripping lance, as godfather for his victim's baptism; how he divided his enemies into two factions, persuading the weaker party to aid in the extermination of their own people; how, after much blood had flowed without a victory, he tempted his foes, swearing on the holy bread that they should unite in a great common expedition against the island of Teneriffe; but the holy bread was unconsecrated and the promise void, so, when the Canarians were secure below decks, they were shipped to a miserable exile in Seville; how, at a desperate shift for funds, he pawned his two sons, the father and uncle of our Cabeza de Vaca, to a Moorish alcaide; how, when the governor of the island of Gómera was slain by the natives, he came gallantly to the beautiful widow's aid, hanging, drowning, and pulling asunder by horses all males over fifteen, and selling the women as slaves. At this last enormity Bishop Juan de Frías, the first of the great line of Spanish ecclesiastics who fought the conquistadores, protested furiously. "Upon this the governor told him that if he gave his tongue such liberty to talk to him in that strain, he would clap a red-hot skull-cap on his head." The bishop returned to Spain with evidence, and an indignant heart swelling with eloquence.[3] As a result, Pedro de Vera was recalled with a mingling of royal displeasure and favor which only a most tactful sovereign could compass. For a new war was in progress which should finally expel the Moor from Granada and the soil of the peninsula, and Don Pedro had gained a rare reputation for his mountain warfare in the Canaries. He held a high command throughout this famous campaign; at its close in 1492 he was apparently again appointed governor of the Canaries, but declined the post, owing to failing strength. He retired to Jerez, and there died, about 1500,[4] and was buried in the monastery of Santo Domingo el Real, whose central chapel he had bought for his family's resting-place.[5]

In the interval between his retirement and his death he had for an auditor the boy Alvar Núñez Cabeza de Vaca, the eldest child of his son Francisco. Telling his fond stories, he recognized in the boy's ardor an early sympathy of spirit, while little Alvar Núñez learned from his fierce old grandfather the honor of courage and fortitude and the scorn of death. Living the clan existence of the old Spanish hidalguía, the lad discovered the world in the words of his elders and from them learned his moral scheme. He shouted with glee as grandfather told of the comic fury of the Guanches, trapped below decks while the caravels plunged toward Spain. In his boyish mind was fixed the purpose to be a soldier and a conqueror when he should grow up, to slay thousands and thousands of naked, pagan savages, to find new Indies like the great Columbus, to rule them as governor, and, at the least indocility, to hang all the males over fifteen and to hold the children as slaves.

When the grandfather tired of story-telling, there were other mentors for the young mind, wielding a more subtle influence. The household

---

[3] Abreu de Galindo, "History of the Canary Islands," 103 *et sqq*. Espinosa ("The Guanches of Teneriffe," 86) says that Fray Miguel de la Serna was the intercessor for the natives.

[4] So states the Enciclopedia Espasa, I know not on what grounds. Parada y Barreto ("Hombres ilustres de Jerez") followed by Yáñez and Allier ("Jerez en lo pasado y en lo presente"), conjectures 1496 or later.

[5] The external signs of the tombs were erased some time before 1750, from the failure of the family to fulfil its contract. Barris Muñoz, Bol. Est. Hist. And., I, 60.

was full of Guanche slaves, chosen by Don Pedro for his personal service.[6] Lulling the boy with island songs, gossiping in the midday quiet, reciting homesick stories of the mountains which stand with their feet in the sea and their heads in the clouds, they poured into his mind a desire for such far countries. More, they gave him a sense of familiarity with inarticulate brown men, the direct, untroubled understanding of a child. This was to be lost with his later education, and was to be recovered only when, on the barbarous coasts of the New World, the brown men were his masters and he the slave.

So the schooling of his spirit proceeded. All the standards of his home, the scale of things honored and things scorned, set toward the praise of cavalier gallantry. The career of an uncle, Hernando de Vera, indicates what yeasty ferments ran in the family's veins. Hernando had wit, which he wielded as ruthlessly as ever his father had the sword. He wrote some satirical verses against Their Majesties, which were handed about until they fell under Their Majesties' own august eyes. Ferdinand and Isabella, though not amused, were deeply interested. Failing to discover the writer, they held the city of Jerez responsible. The lieutenant of the city was beheaded in the market-place, and a number of prominent citizens banished. (So at least the old story runs; I can give you no documents in proof.)

At this point Hernando fled, thus avowing his guilt. He put himself in the hands of that beautiful widow, the mistress of Gómera, whom Don Pedro de Vera had once so lavishly aided.[7] Being faithless as well as beautiful, she confined her guest on a ship to be delivered a prisoner to Their Majesties. On the way he escaped. Later, at his father's intercession, he was pardoned, and sent to Barbary, where he died. I cannot discover—to my despair!—what that jest was which cost one gentleman's life and ruined so many others.

Our subject's father, Francisco de Vera, has left no deep impress

---

[6] "Testimony of Bartolomé de Lobaton, alcalde of Jerez," in Arch. Ind., Justicia, 1131, last document.

[7] She deserves a note in her own right. Her name was Leonor de Bobadilla, sister of Beatriz, the patroness of Columbus. As maid of honor at court, she attracted the benevolent attention of King Ferdinand. The saintly Isabella turned shrewish, married the maid of honor to a courtier, Hernán Peraza, and dowered the pair with the most distant of her islands.

on history. He helped his father in the conquest of the Canaries; he was one of the two brothers pawned to the Moor as security for supplies for that expedition. The records of the city of Jerez show him to have been a chronic objector. He was once condemned by royal decree to lose his property for contumacy, but the decree was never put in force. By 1512 his objections had ceased forever.[8]

Our Alvar Núñez was apparently the eldest of four children. He was born about 1490, in any case between 1487 and 1494.[9] According to a not unusual practice of the time, he was given the name of a distinguished ancestor on his mother's side, Alvar Núñez Cabeza de Vaca, his great-grandfather's grandfather, captain of the fleet of Jerez. The three other children bore, in conformity with the regular Spanish habit, their father's name as the first surname, their mother's as the second. Thus the second brother Juan was named Juan de Vera Cabeza de Vaca. The capriciousness of nomenclature grieves the bibliographers of to-day. The rule tells us to catalogue a Spaniard under his first surname; but so often the subjects themselves violated the rule! Our subject was always called "Cabeza de Vaca" in his own time, and so henceforth we shall term him.

[8] Bol. Est. Hist. And., I, 44.

[9] Vital statistics were not kept in Jerez until the sixteenth century. The date of Cabeza de Vaca's birth may be deduced from a document discovered by Rafael Barris Muñoz, reported in Bol. Est. Hist. And., I, 42. In 1512 Alvar Núñez Cabeza de Vaca, two younger brothers and one younger sister, were confided, as orphans, to *curatela,* a type of guardianship which applied to minors between the ages of twelve and twenty-five. Alvar Núñez, the oldest of the four, must then have been at least sixteen. Most likely he was older. There is good reason to believe that the fourth child, María de Vera, was the daughter of Francisco de Vera's second wife, although in the *curatela* document she is included among the orphaned children of Teresa Cabeza de Vaca. (Private archives of the Marqués de Campo Real, Pleito de Riquelme, *passim.*) If María de Vera was the issue of a second marriage, a decent interval of at least a year must be added to the reckoning. Further, Alvar Núñez went to Italy as a soldier in 1511, and served throughout a grueling campaign. It is fair to suppose, then, that he was at least seventeen in 1511. Enrique de Gandía ("Historia de la Conquista del Río de la Plata," 218, n. 91) asserts, without documentary reference, that Cabeza de Vaca himself states that he was born in 1500. If so, he was mistaken, as people commonly were before the days of records. Alvar Núñez's cousin, Pedro Estopiñán Cabeza de Vaca, testified that he himself was born in 1490 (Torre Revello, in Revista del Ateneo de Jerez, V, 8) and again in 1496 (Archivos de Indias, Justicia, 1131, last document). The importance of birth-dates is something new; deponents in old testimonies usually added to a statement of their own age the phrase "poco más o menos," more or less.

Alvar Núñez's younger sister (or half-sister), María de Vera, was married to Ruy Díaz de Guzmán by 1526 and was still living in 1577. She is mentioned in a record of Dec. 4 of that year, with "her sister, Isabel Cabeza de Vaca." (Archives of Marqués de Campo Real, Pleito de Riquelme, fol. 149.) Who is this Isabel? Perhaps an older sister, not subject to *curatela* in 1512. She must then have been at least ninety in 1577.

Through boyhood years mind and body were prepared for his destiny. With young manhood came the opportunity to serve his king with valor, and to learn the trade of conquest.

In the spring of 1511 the everlasting wars of Italy flared into sudden activity. Pope Julius II appealed to King Ferdinand for aid, and Ferdinand, foreseeing advantage, despatched an ample levy of troops from Seville. In this expeditionary force sailed the youth Cabeza de Vaca, for his first taste of army transport life, of active campaigning, of bloodshed, privation, and disaster.[10]

The troops landed at Naples, then a Spanish province. A great army marched against Bologna and Ferrara; Cabeza de Vaca was there. He was in the terrible bloody rout of Ravenna, on April 11, 1512, when twenty thousand died. Though the Spanish lost the battle, the victorious French, with their leader dead and their host almost annihilated, were obliged to quit Italy. Cabeza de Vaca survived; but he came "muy destroçado," shattered and broken, to Naples.[11] Evidently he had acquitted himself well on the field, and evidently he numbered sufficient years to command respect, for now he was alférez, or lieutenant, of the considerable city of Gaeta, near Naples.

Then for a few years all is dark. No later memories of his own, no business or military records, attest his deeds. About 1513 he returned to Spain,[12] and entered the service of the Duke of Medina Sidonia in Seville. He was camarero, or steward, an employment combining soldierly duties with such business tasks as a gentleman might properly perform.[13]

We hear of him next in the uprising of the Comuneros, discontented factions of nobility and citizens, quaking with the financial purgations administered by the young Emperor Charles V. Cabeza de Vaca's master, the Duke of Medina Sidonia, was a loyalist leader. The rebels of Seville seized the Alcázar on Sept. 16, 1520; on the following day the duke recaptured that stronghold. Cabeza de Vaca,

[10] Various witnesses to Cabeza de Vaca's military record give this testimony. (Arch. Ind., Justicia, 1131, 8A.) His cousin Pedro Estopiñán saw him off. His captain was Alonso de Carabazal; at Ravenna he served in the company of Capt. Bartolomé de Sierra.

[11] "Testimony of Rodrigo León," in Arch. Ind., Justicia, 1131, 8A.

[12] "Testimony of Francisco López Manuel," in Arch. Ind., Justicia, 1131, 8A.

[13] Cervantes was camarero of the Cardinal Acquaviva.

now a veteran of many battles, did his share; after the affray he was set in command of a city gate, the Puerta del Ossario.

The ardent knight bore the full confidence of the duke. He carried important despatches to court; he was at the battle of Tordesillas; he saw the extinction of the Comunero movement in the last stand at Villalar. In that campaign he served his king with four horses. After the Comunero leaders were safely beheaded he fought the French at Puente la Reina in Navarre.

The wars ended, and Cabeza de Vaca reënters his obscurity. Probably about this time he was married. In documents of his old age he twice mentions his wife, and the destitution to which she was reduced for his sake. I have not found her name, nor anything of her character save the fact that, after her husband's fifteen years of absences in the Americas, she loyally spent all her substance to preserve his honor. No record of any children has been discovered.[14]

These few meager facts are all that have been ascertained about our conqueror from his birth until his departure from Spain in 1527, when he was at the most forty, and at the least thirty-three.

The Spain of his young manhood, the Spain of Emperor Charles the Fifth, differed much from the inchoate league of kingdoms of his grandfather's youth. His country was entering upon the difficult Renaissance, the puberty of the modern world. New ideas, new desires, and a new flooding sense of strength animated its collective soul. The Spaniard began to realize the existence of his country as a single and constant creature. In religion, the doubts that afflicted his enemies confirmed him, by contrast, in a more ardent faith. His old good-humored tolerance of Jew and Moor disappeared; he remembered that his Lord brought not peace but a sword. Stout Cortés and many other of the conquerors esteemed themselves as crusaders, engaged in bringing God's revelations to the heathen; and if they lined their pockets in so doing, they were but imitating the first Crusaders. Protestantism gained only rare and furtive converts in Spain, and such few conventicles as did find brief lodgment were soon stamped out by the Inquisition.

[14] Arch. Ind., Justicia, 1131, 8A, also 1131 last document. The learned genealogist Diego Alvaro de Zurita Aveñón (apparently of the seventeenth century) failed to find trace of offspring. (Archives of Marqués de Campo Real, Ascendencia, I, 2, fol. 15.)

But the questioning mind found other subject matters. It was scientific speculation as much as the lust of gold that impelled Columbus across the sea. The useful sciences of cosmography, cartography, and navigation had every encouragement from the government. Modern Spanish literature, architecture, and painting began; critical scholarship came into being. It was a period of excitement and enthusiasm. This world was full of unsuspected marvels, hidden in books, in alchemists' retorts, in far countries. With a little cleverness, faith, and a stout heart one might render any incredible thing true, find a formula for making gold or run afoul of a new continent.

Politically, the Renaissance meant the subjugation of the proud nobles to the power of the king, and the rise of base-born commercial people, independent of the land. Economically, the strangest fact was the abundance of gold, with the popular bewilderment that gold did not bring universal ease. To be sure, it was a fine thing to see the four-ox carts hauling gold and silver bars from the Guadalquivir to the Real Casa de Contratación, in the Alcázar at Seville, and to know how common was the metal in the Indies. Five hundred thousand ounces of gold were brought annually from Hispaniola (now Haiti and Santo Domingo). A piece of gold was discovered there weighing over 320 pounds; a roasted pig was served on it. Ten tons of gold sank in the wreck of one vessel.

But in Spain, gold or no gold, hardship was constant. The Spaniard was ascetic through necessity as well as temperament. Endurance and frugality were assumed of all men of every class. Even My Lord the Duke no doubt followed in his house the custom of his times, of having at noon the one meal of the day, by any modern definition. The evening collation consisted of bread and goat-cheese or sheep-cheese, and perhaps grapes, fresh or dried. Hunger was a common-place to be accepted without surprise and borne without complaint, the more so since the poor gentlemen of Spain might never have recourse to labor. For no stranger could see the void within one's belly, while work for pay was evidence to the world of loss of honor.

Honor! How the word runs through the history, legend, and contemporary news of Spain! Honor is the companion of the Spaniard's life and the determinant of his most trifling actions. His honor is a tangible thing which may be lost or regained, something almost which has weight and extension in the physical world. An insulting word stains the honor; the spot is visible until it is erased in one of three ways: by the blood of the contemner, by the death of the insulted one, or by the intervention of the king, who by a single detergent phrase can cleanse the most grimy honor.

Because of the Spaniard's realistic conception of honor, his country was always the most congenial home of chivalry. The forms of medieval knighthood lingered there beyond their term in other lands. But chivalry had a strange obverse, to wit, mercilessness toward a heathen, hence dishonorable, foe. Joy at the discomfiture of the ungodly mixed with delight in bloody imaginations. The pious pondered gladly on the righteous man in the Psalms, rejoicing as he washed his feet in the blood of the wicked. When the Spanish took Oran in 1509—with the approving sun at a standstill for four hours—they would not cease from slaughter when the city surrendered. Sparing neither age nor sex, they put all to the sword until their arms were wearied, and, drunk with wine and blood, they fell asleep exhausted on the heaps of their victims that weltered in the streets and squares.

The Spaniard has ever been accused of brutality in torture, nay of perverse delight in watching pain. His bull-fights, his blood-stained Christs and Sebastians, the ingenious agonies of his Inquisition, have given him a popular reputation which history does not succeed in refuting. When, during the long reconquest of Spain, a Moorish city was taken, the inhabitants were commonly slain or enslaved. Old records tell how children were thrown into wells and pits, or were flung on the church steps to be the prey of the wolfish scavenging dogs. Returning cavaliers would carry at their saddle-bows the heads of Moors, to be tossed for playthings to the village boys. At the siege of Malaga, in 1487, a Moor who attempted to assassinate Ferdinand and Isabella was shot back into the city by a catapult. To this the pagans whimsically responded by slaying a Galician gentleman and sending his corpse astride a mule out through the gates to the Christian camp.

Cruelty was a daily commonplace. The law of Christian Spain prescribed horrid penalties for misdemeanors. The barbarities of the Spanish troops in Flanders during the wars of religion, however magnified by the afflicted in Zion, are not to be proved false by any such easy phrase as "war psychology" or "atrocity neurosis." And unhappily, there is all too much evidence of the savagery of the conquerors in the Indies toward the timid, gentle, and fawning islanders, wild rather like the hare than like the wolf.[15]

The cruelty in the Spanish character was part of a composite which included allied and harmonious virtues. The Spaniard was merciless to infidel and heretic, believing that his Lord expressly commanded him to be so, and would bless him who should take the children of Babylon and throw them against the stones. An ascetic himself, he could bear the pain of flagellation, and submit to the torture of the flesh, his own or another's. Inhabited more by the fires of passion than his neighbors of the foggy north, he was extreme, fanatical, and wholly unsympathetic with his opponents and their beliefs and feelings. His cruelty was entangled with religion, and induced certain morbid sequels of meditation on the Cross and the varieties of martyrdom. Las Casas saw, in Cuba, thirteen Indians hung in a row "in honor of Christ and his twelve Apostles," and slowly killed by sword-pricks.[16] The *quemadero,* the burning-ground of Seville, whither came finally the victims of the Inquisition, was a stone scaffold with, at each corner, a colossal plaster statue of one of the Prophets. To these the objects of the Church's correction were bound, and in their embrace they died.

Without question Cabeza de Vaca was present at some of these Acts of Faith, for during the heyday of the Inquisition four thousand

---

[15] Patriotic Spaniards protest against the imputation of cruelty to their race. Indeed, all generalizations about national characteristics are statements of minute variations on the ample chart of human nature. But the evidence is against the apologist. Blanco-Fombona, in his splendid eulogy of the Spanish character, says baldly: "The symbolic and representative hero of the Spanish-American race is a man who carried hardness to the point of cruelty." ("El Conquistador español del siglo XVI," 81.) He tells pretty stories of the South American wars of liberation, of the Spanish general Boves, who held bull-fights, using for bulls republicans with horns strapped to their heads, who gave formal balls concluding with the death of all the dancers and the musicians. And Antoñanzas, who sent cases of rebels' ears to the Spanish government. (p. 78.)

[16] "Relation des voyages," 10–11. It is proper to note that Spanish historians challenge Las Casas's stories of atrocities, on the presumption that he was exaggerating mightily for a pious end.

13

of the stiff-necked were there burned. He was accustomed to look, whether curiously or indifferently, on the spectacle of human agony. In the routine of military and courtly life he learned to still all his impulse toward womanish sympathy, he learned to be relentless, hard, and all-enduring in the service of his faith and his king. Thus his spirit was prepared for conquest.

The fact of residence in Seville was in itself a spur to the adventurous mind. The city, holding the monopoly of trade with the two Americas, felt itself the proprietor of the New World. In counting-house and palace, the talk turned forever on the strange lands overseas. When a vessel out of the west was warped alongside the docks of the Guadalquivir, half the citizens, and Cabeza de Vaca among them, would assemble to gaze at the marvels, painted savages, parrots, serpents, curious beasts and plants. Unicorns and dragons could have seemed no stranger than the spitting llamas from Peru.

American Indians were no uncommon sight in the Seville streets. The first shipload of Indian slaves was landed in Spain in 1495, and others followed. They did not thrive, however; many died of homesickness, and many committed suicide, according to the despairing custom of those simple people. (Thus in Cuba great numbers of the natives hung themselves in concert, fifty families in a single village. "Hence it comes that now they pay very dearly for the negroes whom they take to the mines.") [17] More hardy were those Indians who were brought to Seville for training as interpreters. The Venetian ambassador describes a group of chieftains' sons, who were being educated in Seville in 1524.[18] They went about half naked, wearing only a sort of doublet; they had black hair, broad faces, Roman noses, and were not unlike Circassians, though more ashen colored. They were very intelligent and active, and played with much agility a native game of pelota, with a bounding wooden ball the size of a peach, which they would strike not with hands and feet but with their sides, so that it was a marvel to see them. The inquisitive ambassador had also the opportunity to taste some strange foods, particularly the sweet potato and what was apparently the pineapple.

[17] Garcilaso de la Vega, "Historia de Florida," Lib. II, cap. 12.
[18] Navagero, in Fabié, "Viajes por España," 274.

Not impossibly, young Alvar Núñez Cabeza de Vaca saw Christopher Columbus, who dwelt in Seville from November 1504 until May 1505. Nothing could be more natural than that a boy in his teens, with the tradition of conquest behind him and the dream of it before him, should contrive some meeting with the miracle of his times, although the old discoverer was sick in body, heart, and mind, and kept much to his bed. His tall figure had lost its majestic carriage, his red hair was bleached snow white, but in his blue eyes still gleamed the fanatic ardor that had brought a new world to Castile and León.

There is greater likelihood that Cabeza de Vaca met Magellan, who was resident in Seville from 1517 to 1519, preparing the second greatest voyage of history. Magellan's bold imaginations may well have fired in the young man's mind an emulating purpose.

Perhaps, again, he met that striking pair, Lúcas Vásquez de Ayllón and Francisco Chicora. Ayllón was a prosperous official of Hispaniola. An agent of his, landing near Cape Fear, North Carolina, in 1520, invited the natives to visit the vessel, and in the midst of the entertainment set sail, with a hundred and thirty of his guests on board. On returning to Santo Domingo, "the trickery that the Spanish had employed was taken very ill, and the Indians were useless, because almost all died, of anger and woe." [19]

One who did not die was Francisco Chicora. His master, Ayllón, had him baptized, taught him Spanish, and treated him partly as a servant, partly as a son, and partly as the utterer of new gospels.[20] The two went to Spain together, to obtain from the king a grant to Chicora, the country from which Francisco took his surname. Francisco admirably aided his master with his creative imagination. He told of the giant king and queen of his country, and of the method of making giants by kneading the babies' bones and massaging them with magic herbs; of a race of men with skin like fish scales and with flexible tails, which necessitated the cutting of holes in their chairs. Most of all he told of the wealth of his homeland in gold and jewels. Oviedo the historian took from his finger a perfect pearl weighing

[19] González Barcía, "Ensayo cronológico," 5.
[20] Oviedo y Valdés, "Historia general de Indias," III, 626.

twenty-six carats, and asked if there were any such in Chicora. Ayllón cried out that such a petty gewgaw was nothing at all in comparison with the pearls of his desired kingdom. Oviedo, wise after the fact, says in his history that at the time he thought the Indian was lying in order to journey in state back to his own country. Such, at any rate, was the event. An expedition of six vessels with five hundred men landed at Cape Fear in 1526.[21] Chicora and the other interpreters immediately disappeared; Ayllón died; and after a dreadful winter of disease and suffering the survivors retreated to Hispaniola.

Records in disproof of visions make their way slowly. The news of the Cape Fear disaster never overtook the dogmatic rumors of the riches of the North American continent. Cabeza de Vaca, enchanted by the wonder-tales, did not hear the denial of them; before the word could reach Spain, he was pledged to sail to that land of gold, as treasurer to Captain Pánfilo de Narváez.

[21] This expedition was unique among these early enterprises in that it carried agricultural tools, seeds, etc. Ayllón had some vision of a self-supporting colony. Häbler, "Die wirtschaftliche Blüte Spaniens," 30–31.

CHAPTER II

FAREWELL TO SPAIN

PÁNFILO DE NARVÁEZ was born in Valladolid about the year 1480.[1] He was apprenticed to warfare when still a youth, and learned the military virtues of courage, fidelity, doggedness, endurance, brutality, and pious hatred of the foe. Bernal Díaz described him in 1520 as "tall and strong limbed, his face long, with a red beard, and an agreeable presence. His speech and voice was deep as though it came from a cavern. He was a good horseman, said to be brave, a native of Valladolid or of Tudela de Duero, and was married to a lady named Maria de Valenzuela. He was a captain in the Island of Cuba and a rich man, but was said to be very parsimonious. When we defeated him he lost an eye; he made use of good arguments in what he said."[2] To this Las Casas, the apostle to the Indies and their great historian, adds that he was a reputable and honest man, intelligent, though not prudent, of good conversation and behavior, most vigorous in his warring upon the Indians, but with the fault of hasty negligence.

He went out to the Indies in 1500. We find him in Jamaica in 1510, the lieutenant of Juan de Esquivel, under whom he learned the method of pacifying a province by destroying its inhabitants. When Diego Velásquez landed with an expeditionary force in Cuba, in 1511, he appointed Narváez his chief captain, and endowed him with many head of Indians. (The Spanish always reckoned the natives by the "head," counting immortal souls as cattle, says Las Casas.)

His first enterprise was near to being his last. With his thirty archers

---

[1] The Enciclopedia Espasa gives his birth as about 1470; I do not know on what authority. Bernal Díaz says he looked to be about forty in 1520. Oviedo, born in 1478, says "He was as old as I, or older." Herrera (I, 243) and others give his birthplace as Cuéllar.

[2] "The Conquest of New Spain" (trans. Maudslay), V, 258.

he went "pacifying" to Bayamo, about fifty miles northwest of Santiago. He was well received by the natives; indeed, for forcing submission he had no need of anything but his mare, a monster beyond the utmost power of the wildest mythopoeic imagination to conceive. Don Pánfilo played his rôle well; when he would turn her on the forehand she would kick savagely, but without unseating her red-bearded god. For a time the natives were humble and adoring, but as the new yoke began to gall, they were roused by the immolation of a friendly cacique, Hatuey (who, at the stake, was urged to baptism, by a Franciscan friar, that he might end in heaven. "And do the Spaniards go there?" "Those who are good Christians." "Then I will not go to heaven," said the simple savage). Fierce resentment burned because of "the eyes the Spaniards made at the women and girls, and peradventure the hands they laid on them, for this is a much used and ancient custom among our men in those lands," says Las Casas.[3] Seven thousand Indians concerted a night attack, but they paused to rob, and in the interval the Spanish were roused. Narváez hastily bridled his mare, and, clad only in a shirt, sprang to the saddle with a set of bells in his hand, and rode headlong into the mellay. Such was the panic of the Indians—they thought each bell a thousand enemies—that all fled and did not stop till they reached the province of Camaguey.

It was about this time that Bartolomé de las Casas came to Cuba. He whose voice was one of the few crying for justice to the Indian, whose arm already was lifted in defense of the weak, was then a humble priest. He joined Narváez, who was setting forth with a hundred men on an extensive journey into the interior. Las Casas recounts a dreadful story of the madness that seizes on men with shining weapons in their hands.

The expedition halted at noon by a river-bed, where natural whetstones stood by little pools. All the soldiers employed the siesta-hour in sharpening their swords. They came at night to a large village, where about two thousand Indians were assembled, squatting in the square, with five hundred more in the great house. Food was offered to the Spaniards, cassava bread and fish; as it was being distributed,

---

[3] "Historia de las Indias," III, 7.

suddenly a soldier drew his sword, and in a flash all the hundred were upon "those sheep and lambs, slaying men and women, young and old, who were seated heedless, staring at the mares and the Spaniards, all astounded; and within the space of two credos not a man was left alive." Las Casas leaped into the fray in a frenzy, saving some few lives by the respect the madmen still bore to the cloth. And in the midst of it he saw Narváez, calmly sitting his horse and watching, "not speaking nor moving more than if he were of marble." The captain, perceiving the priest, said to him, "And what does your worship think of what our Spaniards have done?" Las Casas answered him: "I offer them and you too to the devil!"

The hatred of the priest and the natives for Narváez was countered by the approval of his superiors. In 1518 he was in Spain, representing Velásquez's claims to the title of adelantado, or governor. In his capacity of envoy he must have become acquainted with the all-powerful Juan Fonseca, bishop of Burgos and head of the Council of the Indies, and may even have knelt before the King and Emperor Charles V. By 1520 he was back in Cuba, enjoying his wealth in land and Indians. In that year he was called upon to do his master an important service.

Velásquez had sent forth an expedition, in November 1518, under the command of Hernando Cortés, to trade with the natives in the new-discovered land of Mexico. Cortés, on coming to land, decided to exceed his instructions, and to appeal for authorization to the king, over the head of Velásquez. While awaiting the king's reply, that boldest and shrewdest captain of history conquered a kingdom with four hundred and fifty men, six field-pieces, and twenty horses.

When Velásquez heard the news "he was taken with cold sweats as of death," says Bernal Díaz, and from fat he became thin. By great exertion he raised a fleet of nineteen ships and fourteen hundred men, set Narváez in command, and sent the expedition to Mexico to enforce his authority by sheer man-power. Don Pánfilo, superb in his new importance, contrived to run from error to error. The provincial authorities in Santo Domingo were suspicious of this threat of civil war, and sent as their representative that Lucas Vásquez de Ayllón of whom we have already spoken as the first colonizer of the present United States. Narváez arrested Ayllón, and sent him back from Vera Cruz to Santo Domingo. Ayllón, having meditated on this affront across the breadth of the Gulf of Mexico, made a report to his superiors which would have filled Cortés with joy.

To Cortés the news of the arrival of Narváez came with a sound of calamity. He left eighty men to garrison the City of Mexico against a hostile nation, and with two hundred and sixty followers he hastened to the coast, to hold his conquest by might or guile. Narváez's agents arrived, defiant and imperious, in Cortés's camp; they were greeted with all courtesy, and rich gifts of gold; and they returned to contrast Narváez's stinginess and sternness with Cortés's warm generosity. For about a month the pourparlers continued. Narváez thought he had rather the better of them, but as a matter of fact he was sadly worsted, for almost his entire army was secretly corrupted by the enemy's promises. Cortés made a night attack on May 29, 1520, and found, as he had expected, little resistance. Only Narváez and his faithful few, on the top of a sacrificial pyramid, fought desperately, bewildered by the desertion of their host. Then Narváez's deep cavernous voice was heard crying: "Holy Mary protect me, they have killed me and put out my eye!" The fighting stopped, and both armies together shouted "Long live the King! Long live Cortés! Victory! Victory!"

For three years Narváez was kept a prisoner, although for some time on parole. Adversity taught him at least outward humility. Early in 1522 he was taken on a tour to the newly pacified interior, and was dazzled by the sight of those cities, "more splendid than any in Spain," which he might so well have seen as master, not as a tourist with an over-attentive personal conductor. Being brought before Cortés, he fell on his knees and would have kissed his hands, had not Cortés prevented him, and raised him up and embraced him and bade him be seated. Narváez then made a humble avowal of his own inferiority to Cortés, and a testimonial to his conqueror's genius. So at any rate says Bernal Díaz, whose memory, for all its exact clarity, is open to suspicion when he sets down speeches uttered forty-five years before his record.

In the following year, Narváez was released, in answer to appeals from his wife. Cortés carried his generosity so far as to give his captive a present of two thousand pesos of gold. When Narváez received this permission and this gift, he humbled himself greatly, and promised in all things to be Cortés's servant.

He did not keep his promise well. He rejoined his wife, who, in her eagerness to aid him, had much increased his substance during his adventures. She had set aside thirteen or fourteen thousand pesos of gold, with the exploitation of his mines and slaves and Indians. But he had seen too much gold in Mexico to regard as of much account the slow product of mines and slaves and Indians. He dreamed of uncountable wealth and the rule of unbounded provinces. After rewarding his wife with a year in her company, he set off again in pursuit of fortune, which now, he thought, lay overseas. In 1525 he was in Spain, bringing accusations against Cortés and seeking favors for himself.

In the long investigation conducted by the Council of the Indies into the deeds and misdeeds of Cortés, Narváez was one of the chief witnesses for the prosecution. He was apparently able to tell the somewhat ignominious story of the loss of his own army in a way that made his defeat seem creditable. He made a good impression at court. He was brave, rich, noble, and well connected; he had an excellent record as a subjugator of Cuba; he knew how to deal with Indians, if not with cunning Christians. His useful testimony in the Cortés case deserved a reward, perhaps according to covert bargains with those important people who were interested in the humbling of Cortés and who needed a willing witness. Narváez's reward cost His Majesty little. Captain Gonzalo Fernández de Oviedo y Valdés, Narváez's friend and the incomparable historian of the Indies, observes with his delightful cynicism:

The prince may be deceived like the poor volunteer, and I have noticed one thing which is not to be forgotten; and that is that Their Majesties almost never put their property or money into these new discoveries, but only paper and fine words, and they say to those captains: "If you should do what you say, we will do this or that," or "our gratitude will be given you." And they give him the title of adelantado or governor, with license and authorization to go wherever it may be by a grant, with those who from ignorance will accompany him with their persons or goods, taken by the sweet smell of his false nobilities.[4]

The Emperor was liberal of undiscovered countries, if chary of cash in hand. He was pleased to grant the petition of his faithful and deserving subject to explore, pacify, and colonize the region known as "Florida," with the accent on the penult. "Florida" extended from the present Florida to the present Mexico. Narváez's heart was high when he was given this opportunity to redeem his military honor and to find a realm of golden cities which, please God, should outshine all the gleaming towers of Mexico.

Those who had not the faith shrugged their shoulders. Oviedo says he told him as a friend that he should bide quiet in his home with his wife and children and give thanks to God that he had sufficient wherewith to pass the ford of this world; "for he was of my age or older, and I wouldn't say that his body was little touched by time. Although he thanked me for my advice, I saw that it did not sit well on his stomach, and I was reminded of what a rustic told me once, when I was a boy; he said: 'You château-people, do you know why one gives an ass the third blow with a stick?' I said it must be to jog him along, but the peasant replied: 'No, but because the ass don't remember the first time you hit him, and because the second time he didn't mend his way.' Well, anyway, there's none of us can dodge God's will."

But Oviedo was a literary man and a mocker. Narváez's simple and ardent mind had never seen adventure with an old man's eyes, had not learned to prize peace above glory and ease above power. Strange tales had been coming out of Florida for years past, and his darling dream was to be the first master of that mysterious world.

Very likely the peninsula was visited and mapped by Spanish adventurers before 1502.[5] It is probable also that there was some intercourse between the Bahaman natives and those of the mainland. The story of the Fountain of Youth on the great Island of Bimini appears in Peter Martyr's "Decades," published in 1511. Juan Ponce de León

---

[4] "Historia General," III, 597.
[5] Lowery, "Spanish Settlements in the U. S.," I, 128.

found the mainland, somewhere near Saint Augustine, on Easter Sunday, 1513; he coasted south, then through the Keys, and ran north along the western shore for an undetermined distance. In 1516 Diego Miruelo, pilot, visited the coast in his trading vessel, exchanged all his toys of glass and iron for gold, but failed to observe the latitudes. Returning to Cuba, "he spread the fame of the riches of that land and the neighboring islands, and he kindled in many the desire to enjoy them." [6] Perhaps especially in Pánfilo de Narváez, then a little restless in his pacified Cuban plantation. Francisco Hernández de Córdova took shelter near Charlotte Harbor in 1517; two years later Alonso Alvárez de Pineda followed the coast from Florida's southern tip to Tampico, Mexico, and back.[7] Ayllón's expeditions, in 1520, 1525, and 1526, have already been mentioned (p. 15). Ponce de León made a serious attempt to colonize in 1521, but when he received from an Indian arrow the wound from which he died, the enterprise was abandoned. In 1525 Estebán Gómez coasted the eastern shore from Nova Scotia to Cuba. In addition to these recorded voyages there must have been many descents upon the coast by bold captains who needed no king's signature to go in search of gold or slaves. Enough, therefore, was known of the mainland to give substance to hopeful dreams. The natives, from whom gold and pearls had been obtained, hinted at a mysterious source of wealth in the interior; and indeed the barbarism of the shore-dwellers could not be alleged in disproof of an Eldorado behind a mountain wall, as the rich highland of Mexico lay all unsuspected by a visitor to the feverish swamp country of its coast. Narváez needed no great eloquence to convince likely candidates for his expedition that they would embark on the surest of certainties.

Narváez's petition to His Majesty, asking permission to occupy the mainland, the annotations of the Council of Indies, and the king's patent, are still in existence.[8] The final document, bearing the great "Yo el Rey," the royal signature, and dated in Granada, 17th No-

---

[6] Barcía, "Ensayo Cronológico," 3.

[7] There is a popular belief, abetted by some school histories, that Soto was the first white man to see the Mississippi. But Pineda apparently remained at the mouth, careening his ships. The river appears on extant maps as early as 1520.

[8] "Colección de Documentos inéditos . . . de Indias," Ser. I, Vol. X, 40, and Vol. XVI, 67. Buckingham Smith, "Relation of Cabeça de Vaca," 210.

vember, 1526,[9] gives Narváez the right to discover, conquer, and people the region from the Río de las Palmas (the present Soto la Marina, in northeastern Mexico) to the Isle of Florida. It makes explicitly clear that the petitioner is to bear all the expense of the enterprise and the crown none. It stipulates further that Narváez is to establish at least two colonies of a hundred men each; that he is to build three forts; that he is to be governor and captain general for life, at an annual salary of 250,000 maravedís (this dazzling sum is only $1000 by the formal tables of conversion; it would buy, however, $10,000 worth of staple goods to-day); that he and his heirs forever shall be alguaciles mayores, high sheriffs; that he and his heirs shall be lieutenants of the forts he may build, with a salary of 70,000 maravedís for each fort; that he and his heirs shall receive four per cent of the tax levies of the province; that he is to have a tract ten leagues square (the league was 2.6 miles) for his private estate; that his companions shall receive various special privileges, including the important one of considering rebellious Indians, once they are admonished and comprehending, as slaves.

The warrant then suddenly abandons the tone of a legal formula and breaks into a stirring and vigorous denunciation of the cruelties practised on the unhappy Indian subjects of His Majesty. The voice is that of Charles the Fifth, but the words are those of Bartolomé de las Casas. The king confesses that he has for a time suspended the granting of licenses for exploration, until he should find a means for punishing past misdeeds and preventing those that might so easily occur again. He stipulates that the crown's representatives in the Indies shall inquire into all cases of official brutality, and forward the reports to the Council of the Indies; that the natives are to be treated not as slaves but as free men, and are not to be taken from their homes nor put to any labor against their will; that at least two clerics are to accompany every expedition in order to instruct and convert the natives, and to protect their charges against any presumption of the military or civil authorities; that the first action of

[9] A cedula, dated 15 Nov., 1526, in Valladolid, orders a reënquiry into the 600 peso fine paid by Narváez to Ayllón. The king was in great good humor toward Narváez. As the king's person was in Granada, the cedula must have been signed by his proxy. (Col. Doc. Ined., Ser. II, Vol. I, 361.)

A CARAVEL

An illustration for Hans Staden's Journey to Brazil in 1547, and his account of the flying-fish pursued by great fish. Notice the rigging with spritsail and lateen mizzen. Though his ship was in fact Portuguese, she seems to fly the French fleur-de-lis.

the conquistadores on disembarking must be to explain to the natives that they come as friends, to save their souls, "that our conscience may be disburdened"; that fortresses may be built, only for security, not for aggression; that barter shall not be forced; that war shall not be declared on the natives without the consent of the clerics; that the Indians shall not be forced to work in mines or pearl fisheries, and shall be paid for their labor; but that, with the consent of the clerics, the Indians may be assigned, as an *encomienda,* to the benevolent supervision of individual masters.

What Narváez, with his twenty-six years' experience in handling natives, thought of this document, and what inward reservations he made, we are not informed. He certainly signed readily enough; it would go hard with him if he could not bring a pair of pasty-faced priests to a sensible way of thinking.

He spent the winter in choosing and instructing his personnel, in chartering ships, and in providing the equipment for an expedition into a world whose climate, physical conformation, and resources were unknown. On this problem the outfitters of Seville were able to give well-pondered advice. The one matter beyond his control was the appointment of the clerics and of the three king's officers, the treasurer, the quartermaster *(factor)* and the inspector *(contador).*

At this point Cabeza de Vaca reënters the story. He was made treasurer of the expedition by a royal warrant dated 15 February, 1527. The fact of his selection for this post, of the most urgent interest to the crown, indicates sufficiently well that he had given evidence of probity and of sober good sense in handling money and men. Though certainly officialdom might recommend gay scapegraces, cardinals' nephews and such, for hazardous and distant explorations, they would appoint as treasurer one who would make no errors of arithmetic, who would be wise in the weighing and testing of gold and goods and the chattels of the visible world.

His duties were to be those primarily of a collector of revenue. He was to be diligent in gathering the king's five per cent of all gold obtained by barter or otherwise, and the five per cent tax on gold and silver melted down; to collect the rent on salt works; to collect the seven and a half per cent import duty, when it should be established; to account for the income from the royal fields and live-stock; to pay to the officers their salaries and indemnifications; to aid in every way the peopling and pacification of the country, "inform-ing us . . . especially of how our commands are obeyed and executed in those lands and provinces, of how the natives are treated, our in-structions observed, and other of the things respecting their liberties that we have commanded; especially the matters touching the service of our Lord and divine worship, the teachings of the Indians in the Holy Faith." Finally he was required to deposit two thousand ducats with the Seville treasury, as a bond of proper conduct in office.

As if these duties were not enough, he was made in addition alguacil mayor, to be translated perhaps as provost marshal, in charge of the army's discipline.

At length a proper band of volunteers was assembled, including plenty of bold men-at-arms, and not one who could sail a boat, plenty of good marksmen with the cross-bow but hardly one who knew an ax from an adz. Belike the captain's review of his men resembled that of Soto eleven years later, when the Castilians appeared in silk over silk, pinked and slashed, but, when commanded to show their fighting gear, could produce only very sorry and rusty shirts of mail.

When a captain or a man of reputation or importance of these Indies goes to Spain [says Oviedo, my delight] and especially those who go to plead for governorships and new conquests, and know how to use their tongue middling well to attract people, he utters a flood of promises among those who know nothing of it, and all those who listen to him think that he knows and has seen and visited and explored everything there is out there, not omitting a single island or hand's-breadth or cranny of the main-land and the Indies. And at that these loud speakers don't fail to talk in just such a way about everything. And the ignorant people, hearing them, imagine and believe that the Indies must be like the kingdom of Portugal or Navarre, or at least a compact and narrow country, wherein every in-habitant knows everybody else and can communicate with the same ease as from Cordova to Granada or Seville, or at the outside from Castile to the Biscay region. Thus letters arrive out there from ignorant mothers and wives seeking and writing to their sons and husbands, and for other rela-tives, and they are addressed thus: "To my beloved son Pedro Rodríguez, in the Indies," which is like saying, "To my son Mahomet, in Africa," or "To Juan Martínez, in Europe," which is as good as saying "In the next

26

world." Because all those who understand something of the form of the world and its geography don't fail to suspect that it is divided into two parts, of which our continent and Asia make one, and the other is that new world, or as some call it, *Orbe Novo*. And, as I have said several times in this history, I call it a half of the same world, and Africa, Europe, and Asia have nothing to do with it.

Well, I want to say that many people come to these Indies just as benighted as those who addressed the letters I spoke of, not knowing nor understanding whither they are bound. And Narváez caught plenty of them, and other captains find as many as they wish, or at least more than they need, because the poverty of some and the greed of others and the craziness of nearly all doesn't let them realize what they are doing nor whom they are following. . . .

The organizer, once dispatched from the Court, comes to Seville with less money than he would like. He sends out a drummer and a couple of friars or a few priests, who join with him under color of the conversion of the Indians, and go here and there upsetting people's minds and promising riches that they know nothing about. Meanwhile the Captain is busy borrowing money and buying old and worn-out ships which have come to port by the grace of God and double pumping, and not only are in no shape to return but they will never bring back to Castile a report of the cargo they carried out. And he sends out a young man who is appointed his "Secretary," and who has never learned what a "secret" is, with other cunning and smooth-tongued fellows, the best schemers the captain knows, who know how to talk over the poor volunteers and persuade them to two things: first, to lend the captain money on the vain hopes they are promised, and on a receipt which the recipient thinks to be like a bank note. Thus the poor volunteer gives up the little money that is left him, and if the trap is well sprung, he will sell his cape and his doublet and go in his shirt like Guillote, because he thinks that when he comes to the tropics he will be finely dressed with all the favor he awaits and which has been offered him.

The other thing is that each ten volunteers, more or less, shall obligate themselves jointly to pay each one at a certain time ten or twelve ducats or pesos of gold for their food and transport whither they are going, but what they get can only be told by those dupes who have returned again to Spain, and they are few; because, as the voyage is long and life is short, and the chances to lose it are innumerable, most of those who come there settle down, never to return to the homeland. And it is all very contrary to what they had imagined in Spain, as now you will hear, and as you have learned already if you have read this history from its beginning.[10]

[10] "Historia general," III, 597.

Oviedo spoke with full knowledge; he crossed the ocean twelve times before his death. The cynic may listen to his cynic speech, as the believer hearkened to Narváez and Cabeza de Vaca. The drummers went forth and the friars preached, and volunteers stepped forward with their passage money in hand, and, I am convinced, all were filled with high purpose and virtuous dreams, the captain and treasurer, the drummers, friars, and volunteers.

The ecclesiastical staff consisted of five Franciscan monks for the spiritual care of the soldiers and for the conversion of North America. Their leader, Father Juan Juárez, was the commissary, or clerical delegate. He and his companion, Juan de Palos, a lay brother, had gone out to Mexico with the first group of clerics to answer Cortés's call. Juan Juárez became superior of the Convent of Huexotzinco. His portrait and that of Brother Juan de Palos still hang in the Convent of Tlaltelalco. The faces show forth the minds of intelligent men; the deep-sunk eyes, even though by painter's artifice, suggest vigils and ardor and gladness in martyrdom.[11]

The monks brought from Mexico a strange companion for the expedition, Prince Tetlahuehuetzquititzin of Tezcuco. Heir to the throne of that important region, he had joined Cortés in order to throw off the yoke of Montezuma upon his people, and had led one of the auxiliary armies in the assault on the City of Mexico. The Spaniards, in the manner of all soldiers at odds with strange names in foreign lands, re-christened Prince Tetlahuehuetzquititzin "Don Pedro."

Five caravels made the fleet. They slipped with the current down the Guadalquivir from Seville to the port of San Lúcar de Barrameda at the river's mouth. While they waited there for government inspection [12] and a fair wind Cabeza de Vaca must have ridden the fifteen miles to Jerez de la Frontera. There he bade farewell to his kinsmen, with the special gravity of Spanish leave-takings. Even in the polite everyday formula, "Go with God," the Spaniard is conscious of the meaning of his words. There is a sense of God in "Vaya Usted con

---

[11] Reproduced in Buckingham Smith's "Relation of Cabeça de Vaca" (1871).
[12] For the description of these inspections see F. de Castro y Bravo, "Las Naos Españoles," 17.

28

Dios" which has disappeared in "good-by." As the clan of the Veras uttered their words of parting, they spoke more to the Deity than to Alvar Núñez. It is to be presumed that the Deity was moved at the thought of the doom prepared for Narváez and his men, and chose to make a special exception in the case of their Treasurer.

The expedition, five caravels and some six hundred men, set sail on June 17, 1527,[13] from San Lúcar. Rounding the bar that shelters the river from the sea, the ships filled their sails with ocean winds and turned westward.

Waving farewell from the shore stood the cousin of Alvar Núñez, Pedro Estopiñán Cabeza de Vaca, of whom we shall hear again after many days.[14]

In the capilla mayor of the convent of Santo Domingo in Jerez de la Frontera, beside the tomb of old Pedro de Vera, the monks pattered through their masses for the safety of his grandson, out on the western ocean, fulfilling his boyish dreams.

---

[13] Seven hundred men, according to the "Relación del viaje de Narváez, hecha por Cabeza de Vaca," in "Colección de Documentos inéditos . . . de Indias," Ser. 1, XIV, 269. The date is given as June 7 in this Relación, June 27 in the 1542 edition of the "Naufragios."

[14] "Testimony" in Arch. Ind., Justicia, 1131, 8A.

CHAPTER III

FROM SPAIN TO FLORIDA

THE journey from Spain to Santo Domingo passed without recorded incident. Probably the fleet followed the usual route: southwest to the Canaries, then directly west until the Antilles rose ahead. By pursuing this course the navigator spared himself the distress of taking the longitude, a tricky business before the days of accurate chronometers.

The Canaries loomed before Cabeza de Vaca's eyes, troubling his clear youthful imaginations of these scenes. Here was the Grand Canary, where his grandfather had harried the naked warriors; there the monstrous Teneriffe, enveloped with its clouds and the legends told by the household slaves of his boyhood. Looking back with a man's tenderness for his tiny self, his memory's child, he felt the old ardor with the strength of manhood. These islands were the province of his grandfather; his own destined kingdom lay far toward the sunset.

The crossing of the Atlantic must have been, at best, a cruel trial of the adventurous temper. Some hundred and twenty men were apportioned to each caravel, of about one hundred tons burthen. The high-pooped, high-forecastled, top-heavy craft rolled and pitched tumultuously in the calmest sea. There was no deck-space for the passengers to sit or stand, even when the decks were not cleared for the handling of the ship. Exercise was entirely out of the question. With the human cargo packed body to body between decks, one seasick landsman could poison life for a hundred, one verminous member could infect the whole ship's complement. The seasick landsman, the verminous member, were never lacking. The sea-going rats, says a contemporary, stand at bay against their hunters like wild boars, and cockroaches grow to be ocean wildfowl.[1] The food, cooked

[1] Castro y Bravo, "Las Naos españoles," 138.

in a brick galley amidships when weather permitted, set the old evil tradition of transatlantic cuisine. The prescribed ration in the fleet at this time was—a pound and a half of biscuit and a quart of wine daily to each man; on Sunday and Thursday a pound of meat and two ounces of cheese; on Monday, Wednesday, Friday, and Saturday, soup of beans and chick-peas, and a third of a pound of salt fish; on Tuesday, rice soup with oil, and two ounces of salt pork; also garlic, oil, and vinegar in liberal quantities.[2] Obviously this diet was an ideal often not attained, through necessity or the parsimony of the commander. It will be remembered that Don Pánfilo's reputation for stinginess covered the Gulf of Mexico.

The fleet came to shore, probably in early August. The men lingered in Santo Domingo for forty-five days, collecting provisions, and especially horses. These, we may surmise, were of the great Andalusian breed, round-quartered, small-barreled, broad-chested, paced to the *paso castellano,* "which is something more than a walk, and less than a trot, and is truly sedate and sedan-chair like, and suits a grave Don, who is given, like a Turk, to tobacco and contemplation." [3] They are hardy beasts, and trained to an austerity in food to match that of their masters. A number of them bore Soto's men on their great three-year journey from Florida to North Carolina, west to Texas, and back to the Mississippi, where, unable longer to serve with their strength, they gave their flesh for their masters' food and their hides for clothing. O patient eyes, courageous hearts! [4]

In Santo Domingo a hundred and forty men deserted the expedition, tempted by the wealth of the country and by the handsome promises made them by the inhabitants. It is permissible to believe that, to cause such a considerable desertion, Don Pánfilo had aroused personal dislike among his followers, or perhaps an alarmed distrust of his prediction of Floridan gold. Better the tangible good of a com-

[2] Castro y Bravo, "Las Naos españoles," 166.

[3] Ford, "The Spaniards and their Country," 69. Also Graham, "Horses of the Conquest."

[4] There is a pretty legend that his steeds, set free, gave America its wild plains horses. See Mark van Doren's poem in Untermyer's "Modern American Poetry," 690. But Garcilaso says: "The Indians pulled off their halters and saddles, set them running through the field, and hunted them down with arrows until they had slain them all. Thus perished the last of the three hundred horses which had entered Florida." "Historia de Florida," Lib. VI, cap. 5.

fortable sugar plantation in Hispaniola, with a few fruitful black couples to work it, than iridescent hopes of a land out of which nothing but disaster had yet come. Better almost anything, perhaps, than a continuance of the journey in the caravels' 'tween-decks, with a herd of horses for bedfellows.

The faithful ones sailed for Santiago de Cuba, and there remained some days, taking on men, arms, and horses. Cabeza de Vaca and Captain Pantoja, each in charge of a vessel, were ordered to the town of Trinidad, midway along the southern coast of the island, to load provisions, offered them by a celebrated Cuban gentleman, Vasco Porcallo, who was later to accompany Soto. While Cabeza de Vaca was on shore, concerned with his financial duties, a terrible hurricane came on to blow. All the houses and churches fell down, and men had to go seven or eight abreast, with arms linked. And all that night they heard a great roaring and a great noise of voices and the sound of bells and flutes and tambourines, the favorite instruments of demons and spirits, then as to-day. In the morning the tempest ceased; the ships had disappeared and nothing could be found of them, only a ship's dinghy on the top of some trees, a mile from shore, and two faceless bodies, beating against the rocks, some box lids, a cloak and a ragged coverlet. Sixty men and twenty horses were never seen again. They were spared much, those sixty men and twenty horses.

When the governor arrived, on November 5, he was determined, not only by the material damage of the hurricane, but also by the terrors of the expeditionaries, to go into winter quarters in Cuba. He gave Cabeza de Vaca command of the fleet, thus manifesting that the treasurer, a king's appointee, had proved his competence to his new superior. The vessels spared from the storm moved west along the coast to Jagua, and encamped by the beautiful landlocked bay of Cienfuegos. The governor, we may be assured, rode westward to the province of Guaniguanico, to pay his triennial visit to his wife.

The expeditionaries remained in Jagua for the winter, amusing themselves as idle gentlemen in barracks do. In the long discussions about the evening fires, many commented on the bad luck that pursued their leader. Herrera, the historian who notes this fact, most

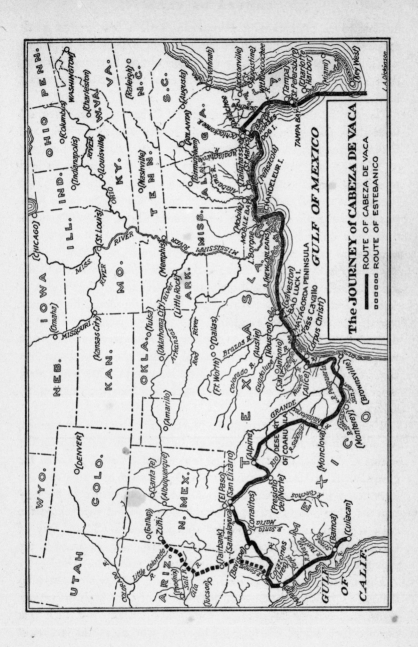

The JOURNEY of CABEZA DE VACA

━━━ ROUTE OF CABEZA DE VACA

□□□□ ROUTE OF ESTEBANICO

J. A. Dickinson

aptly quotes Cicero: "Ad amplitudinem, et gloriam, et ad res magnas bene gerendas, divinitus advincta fortuna." [5] Or, "For positions of consequence, and fame, and the management of great matters, one must be a lucky man, by God's help."

On February 20, 1528, the governor arrived with a ship he had bought in Trinidad, and with a pilot, Diego Miruelo, a nephew of the Diego Miruelo already mentioned (p. 23). The uncle had visited the Florida coast three times, if not more, before his death in Ayllón's expedition; the nephew, who had been on Pineda's cruise, inherited at least the prestige of his uncle's name. On the 22nd the fleet, four ships and a lugger, four hundred men and eighty horses, set sail, heading west southwest to clear the western cape of Cuba. The pilot promptly ran the vessels on the Canarreo shoals, and there they remained, scraping bottom, for two weeks, until a strong south wind brought high water and set them free. Two more storms smote them before they could weather Cape Antonio. Thence they ran northeast against contrary winds to Havana, but when they would enter the harbor a south wind drove them away. Decidedly God was in no very helpful mood, unless, as one may always reflect, his adverse blasts are sent as a test of character. Well, the wind blew toward Florida; the flagship trimmed its yards to run before it, and the others followed. On Tuesday, the 7th of April, land was sighted.[6] Under the Florida sun, the world shone blue and white, Christ's color and the Virgin's. The quiet surf edged the shining sand of the seaboard islands, behind which a thin green line marked the mangrove swamp and the salty marshes. Here and there the peninsula's island wall was broken, and through the gap one could see the mainland, with a brush of heavier green, live-oaks, palms, and magnolias. The pilot gazed anxiously at each succeeding island, trying to evoke an old memory of an inland channel and to compare it with the bewildering realities succeeding each other, so serenely identical. He was searching for that great land-locked bay of Espíritu Santo, the

---

[5] Herrera, "Historia," I, 243.
[6] His own relation says "Tuesday the 12th of April," and Oviedo agrees. But Easter fell on the 12th of April; it seems to me more likely that he remembered the events of Easter week by the special character of the sacred days than that he preserved the reckoning of the days of the month.

Holy Spirit, now reduced to be Tampa Bay. On Holy Thursday, a day of good promise, he found the entrance to a little bay, and on the mainland at its head some Indian houses.

The inspector, Alonso Enríquez, went off in a boat to one of the islands. He found some Indians and called to them, making signs of amity. The two parties met and uttered friendly sounds; the Indians proved their good will by making the inspector a present of fish and venison. The governor, encouraged by these indications, made a landing on the next day, Good Friday, the 10th of April, 1528. On Easter Day, fifteen years before, Ponce de León had discovered the mainland and had christened it Florida.

The statements of Cabeza de Vaca make it possible to settle his landing place with a good chance of accuracy.[7] He turned in from the gulf at St. John's Pass, just north of St. Petersburg. The Indian village he saw stood on the mainland, in line with the pass; it is marked to-day by the large shell mounds cast away by oyster-eating Carlos Indian villagers of the sixteenth century. The spot is known as the Jungle, because of its dense tropical growth. There is no monument or tablet, nothing to indicate that here, four hundred years ago, Narváez and his men landed on the short journey to their doom.

[7] See Lowery, "Spanish Settlements," I, 453. Since Lowery's book appeared, Dr. A. D. Phinney investigated the question on the spot. (Florida Hist. Soc. Quarterly, Jan., 1925.) I follow his conclusions.

CHAPTER IV

THE JOURNEY BY LAND

THE moment of disembarkation was to Cabeza de Vaca and his companions the true beginning of their adventure. They stood upon a continent, theirs by the gift of the emperor, who had it from the Pope. All its wealth was theirs; and all its inhabitants, in spite of the ludicrous provisions of His Pious Majesty, were their servants. If the natives did not come to the shore with gifts of gold nuggets, one had no need of discouragement. Father Juan Juárez, Brother Juan de Palos, Captain Pantoja, and others who had been in Mexico testified that this pleasant country lacked nothing in promise.

The Good Friday landing party headed for the Indian village visible from their anchorage. Although it appeared deserted, the governor formed his men in good defensive order on the beach and marched in with Cuban cries of good will but with crossbows flexed and swords loose in the scabbard. The village was indeed empty, and the Spaniards scattered through it, curiously examining the abandoned tools and cooking pots, and turning over everything in the hope of finding gold. The dwellings of the village were small and round like pigeon houses, with trees for uprights, and thatched with palmetto leaves. In the center was a large barn-like house with whole trees for rafters; this, the "town house" of other observers, was said to hold more than three hundred persons. If it resembled one that Hernando de Soto later saw, it bore on its roof-tree a wooden fowl with gilded eyes.

Suddenly a great shout arose. One of the soldiers, poking among some fish-nets, had discovered a golden rattle.

If there had been some doubt of the wisdom of making a landing here, it was now at an end. On Saturday, Easter Eve, the governor raised the flag of Spain in honor of the king, and the friars set up a cross to the Heavenly Sovereign. Cabeza de Vaca and the other royal appointees in turn publicly recognized the authority of the governor. As they laid their commissions before him, he took them in his hand, acknowledged them, and returned them. The notary, Jerónimo de Alañiz, busily recorded the governor's acceptance, and took the signatures of witnesses thereto. The governor then stepped forward, and read aloud, as he was required, the King's Summons to the Indians.[1]

In behalf of the Catholic Cæsarian Majesty of Don Carlos, King of the Romans, and Emperor ever Augustus, and Doña Juana his mother, Sovereigns of León and Castilla, Defenders of the Church, ever victors, never vanquished and rulers of barbarous nations, I, Pánfilo de Narváez, his servant, messenger, and captain, notify and cause you to know in the best manner I can, that God our Lord, one and eternal, created the heaven and the earth, and one man and one woman of whom we and you and all men in the world have come, are descendants and the generation, as well will those be who shall come after us: but because of the infinity of offspring that followed in the five thousand years and more since the world was created, it has become necessary that some men should go in one direction and others in another, dividing into many kingdoms and provinces, since in a single one they could not be subsisted nor kept.

All these nations God our Lord gave in charge to one person, called Saint Peter, that he might be Master and Superior over mankind, to be obeyed and be head of all the human race, wheresoever they might live and be, of whatever law, sect, or belief, giving him the whole world for his kingdom, lordship, and jurisdiction. And he commanded him to place his seat in Rome, as a point most suited whence to rule the world; so he likewise permitted him to have and place his seat on any part of the earth to judge and to govern all people, Christians, Moors, Jews, Gentiles and of whatever creed beside they might be: him they call Papa, which means admirable, greatest, father, and preserver, since he is father and governor of all men. Thus Saint Peter was obeyed and taken for King, Lord, and Superior of the Universe by those who lived at that time, and so likewise have all the rest been held, who to the Pontificate were afterward elected: and thus has it continued until now, and will continue to the end of things.

One of the Popes who succeeded him to that seat and dignity of which I spake, as Lord of the world, made a gift of these islands and main of the Ocean Sea, to the said Emperor and Queen, and their successors, our Lords, in these kingdoms, with all that is in them, as is contained in certain writings that thereupon took place, which may be seen if you desire.

---

[1] Buckingham Smith's translation, "Relation of Cabeça de Vaca," 215.

Automatically Don Pánfilo looked up and gazed around. If there were any Indians peering from behind distant live-oaks, they did not ask a citation of the Bull *Inter Cetera*. The governor resumed his reading.

Thus are their Highnesses King and Queen of these islands and continent, by virtue of said gift; and as Sovereigns and Masters, some other islands and nearly all where they have been proclaimed, have received their Majesties, obeyed and served, and do serve them as subjects should, with good will and no resistance, and immediately without delay, directly as they were informed, obeying the religious men whom their Highnesses sent to preach to them and teach our Holy Faith, of their entire free will and pleasure, without reward or condition whatsoever, becoming Christians which they are; and their Highnesses received them joyfully and benignly, ordering them to be treated as their subjects and vassals were, and you are held and obliged to act likewise.

Wherefore, as best you can, I entreat and require you to understand this well which I have told you, taking the time for it that is just you should, to comprehend and reflect, and that you recognize the Church as Mistress and Superior of the Universe, and the High Pontiff, called Papa, in its name, the Queen and King, our Masters, in their place as Lords, Superiors, and Sovereigns of these islands and the main by virtue of said gift, and you consent and give opportunity that these fathers and religious men, declare and preach to you as stated. If you shall do so you will do well in what you are held and obliged; and their Majesties, and I, in their royal name, will receive you with love and charity, relinquishing in freedom your women, children, and estates without service, that with them and yourselves you may do with perfect liberty all you wish and may deem well; you shall not be required to become Christians, except when, informed of the truth, you desire to be converted to our Holy Catholic Faith, as nearly all the inhabitants of the other islands have done, and when his Highness will confer on you numerous privileges and instruction with many favors.

If you do not do this [and here Don Pánfilo's voice lost its painful effort to convey benevolence, and resumed the tone of a Conqueror to Indians] if you do not do this, and of malice you be dilatory, I protest to you, that, with the help of Our Lord, I will enter with force, making war upon you from all directions and in every manner that I may be able, when I will subject you to obedience to the Church and yoke of their Majesties; and I will take the persons of yourselves, your wives, and your children to make slaves, sell and dispose of you, as their Majesties shall think fit, and I will take your goods, doing you all the evil and injury that I may

37

be able, as to vassals who do not obey but reject their master, resist and deny him; and I declare to you that the deaths and damages that arise therefrom, will be your fault and not that of His Majesty, nor mine, nor of these cavaliers who came with me. And so as I proclaim and require this, I ask of the Notary here that he give a certificate; and those present I beseech that they will hereof be the witnesses.

No answer was heard, only the ironic applause of the little waves along the shore. Jerónimo de Alañiz gave his certificate that the natives were properly informed of the legal status of their lands, their bodies, and their souls. The witnesses signed. The party returned to the ships with a feeling of work well done. They had given their master title to a continent, with the attested signature of a notary.[2]

The remainder of the day was spent in the landing of the horses. The forty-two remaining alive from the eighty that had left Cuba were, after their two months in the hold, too weak and lean to be of service.

The next day, Easter Sunday, the monks set up their portable altar on the shore, and celebrated a solemn high mass of thanksgiving, with their precious wine and wafers of Spanish flour.[3] The festival was marred by a committee of Indians, who came and talked angrily and made menacing signs which seemed to mean "go away."

Father Juan Juárez and Brother Juan de Palos, for all their Franciscan humility, could not but recall with a twinge of disappointment their reception in Mexico in 1524, when twelve friars had been met by Cortés, King Quauhtemotzin, and all the kings and chiefs;

[2] This Requisition, or *Requirimento*, was first used by Pedrarias de Avila in the Conquest of the Isthmus of Panama in 1514. He read the document through while the Bishop listened from safety on the ship. The interpreter had difficulty in interpreting, and the savages no less in comprehending. Pedrarias returned to the ship and reported in disgust to the Bishop: "My Lord, it appears to me that these Indians will not listen to the theology of this Requisition, and that you have no one who can make them understand it. Would your honor be pleased to keep it until we have one of these Indians in a cage, in order that he may learn it at his leisure and my Lord Bishop may explain it to him?" A later method of reconciling expediency with the law was for the soldiers of the King to crawl up to an Indian village in the dead of night, read the Requirimento in a whisper to the trees, have the notary duly witness it, and then rush to massacre with the cry of "Santiago!" (MacLeod, "The American Indian Frontier," 73–74.)

[3] When Soto's priests lost their white bread, near Mobile, they decided that the miracle of transsubstantiation could not be performed with corn-bread.

A LANDING MASS

Christopher Columbus and Father Boil celebrating a mass of thanksgiving on the island of Jamaica, in 1494. This sweet island could be smelt four leagues off shore. Notice the parrot-feather cloaks.

and Cortés himself had knelt in the dust and kissed the hems of their patched and ragged robes!

On Monday the serious business of exploration began. The governor and forty men, including Cabeza de Vaca, went ten miles north to "a very large bay which appeared to stretch far inland." This was Old Tampa Bay. Two days later they repeated the expedition. On the way they captured four Indians, to whom they showed some Indian corn, with inquiring inflexions. The Indians led the Spaniards to a village at the head of the bay where they found growing corn, and to another village, ten leagues farther. There the explorers remained two days.

Their talk with the Indians was all of food and gold. They found in the villages pieces of linen and other cloth, and bits of gold. Holding the gold before the natives' eyes, they would inquire, by word, intonation, and gesture, whence it came. At last the Indians seemed to understand; they pointed to the north, and cried "Apalachen! Apalachen!" Were they not saying that in "Apalachen" one would find much gold and much food?

If indeed that was their meaning, it was sincere, and not the utterance of savage duplicity. What gold they had—until shipwrecked galleons came to provide a readier source of supply—came from Apalachee Indians in Georgia and West Florida. A considerable amount of gold was washed in the streams of North Georgia, and served as a prized article of commerce before the introduction of European economics. As for the final "n" on Apalache, it is perhaps to be interpreted as the Muskhogean objective ending.[4] Either the Timucua Indians, misunderstanding the Apalachees, or the Spanish, misunderstanding the Timucuas, took the objective "Apalachen," "to Apalachee," for the nominative case. And now we can correct a grammatical confusion made in a Florida jungle by savages whose tongue is hardly known, whose race has been extinct these two hundred years! What curious veins run back into time!

These Timucua Indians, a race of sturdy savages, resisted the white man's arms and his diseases until the eighteenth century. They were described by Jean Ribaut, in 1562, as "of good stature, well shaped of

[4] Swanton, "Early History of the Creek Indians," 113.

body as any people in the world; very gentle, courteous, and good-natured, of tawny color, hawked nose, and of pleasant countenance." [5] The men wore breech-clouts of painted deerskin, while the women's single garment was of Spanish moss. The breech-clouts were often ornamented with strings of metal plates, which jingled merrily. Perhaps Cabeza de Vaca's mention of a "golden rattle" refers to these. Their bodies presented a brighter interest than our sun-tanned forms; says Ribaut: "The forepart of their bodies and arms they also paint with pretty devices in azure, red, and black, so well and properly, that the best painters of Europe could not improve upon it." These colors were permanent, pricked in with thorns, and supplemented by temporary painting of the face, for state occasions and for war. "Men and women have their ears pierced, and fix in them little inflated fish-bladders, shining like pearls, colored and looking like wet carbuncles. It is astonishing that such barbarous men have found out such pretty things." [6]

Meanwhile the lugger had been sent north along the coast in search of the deep bay "extending a dozen leagues inland," which the pilot insisted that he knew—and which he would have found by running only a few miles south. The Spanish judicial league equaled 2.634 miles; it will be noticed that Cabeza de Vaca constantly over-estimates distances. The lugger's orders were to find the bay and return to report; or if it should not be found, to sail direct to Havana and return with the supply ship there in harbor.

No news had come by the first of May. Food was short and the men were restless, begrudging every day that went by without gold, women, and lordships to be won by the sword. On that day the governor called into conference Father Juan Juárez, the quartermaster, the inspector, the notary, a sailor named Bartolomé Hernández, and Cabeza de Vaca. He proposed that the expedition set forth into the interior, following the coast until it should reach the great bay, which, according to the pilots, was very near on the way to the River of Palms, in Mexico. And he asked the opinions of those present. Cabeza de Vaca later reported:

[5] Quoted by Swanton, "Early History of the Creeks," 345.
[6] Jacques Le Moyne, in Ningler, "Voyages en Virginie," 302.

I said that it seemed to me that by no means should we leave the vessels until they were in a secure and inhabited harbor, and that he should note that the pilots were not certain, nor did they agree in any one thing, nor know where we were; and that in addition the horses were in no state to serve us well in any emergency that might arise; and that beyond all this we were dumb and speechless, whereas we could ill understand the Indians, nor learn what we wished about the country; and that we were entering upon a region of which we had no information, nor did we know what it was like, nor what there was in it, nor by what race it was inhabited, nor where we were in it, and that above all we did not have enough supplies to set off we knew not where. And because, considering what there was in the ships, one could not give as rations to each man setting out into the country more than a pound of hardtack and one of bacon, my opinion was that we ought to reembark and go and look for a harbor and a region that would be better to settle, because the one we had seen was uninhabited and poor like none that had ever been found in those parts.[7]

The clerical delegate, Fray Juan Juárez, took the opposite view. He thought it very simple to journey north along the coast, in touch with the ships, until they should come to the great bay. Did not the pilots insist that it could not be more than ten or fifteen leagues to northward, and as it stretched a dozen leagues inland, one could not miss it? Whichever of the two, the land party or the sailors, should arrive first would wait for the others. And—to interpret the divine will, as was his profession—"to embark would be tempting God, since we had undergone so much travail since we had left Spain, and so many storms, and we had lost so many ships and men."

The others agreed, all but the notary, who, with his notarial liking for security and tidiness, thought that they should not leave until the ships were in a known, safe, inhabited harbor.

The governor made clear that he would follow his own opinion, which was that of the majority. Cabeza de Vaca, looking at the exulting illumination in his chief's single eye, was filled with foreboding. What was his own amateurish opinion worth, to be set against that of the veteran of twenty-six years' service in the Indies, and against

---

[7] I follow, here and elsewhere, the mellow prose of Buckingham Smith's translation, making some changes in favor of what seems to me lucidity and accuracy.

that of Father Juan, who had labored in Mexico? And yet, as the king's chief representative, he had a clear obligation.

I required him on the part of Your Majesty that he should not leave the ships until they were safe in harbor, and I asked a certificate of my statement from the notary. He answered that since he was conforming with the opinion of the majority of the other officials and the clerical delegate, I had no right to make these requirements, and he asked the notary to give him an attestation that as there was not in that region the means for colonization, nor any harbor for the ships, he was raising the settlement he had made there, and was going in search of a better harbor and country. He then sent to inform the people who were to go with him that they should provide themselves with all that was needful for the journey. And when this was done, in the presence of those who were still there he said to me that since I interfered so much and since I was so afraid of going into the interior, I should remain behind and take charge of the ships and their complement, and should go ashore if I should reach the bay before him.

At his commander's sneer of cowardice Cabeza de Vaca's hand twitched on his sword-hilt. He remembered his duty to his sovereign, and soberly refused the post. But never, in good fortune or bad, would he forget this public dirtying of his honor.

That evening Don Pánfilo's anger had cooled. He repeated his request that Cabeza de Vaca take charge of the ships, for there was no one else to whom he could intrust the post.

Seeing that for all he importuned me [Cabeza de Vaca] I still excused myself, he asked me why I refused to accept it. Thereto I answered that I refused to take it upon myself because I held it a certain thing and I knew well that he would never see those ships again; nor would the ships see him, and this was clear from our entering so ill equipped into the country, and that I would rather venture into the danger where he and the others were venturing, and go through, than to take charge of the ships and let people say that as I had spoken against the journey I was staying behind out of fear, and my honor would be in question, and I would rather venture my life than put my honor in such a pass.

This declaration considerably eased his spirit. He refused the persuasions of various envoys the governor sent to him to urge him to a change of mind. Finally an alcalde named Caravallo was made lieutenant of the fleet.

(I have quoted here from the report which Cabeza de Vaca wrote of his adventures when at length he returned to Spain. This report he presented to the king; it was printed in 1542. One other primary source of information exists. Cabeza de Vaca and Dorantes, another survivor of the expedition, made a first joint report to the Audiencia of Hispaniola. Although this has disappeared, it was consulted by the historian Oviedo y Valdés, who made large extracts from it for his third edition of the "Historia de las Indias," published in 1547. This valuable supplementary material will be referred to briefly as the Oviedo record. A third source, a fragmentary "Relación," differs only slightly from Cabeza de Vaca's report to the king.)

On the first of May, as Cabeza de Vaca reëstablishes the dates, the expedition set forth. They were three hundred in number, with forty horses. The total rations were two pounds of hardtack and half a pound of bacon per man. They marched north through a level sandy country, with clumps of hammock land tufted with tall pines. They saw no human creature, no lodging of man, no tilled field. The region was not, apparently, heavily overgrown; they could have made good progress had it not been for the swamps and creeks blocked with fallen trees and tangled swamp-growth, the lurking-places of alligators. They found nothing to eat except the fruit of the dwarf fan-palm. After a fortnight's travel they came to a river, evidently the Withlacoochee, with a strong current. They built rafts to carry the shirts of mail, the weapons, what other baggage they bore, and the non-swimmers; the others made the sign of the cross, and plunging in, came safe to the other side. There they were met by a band of two hundred Indians, who made such menacing gestures that the Spanish seized five or six. The captives led the way to their village, where a large quantity of corn stood in the fields, ready for harvest. This the ravenous Spanish immediately gathered, giving infinite thanks to God, and none to the cultivators.

Cabeza de Vaca's mind was haunted by concern for the ships so long unseen. He urged the governor to send an expedition downstream to the seaboard, and was rewarded by the leadership of such a party. No ships were found, and no harbor at the river's mouth, only shoal water for miles off shore, no hint of a haven that would tempt a sailor to land. Retreat was cut off; there remained no course but to follow the mysterious adjuration of the Indians, and seek "Apalachen! Apalachen!"

Crying this name to the Indians, and following their pointing fingers, the Spanish turned northwest, journeying through pine forests and over level sand. And one day the scouts halted in fear, hearing the sound of strange music. Among the dark tree trunks a group of flute-playing Indians appeared; their instruments were apparently reeds without stops, like whistles. Behind the musicians was a chief named Dulchanchellin, carried on the shoulders of another Indian, and wearing a painted deerskin. He was brought to the presence of the governor, and the two conversed by signs. To Narváez's indication that he would go to Apalachen, the chief made clear that he was a foe of those people, and would join the Spanish in a war upon them. "We gave him beads and bells and other trade goods, and he gave the governor the deerskin he was wearing, and we turned and followed him."

That night they came to the Suwanee River, and crossed it with the aid of the Indians and improvised boats. One man was lost with his mount, attempting to swim the river. All were much grieved at this, their first casualty, although the feast of horse meat somewhat mitigated their sorrow. The next day they came to the chief's village, whither he sent them corn. Some felt that the worst of their trials were over. But that evening, as a party went for water, an arrow flew by them, out of the twilight. All the natives suddenly disappeared, and were no more seen.

Next day the march was resumed, but with precautions against attack. Three or four Indians were taken in an ambush and forced to serve as guides. They led the way through a strange and difficult country, under deep forests of tall trees, many of them fallen, many of them riven by thunderbolts. Finally, on the day after St. John's Day, June 25, they came gladly in sight of their goal, the village of Apalachee. There they would find food and gold and rest for their bodies galled with armor. "Already it appeared to us that we had got rid of a great part of our labor and weariness."

Cabeza de Vaca, with nine cavalrymen and fifty foot-soldiers, attacked the town. Meeting with no resistance, he entered, and found only women and children.

The soldiers looked about them with sinking hearts. The aspect of the village did not belie its appearance from the distance. Far from being the great and shining city of stone and perfumed woods which they had imagined as a rival to Mexico, it was a wretched huddle of forty thatched huts. There was no sign of gold, no amethysts, emeralds and turquoises. All their booty was ripe corn and many deerskins. In dirty paths of the Indian village the Spaniards spat and upbraided their patron saints.

Apalachee stood, probably, on Miccosukee Lake, in Jefferson County, Florida, just south of the Georgia line. Cabeza de Vaca describes the lakes, the deep and varied forests, and the abundance of game: deer, rabbits, hares, bears, and lions, and geese, ducks, partridges, and other birds. Strangely enough, he omits the turkey and the alligator in his description of wild life. But he includes "an animal which carries its young in a pocket in its belly, and while they are young they are there carried until they can seek food, and if perhaps they are out looking for food and some one appears, the mother will not flee until she has got them in her pocket." This is history's first reference to the opossum.

Here the expedition made its headquarters. Three exploring parties were sent forth, and returned with reports only of a poor and unwelcoming country, well-nigh impassable with its lakes, marshes, fallen trees, and tangled underbrush. The natives were few and hostile. From their allies and from a captured chieftain the Spaniards could learn no more encouraging news. (During their four months in Florida, a means of communication had been devised with the Indians.) Apalachee, the natives persisted, was the largest town of all that region; farther on to west and north were great lakes and thick forests and great deserts and solitudes. Only, to the south there stood a town called Aute, well supplied with corn, beans, and pumpkins, and with the fish that abound along the coast.

Life in Apalachee became unendurable. The stores of food were soon consumed. The Indians practised a guerilla warfare that shook the stoutest nerves. Arrows would fall from nowhere, would suddenly stick quivering in a tree-trunk by a man's head. To take the horses to water was a dangerous ordeal. A volley of arrows would fly from a clump of rushes; and when the soldiers had beaten their way to the ambush, they would find no living soul. The marauders had swum away under water, or had slipped off through the impenetrable marshes. These tactics were repeated eleven years later, in the same place, against the troops of Soto, but with less success.

Men and horses were wounded in this maddening war. An arrow killed Don Pedro, the Mexican prince. He who had led his army across the lakes surrounding the City of Mexico, and who had triumphantly scaled those walls, now fell ignobly, picked off by a native sharpshooter. Some day, perhaps, the skull of an Aztec prince will be turned up by Lake Miccosukee, to provide a puzzle for ethnologists.

The mood of the men turned to the profoundest discouragement. Their dream of gold and glory had led them only to this evil wilderness. Instead of lordships to reward their valor, they had won only some handfuls of parched corn. There was nothing to fight for and no one to fight, for no hand could be seen to loose an arrow. Many a sour jest was uttered about the camp-fires, as when Miguel de Lumbreras, with his commission as lord lieutenant of the first city to be established, would mockingly protest against Cabeza de Vaca's collections of the royal share in gold mines.

There seemed no course but to turn southward to Aute and the sea, with the wild hope that they might there descry their ships at anchor, brought thither by some saint's special instructions to the pilot. Therefore, after twenty-five days in Apalachee, the expedition set forth on what they knew to be their retreat. "Well do I think," says Oviedo in his history, "that Pánfilo remembered, and that more than once, the advice I gave him in Toledo."

It was a dreadful march. On the second day, while fording a lake with water to the breast, they were attacked by showers of arrows from the wooded shore. The Indians wounded men and horses, and captured the guide. As the Spaniards emerged from the water and prepared to charge, the Indians leaped into the lake, and continued to shoot from the shelter of rushes and fallen trees.

46

In this conflict some of our men were wounded, for the good armor they wore was of no use. There were men that day who swore that they had seen two oaks, each as thick as a man's lower leg, pierced entirely through by the Indians' arrows; and that is none so marvellous, seeing the strength and skill with which they shoot them. I myself have seen an arrow buried in a poplar stump a good half a foot. All the Indians we had so far seen in Florida were archers, and as they are so large of frame and go naked, from a distance they seem to be giants. They are a marvellously well developed race, very lean-limbed and strong and agile. Their bows are as thick as one's arm, eleven to twelve hand-spans in length, which they shoot at two hundred paces with so much sureness that they miss nothing.

The Indians' skill with the bow, at which the Spanish crossbowmen wondered, seems even more marvelous to us who know only the fluttering marksmanship of college women's archery clubs. Soto's veterans remembered that these natives shot six or seven arrows while a Spaniard was reloading his musket. A shaft loosed at close range penetrated a horse's breast and heart and lodged in the bowels. Another having pierced a coat of mail worth a hundred and fifty ducats, a test was made; a fine chain-mail jacket was fitted on a cane basket, and a prisoner promised his liberty if he could break it at a hundred and fifty paces. He did so; a second coat of mail was put over the first; the arrow penetrated the two with force enough to kill a man, though the point did not emerge on the other side. Thereafter Soto's Spaniards termed their chain-mail Holland cloth, and protected themselves and their horses with thick, soft, wadded doublets.

The Indians' bows were made of hard wood, with a string of deer-gut or deerskin; the arrows were of reed, feathered, and pointed with snake-teeth, fish-bone, or flint. Some had no point but the sharpened reed, and these were the most dangerous, for they would split on the meshes of a mail shirt and inflict a deep double wound.

Amid such missiles winging out of the dark forests, Pánfilo de Narváez and his men made their way to the sea. A hidalgo named Avellaneda was struck just above his steel cuirass; the arrow passed almost entirely through his neck, and he presently died. Cabeza de Vaca himself was wounded in a sortie.

With wounds, terrors, short rations, heat, and hardship, it was a grievous journey. One need only think of the plague of flies, red bugs, and wood ticks burrowing under the soldiers' armor to picture the distresses of the harried legionaries. William Bartram, who visited this region in 1774, gives a graphic description of insect affliction which I cannot forbear to quote:

The heat and the burning flies tormented our horses to such a degree as to excite compassion even in the hearts of pack-horsemen. These biting flies are of several species, and their numbers incredible; we travelled almost from sunrise to his setting amidst a flying host of these persecuting spirits, who formed a vast cloud around our caravan so thick as to obscure every distant object; but our van always bore the brunt of the conflict; the head, neck, and shoulders of the leading horses were continually in a gore of blood: some of these flies were near as large as bumble bees; this is the hippobosca. They are armed with a strong sharp beak or proboscis, shaped like a lancet, and sheathed in flexible thin valves; with this beak they instantly pierce the veins of the creatures, making a large orifice from whence the blood springs in large drops, rolling down as tears, causing a fierce pain or aching for a considerable time after the wound is made; there are three or four species of this genus of less size but equally vexatious, as they are vastly more numerous, active and sanguineous; particularly, one about half the size of the first mentioned, the next less of a dusky color with a green head; another yet somewhat less, of a splendid green and the head of a gold color; the sting of this last is intolerable, no less acute than a prick from a red-hot needle, or a spark of fire on the skin; these are called the burning flies. Besides the preceding tormentors, there are three or four species of the asilus or smaller biting flies; one of a greyish dusky color, another much of the same color, having spotted wings and a green head, and another very small and perfectly black: this last species lie in ambush in shrubby thickets and cane brakes near water; whenever we approach the cool shades near creeks, impatient for repose and relief, almost sinking under the persecutions from the evil spirits, who continually surround and follow us over the burning desert ridges and plains, and here in some hopes of momentary peace and quietness, under cover of the cool humid groves, we are surprised and quickly invested with dark clouds of these persecuting demons, besides mosquitoes and gnats (culex et cynips).[8]

At length the afflicted wanderers came to Aute village, near the site of the present St. Marks, in Wakulla County, on the St. Marks River and not far from the sea. The village was abandoned and the

8 "Travels through . . . Florida," 385.

houses burned, but corn, beans, and squash were ripe and ready for gathering in the Indians' fields. After two days' rest, the governor sent forth Cabeza de Vaca and sixty men to hunt for a harbor. Two of his companions were Captain Alonso del Castillo Maldonado and Captain Andrés Dorantes. Except these three and Dorantes's negro slave, all Narváez's men were destined to imminent death.

Cabeza de Vaca's party journeyed, apparently, southwestward along Apalachee Bay, where the low, marshy shore, barely rising from the lagoons, gives way imperceptibly to the shallow main. Little elevations of the gulf's floor make reefs, bars, and islands in this indeterminate margin, neither land nor sea. For two days they followed the coast, feasting upon oysters, until they were blocked by the Ocklocknee River, whose deep channel opens eastward into Apalachee Bay.

Returning to Aute, they found the governor and many others sick, no doubt from malaria. In this condition they had sustained a night attack from the Indians. The entire band, almost hopeless but desirous at least of contact with the open sea, set forth for the river mouth.

The journey was extremely difficult; for neither did we have enough horses to carry the sick, nor did we know what remedy to give them, and more were falling sick every day, and it was a matter of great grief and pain to see the hardship and need in which we were. When we had arrived, we saw how little use there was in going farther, for there was no place to go, and even if there had been our men could not have gone forward, for most of them were sick and in such state that there was little they could do.

It was a desperate pass, and the counsels were those of despair. The mounted men plotted secretly to abandon the governor, the foot-soldiers, and the sick, and to make a dash for safety. Better that a few should survive than that all should die together on this pestilential coast. But the hidalgos, the gentlemen among them who could not forget the lessons of honor learned in Spain, insisted on disclosing the plot to their chief. Narváez, far from punishing the mutineers, argued with them. "We put their purpose in an evil light," says Cabeza de Vaca, "pointing out to them at what an untimely moment they were abandoning their captain and their sick and helpless comrades, and especially how they were quitting the service of Your Majesty." They yielded to persuasion, not to force, resolving to share the common fate.

The curiously democratic constitution of these conquering bands of Spaniards appears in this incident. Just so Cortés had always addressed his men as comrades, and had appeared always to accept their decisions. Cortés having, however, first skilfully implanted in the minds of his men the conclusion which he wished them to adopt, gained the right to act as the humble agent of their will. Cortés might serve as a model for dictators in a democracy.

After the accomplishment of this, the governor called them all to him, and of each apart he asked advice as to what he should do to get out of a country so miserable, and seek that assistance elsewhere which could not here be found, a third part of the people being very sick, and the number increasing every hour; for we regarded it as certain that we should all become so, and could pass out of it only through death, which from its coming in such a place was to us all the more terrible. These, with many other embarrassments being considered, and entertaining many plans, we coincided in one great project extremely difficult to put in operation, and that was to build vessels in which we might go away. This appeared impossible to every one; we knew not how to construct, nor were there tools, nor iron, nor forge, nor oakum, nor pitch, nor rigging; finally, no one thing of so many that are necessary; nor any man who had a knowledge of their manufacture; and above all, there was nothing to eat, while building, for those who should labor. Reflecting on all this, we agreed to think of the subject with more deliberation, and the conversation dropped from that day, each going his way, commending our course to God, our Lord, that he would direct it as should best serve him.

The next day it was his will that one of the company should come saying that he could make some pipes out of wood, which with deerskins might be made into bellows; and, as we lived in a time when anything that had the semblance of relief appeared well, we told him to set himself to work. We assented to the making of nails, saws, axes, and other tools of which there was such need, from the stirrups, spurs, crossbows, and other things of iron there were; and we determined that for our support, while the work was going on, we would make four raids into Aute, with all the horses and men that were able to go, and that on every third day a horse should be killed to be divided among those who labored in the work of the boats and the sick. [Our author confesses that for all his hunger he could never bring himself to eat the horse flesh.]

The incursions were made with the people and horses that were avail-

50

able, and in them were brought back as much as six hundred and forty bushels of maize; but these were not got without quarrels and contentions with the Indians. We caused many palmettos to be collected for their fibre and husk, twisting and preparing it for use in the place of oakum for the boats.

We commenced to build on the fourth of August, with the only carpenter in the company, and we proceeded with so great diligence that on the twentieth day of September five boats were finished, thirty-three feet in length, each caulked with the fibre of the palmetto. We pitched them with a certain resin, made from pine trees by a Greek, named Don Theodoro; from the same husk of the palmetto, and from the tails and manes of the horses we made ropes and rigging, from our shirts, sails; and from the junipers growing there we made the oars that appeared to us requisite. Such was the country into which our sins had cast us, that only by very great search could we find stone for ballast and anchors, since in it all we had not seen one. We flayed the horses, taking the skin from their legs entire, and tanning them to make canteens wherein to carry water.

It is a pity that our chronicler did not report in more detail the devices and ingenuities, the discouragements and triumphs, in the building of the boats. First the making of air-tight bellows with sheath-knife, bone needle, gut thread, the seams being sealed with evergreen pitch. The whittling of pipes, probably by splitting straight saplings in four, cutting away the right angles, and sealing the four parts. Such pipes would burn after two or three contacts with a bed of coals. The artificer, before proceeding to the making of his tools, must build kilns wherein to reduce wood to charcoal. This done, he would perhaps make earthen molds, in which to melt his iron and steel, even the precious ratchet-wheels of his crossbows. Though they melted and fused, he had no hammer and anvil with which to work them, no tongs wherewith to hold them. Perhaps with clay-surfaced wooden ladles he could remove his hot metal and drop it in water to temper it to steel. But to whatever devices he resorted, his ax-head must have emerged dull and brittle, his saw must have been thick and inflexible, with teeth that rubbed vainly on the knots in pine wood. And yet somehow, by sheer muscle and fury and the ingenuity of despair he built himself these arks for his salvation.[9]

[9] Compare the building, under similar circumstances, of the craft in which Orellana descended the Amazon in 1542. (Bayle, "El Dorado Fantasma," 200.)

One pictures them as something between a raft and a boat. (With such tools as the builders possessed, they could not have shaped timbers nicely.) Probably they were square-ended scows, made of the straightest pine-trees obtainable, laid side by side, squared willy-nilly, lashed together with fibers and plentifully calked. Cross pieces or thwarts held the sides rigid and served as seats for the rowers. The slightest problems of construction which a ten-year-old boy with half a dozen tools could solve must have reduced the entire camp to desperation. How, for instance, can one make rowlocks rigid enough to bear the constant pressure of the oars, if one has no nails to spare, and no auger to drill holes for thole-pins? Perhaps they contrived some sort of a bow-string drill; perhaps their gunwales were chosen from tree trunks with a succession of projecting branches.

Meanwhile the camp was fed with shell-fish, gathered in the near-by coves and creeks. Ten men were killed by Indians within sight of the camp, while at this employment. Although some wore armor, their bodies were found completely transfixed by arrows.

Before we embarked there died more than forty men of disease and hunger, without enumerating those destroyed by the Indians. By the twenty-second of the month of September, the horses had been consumed, one only remaining; and on that day we embarked in the following order: In the boat of the governor went forty-five men; in another, which he gave to the inspector (Alonso Enríquez) and the clerical delegate (Fray Juan Juárez), went as many others; the third, he gave to Captain Alonso del Castillo Maldonado and Andrés Dorantes, with forty-eight men; and another he gave to two captains, Téllez and Peñalosa, with forty-seven men. The last was given to the quartermaster (Alonso de Solís) and myself, with forty-nine men. After the provisions and clothes had been taken in, not over half a foot of the gunwales remained above water; and more than this, the boats were so crowded that we could not move: so much can necessity do, which drove us to hazard our lives in this manner, running into a turbulent sea, not a single one who went having a knowledge of navigation.

If the barges were thirty-three feet long, as Cabeza de Vaca states, trusting to an eight-year-old memory, the men must have huddled three and four abreast; for we must allow at least three feet by two for a man's body pulling at an oar. Naked under the Florida sun, or clad in deerskins—for their shirts flapped overhead as sails—with a little dried deer meat for food and with their water oozing from their canteens of fresh horsehide, two hundred and forty-seven Spaniards commended their souls to their various saints and turned their leaky craft toward Mexico. "Pánuco" was the word on every lip. Pánuco, the northernmost Spanish settlement in Mexico (near the present Tampico), was the symbol of their deliverance. Witting so little of this world's geography, they thought it might lie around the next headland, or a dozen leagues away.

Eleven years later a party of Soto's men were led by Indians to the spot where Narváez built his boats. They saw there the remains of his iron works, scattered charcoal, the stump of a great felled tree, with the trunk split up into stakes, and the limbs made into mangers. They found also the skulls of horses. Therefore this bay was known to the Spaniards as Bahía de los Caballos, the Bay of the Horses. It gave Soto's men a grim feeling, and perhaps a premonition. Those who were not destined for death in the American forests would in their turn build boats beside the Mississippi and flee to Mexico, under a farewell of arrows.

CHAPTER V

THE JOURNEY BY SEA

For several days the little fleet floundered among the bars and shallows of that vague coast, thrusting aground, pulling loose, and making a new cast for a clear channel. They approached an island, which would seem to be Dog Island, in Franklin County. Some Indians in five canoes came paddling toward them, but at sight of the strange craft swarming with white and bearded men, they fled to shore, leaving their canoes on the beach. The Spaniards landed, and found in the Indian settlement a large provision of dried mullet with their roes. After a memorable banquet, they constructed waistboards from the Indian craft. Thereby they raised the sides of their barges two spans, or sixteen inches, further above the water.

Emerging from St. George's Sound, at the mouth of the Appalachicola River, they saw before them no sheltering islands, only the open Gulf. Though their clumsy, overloaded barges rose heavily on the waves, though they surely leaked as the strain of travel worked their calking loose, though they took water overside in the slightest sea, though in a north wind they would inevitably be carried out to open water, only one course lay open to the mariners.

Again we began to move along the coast in the direction of the River Palmas, our hunger and thirst continually increasing; for our scant subsistence was getting near the end, the water was out, and the bottles made from the legs of the horses, having soon rotted, were useless. Sometimes we entered coves and creeks that lay far in, and found them all shallow and dangerous. Thus we journeyed along them thirty days, finding occasionally Indian fishermen, a poor and miserable lot.

The thirty days which Cabeza de Vaca estimated for his journey from the Bay of Horses to Pensacola Bay, the next identifiable spot, seems far too much, as the single day's journey from Mobile Bay to the Mississippi is far too little. When, eight years after these adventures, he wrote them down, he had no reference but memory, and there was little in the thought of those endless, thirsty, burning, half-mad days of toil along a changeless shore to mark a beginning and an end. What maps he might have seen were the work of theorizing cartographers, based on the experience of two or three explorers in little better case than his own.

They worked northwest and west along a tidal shore. Probably they missed the difficult entrance to Santa Rosa Sound, or, seeing it, dared not enter upon it. At an island which I should guess to be the western end of Santa Rosa Island, they were caught by a storm. They could find no water, and dared not put to sea. "As it was now five days since we had drunk, our thirst was so excessive that it put us to the extremity of swallowing salt water, by which some of the men became so crazed that three or four suddenly died. I state this so briefly, because I do not believe there is any necessity for particularly relating the sufferings and toils amidst which we found ourselves; since, considering the place where we were, and the little hope we had of relief, every one may conceive much of what must have passed." So says our author, with a decent man's disinclination for prolonging pity.

The storm continuing on the sixth day, it became evident that unless they stirred, death from thirst was certain and imminent. The men, fidgeting with inaction, chose to venture out to sea, to die suddenly of a great draught of salt water, rather than to linger at anchor dying of the dry breath in their throats. Commending their souls to God, they hauled in the anchor stones and pulled in the direction of a canoe they had once seen passing. God manifested his capricious favor; at sunset they doubled a point of land, and came into shelter and calm. This welcome haven was, no doubt, Pensacola Bay.

Here many canoes appeared, filled with Indians, large and well-proportioned men. They were unarmed, and gave signs of amity. The Spaniards followed them to their villages near by, at the water's edge, and, on the savages' invitation, jumped out on the shore. Before each dwelling stood earthen jars full of water, and a large quantity of cooked fish. The Indian chief, magnificent in a fragrant coat of marten skins, well recognized the wild eyes of thirst, and waved his visitors to the stored water. With a gesture of invitation he bade the governor and his staff enter his house, a permanent structure of matting laid on a wooden frame.

The Spaniards were treated with Indian courtesy; fish was brought forth and put in their hands. The governor, unaccustomed though he was to this sort of parleying with naked heathens as one would with Catholics, responded in good kind. He had some of the expedition's parched corn brought, and this he presented to the chief. The Indians ate the corn with gusto, and appeared to ask for more. This too the governor gave them; and to the chief he presented many of the trading trinkets with which he was supplied. Some one screamed outside; the village was filled with yells and shouts. Whether by cunning design or by sudden panic at a misunderstood gesture or from anger or dog-like hate the natives fell upon their guests. Three of the sick were killed in this onslaught. Within the chief's house the Indians attacked the governor, wounding him in the face with a stone. Several of the Spaniards clutched at the Indian chief; his braves sprang to his aid and freed him, hustling him out the door and leaving in the Spaniards' hands only the fine marten coat.

In the darkness and confusion it was not difficult to escape to the boats. The governor and the majority of the men embarked and pulled out beyond an arrow's flight from shore. Cabeza de Vaca and fifty of the men in best condition remained on shore to cover the retreat.

Three times the Indians attacked that night, each time so furiously as to drive the Spaniards back more than a stone's throw. Not one of the defenders escaped injury; Cabeza de Vaca was wounded in the face. But fortunately the wounds were slight, such as might be caused by thrown missiles, for the Indians had very few arrows. After the second attack was repulsed, Captains Dorantes, Peñalosa, and Téllez with fifteen men stealthily followed the retreating Indians through the dark, and formed an ambush. When the third wave of the assault surged forward, the hidden Spaniards took the attackers in the rear, so effectively that they turned and fled.

The next morning Cabeza de Vaca broke up more than thirty canoes upon the shore. The men built great fires with the wood, for a cold north wind was blowing, and the sea was too high for their queasy craft. Next day the storm subsided; the expedition set forth, and after three thirsty days came to Mobile Bay.

Turning into an inlet, the wanderers perceived an Indian canoe. They set up a great hallooing, which the natives could recognize as friendly in intention. The Indian canoe approached the governor's flag-ship; he made the sign of a thirsty man drinking; the natives indicated that they would fill containers that the visitors must provide. Suddenly the Greek, Don Dorotheo Theodoro, he who had made pitch from the pine-trees in the Bay of Horses, became uncontrollable. He had had enough of crouching in a thirsty boat; he was bound that he would go with the Indians. In spite of the governor's rebukes and the remonstrances of his friends, he insisted on clambering into the Indian's pirogue, taking with him a negro. The natives allowed two of their number to be taken as hostages by the Christians.

The voyagers moored their barks on some sandy spot. At nightfall the Indians returned; they brought no water, nor did they bring Theodoro and the negro. They cried some words to their two friends on shore, who then suddenly attempted to throw themselves into the sea and return to their own. But the Spaniards caught the hostages and held them fast, and the Indians fled, "leaving us sorrowful and much dejected for our loss."

In the morning a great many natives appeared in canoes, and asked for the return of their hostages. The governor made clear that the surrender of the Spaniards must precede the deliverance of his captives.

With the Indians had come five or six chiefs, who appeared to us to be most comely persons, and of more authority and condition than any we had hitherto seen, although not so large as some others of whom we have spoken. They wore the hair loose and very long, and were covered with robes of marten such as we had before taken. Some of the robes were made up after a strange fashion, with inserted patches of fawn-colored fur, making a brave show. They entreated us to go with them, and said they would give us the Christians, water, and many other things. They continued to collect about us in canoes, attempting in them to take possession of the mouth of that entrance; in consequence, and because it was hazardous to stay near the land, we went to sea, where they remained by us until about midday. As they would not deliver our people, we would not

57

give them theirs; so they began to hurl clubs at us and to throw stones with slings, making threats of shooting arrows, although we had not seen among them all more than three or four bows. While thus engaged, the wind beginning to freshen, they left us and went back.

Cabeza de Vaca does not tell us of the fate of the native hostages. Perhaps the manner of their death was not important. Don Theodoro and the negro, who may well be thought to have voluntarily chosen life among the natives in preference to further seafaring, appear once more in history. In 1540 Soto and his men, who had sought gold in vain from Tampa to North Carolina, were working southwestward through Alabama, by way of Coosa County toward Mauilla or Mobile.

We came to a river, a copious flood, which we considered to be that which empties into the Bay of Chuse. Here we got news of the manner in which the boats of Narváez had arrived in want of water, and of a Christian, named Don Teodoro, who had stopped among these Indians, with a negro, and we were shown a dagger that he had worn.[1]

Thence the voyagers continued west, probably until the increasing shoal water of Lake Borgne warned them of their impasse. Evidently then they retraced their course and found their way into Chandeleur Sound, keeping the low sandy line of the Chandeleurs to port and the amphibious marshes of the mainland to starboard. Finally Cabeza de Vaca found a point of land forming one lip of a great river's mouth. This, at last, was the Mississippi.[2]

The determination of the exact spot at which Cabeza de Vaca paused to look upon the brown waters of the enormous flood is no easy matter. His description does not fit the aspect of the delta to-day, and naturally enough, for during four hundred years the river has been bringing the soil of mountain and prairie to the sea, and the waves and tides of the gulf have been moving the bar sands vaguely to and fro.[3]

[1] The Biedma narrative, in Buckingham Smith, "Narratives of De Soto," 242. The Bay of Chuse was Pensacola Bay, but Soto could not have reached its affluents. The "great river" was either the Coosa or the Alabama. Thus the scene of Don Theodoro's adventure is fixed as Mobile Bay. According to Oviedo (I, 568) Theodoro was put to death by the Indians.

[2] Cabeza de Vaca says, in his narrative, that he arrived here in the afternoon after leaving Mobile Bay. This is an impossibility. Oviedo says "two days," equally impossible.

[3] Now the great rush of water empties into the gulf through South Pass and Southwest Pass, with a secure ten-fathom depth beyond the jetties' end. On the eastward side of the

Enough that Cabeza de Vaca found one of the main mouths of the river, pouring eastward into the gulf. The governor joined him; they dipped fresh water from the sea and drank it. The slaking of thirst brought hunger, and the party disembarked on an island, to parch their corn, which, for two days, they had eaten raw. Finding no firewood there, they decided to cross the river. But once in the stream, they could not by their utmost effort win to the farther shore. The current and a rising north wind bore them steadily from the land. Half a league out they cast the lead, and could not find bottom at thirty fathoms. They recognized, however, that the force of the current disturbed their cast. For two days they struggled to sight the land again, and on the third, a little before dawn, they saw many fires and columns of smoke rising from the shore. They headed toward them, and found themselves in three fathoms of water. On account of the darkness and the dangers of the unknown coast and the possible menace of the fires, they decided to wait till morning before attempting a landing. But a strong offshore current dragged their anchors, mere bags of stones, out again into the deeps.

When day came, the boats had lost sight of each other. I found myself in thirty fathoms. Keeping my course until the hour of vespers, I observed two boats, and drawing near I found that the first I approached was that of the governor. He asked me what I thought we should do. I told him we ought to join the boat which went in advance, and by no means to leave her; and, the three being together, we must keep on our way to where God should be pleased to lead. He answered saying that could not be done, because the boat was far to sea and he wished to reach the shore; that if I wished to follow him, I should order the persons of my boat to take the oars and work, as it was only by strength of arm that the land could be gained. He was advised to this course by a captain with him named Pantoja, who said that if he did not fetch land that day, in six days more they would not reach it, and in that time they must inevitably famish. Seeing his purpose I took my oar, and so did every one his, in my boat. We

delta, North Pass, Pass à Loutre, Northeast Pass, and Southeast Pass do their share. Of these Pass à Loutre alone is held navigable, and that only by small local craft with less than seven-foot draft. But eighteenth-century maps (as in Thomas Jefferys, "History of the French Dominions," 148) show the main exit of the river to be East Pass. Le Page du Pratz ("Histoire de la Louisiane," I, 161), writing in the mid-eighteenth century, says that shipping had abandoned Southeast Pass in favor of East Pass. He adds that nowhere south of Pass à Loutre can one set foot ashore, for the land is only "trembling marshes." The land gains two leagues a century on the sea, he avers.

rowed until near sunset; but the governor having in his boat the healthiest and strongest of all the men, we could not by any means hold with or follow her. Seeing this, I asked him to give me a rope from his boat, that I might be enabled to keep up with him; but he answered that it would be no small task for them to come unhampered to land that night. I said to him, that since he saw the feeble strength we had to follow him, and do what he ordered, he must tell me how he would that I should act. He answered that it was no longer a time in which one should command another; but that each should do what he thought best to save his own life; that he so intended to act; and saying this, he departed with his boat.

As I could not follow him, I steered to the other boat at sea, which waited for me, and having come up, I found her to be the one commanded by the Captains Peñalosa and Téllez.

Thus we continued in company, eating a daily allowance of half a handful of raw maize, until the end of four days, when we lost sight of each other in a storm; and such was the weather that only by God's favor we did not all go down. Because of winter and its inclemency, the many days we had suffered hunger, and the heavy beating of the waves, the people began next day to despair in such a manner that when the sun sank, all who were in my boat were fallen one on another, so near to death that there were few among them in a state of sensibility. Of the whole number at this time not five were on their feet; and when night came, only our boatswain and myself were left, who could work the boat. Two hours after dark, he said to me that I must take charge of her as he was in such condition he believed he should die that night. So I took the steering-oar, and going after midnight to see if the boatswain was alive, he said to me he was rather better, and would steer until day. I declare in that hour I would more willingly have died than seen so many people before me in such condition. After the boatswain took the direction of the boat, I lay down a little while; but without repose, for nothing at that time was farther from me than sleep.

Near the dawn of day, it seemed to me I heard the tumbling of the sea; for as the coast was low, it roared loudly. Surprised at this, I called to the boatswain, who answered me that he believed we were near the land. We sounded and found ourselves in seven fathoms. He advised that we should keep to sea until sunrise; accordingly I took an oar and pulled on the land side, for we were about a league distant from it, and then we turned her stern to the sea. Near the shore a wave took us, that knocked the boat out of water the distance of the throw of a crowbar,[4] and from the violence with which she struck, nearly all the people who were in her

---

[4] *Juego de herradura*, a game played with an iron bar, often a crowbar, which is grasped at the middle and cast as far as possible. (*Note by Buckingham Smith.*)

like dead, were roused to consciousness. Finding themselves near the shore, they began to move on hands and feet, crawling to land into some gullies. There we made fire, parched some of the maize we brought, and found rain-water. From the warmth of the fire the people recovered their faculties, and began somewhat to exert themselves. The day on which we arrived was the sixth of November.

The memory of many thirsty, laboring, mad days has disappeared from this record. Modern students have located the landing-place as San Luis Island, on the Texas coast, southwest of Galveston Island. The seven days the narrative allows for the journey thither from the Mississippi will not suffice; a storm great enough to blow them so far would have sent their rickety craft ashore as driftwood. Cabeza de Vaca's landing-date, November sixth, may be taken as the fallacious result of retrospection. Perhaps one may make a likely correction by subtracting a dozen days from the excess allowance from Florida to the Mississippi and adding them to the insufficient reckoning west of the great river.

These doubts and emendations belong to our critical time. Cabeza de Vaca's grandnephew, writing in the distant Argentina, was deeply impressed by the wanderer's accuracy of reckoning. Cabeza de Vaca, he says, in his eight years' journeying, "never lost the Dominical or Sunday letter, nor the account of the days of the calendar, a proof of his great memory and Christianity." [5]

The counting of those desolate days need not detain us. The voyagers gave thanks to God for warmth and water and his strange caprice in still preserving them alive. Perhaps even hope was in their hearts. If so, it was soon extinguished. This refuge to which they had come was to be christened "la isla de Mal Hado," Bad Luck Island.

[5] Ruy Díaz de Guzmán, in Angelis, "Obras y Documentos del Río de la Plata," I, 50.

CHAPTER VI

BAD LUCK ISLAND

Wᴴᴇɴ the fleshless, bloodless grotesques of men had swallowed their small allowance of parched corn and had got from the driftwood fire a transfusion of warmth which seemed for a moment to be life itself, Cabeza de Vaca, as commander, took what measures of welfare were possible. Near by some trees rose from the sand. Cabeza de Vaca chose Lope de Oviedo as the most vigorous of his ghosts, and bade him climb one of them and see, if he could, some solace or a quick doom. Soon Lope de Oviedo (who is not, by the way, to be confounded with the historian) returned with the news that they were on an island; but—and at this the sodden figures about the camp-fire stirred to attention—the ground was pawed as though by cattle, and hence he judged that it was a land of Christian men! "Go back," said the chief; "go back and look for a path; but beware of going far, into some danger from which we are too weak to rescue you." Oviedo disappeared. "Pánuco!" murmured the men about the fire. "Have we come at last to Pánuco and the home of Christian men?"

Oviedo went again and found a path. He followed it half a league to some huts, with no occupants, for they were out in the shoal waters, pulling roots for food. Searching for some edible thing, he discovered only a little dog and a few mullets. These he put under his arm, and seizing a cooking pot, started back to his companions. Before he had gone far, he was halted by shouts. Turning, he saw three Indians, armed with bows and arrows. Too weak to escape with his spoil, he faced the natives, beckoning them to approach.

Meanwhile Cabeza de Vaca had grown uneasy at Oviedo's long absence. He sent out two other men, who joined Oviedo as he was making his propitiatory signs to the Indians. And these warriors, evidently puzzled and uneasy at the sight of bearded white faces and

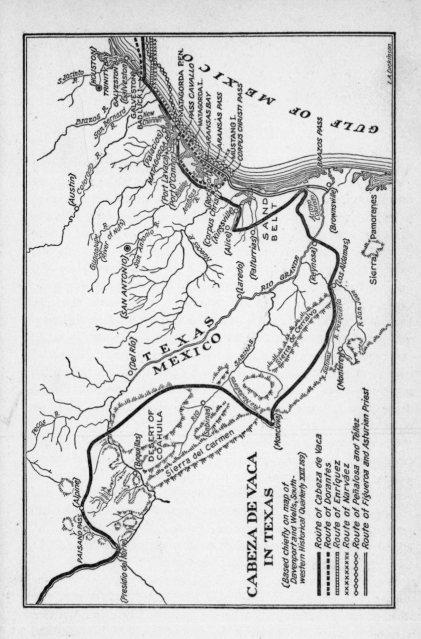

I.A. Dickinson

GULF OF MEXICO

S. Jacinto R. / {HOUSTON} / {Galveston} / GALVESTON TRINITY / Galveston B. / BAD LUCK / New Channel / MATAGORDA PEN. / PASS CAVALLO / MATAGORDA B. / MATAGORDA I. / ARANSAS PASS / ARANSAS BAY / USTANG I. / CORPUS CHRISTI PASS / BRAZOS PASS / Sierra Pamoranes

Brazos R. / San Bernard R. / Colorado R. / {Austin} / Guadalupe R. / (River of Nuts) / San Antonio / {SAN ANTONIO} / {Del Rio}

{Palacios} / MATAGORDA BAY / {Port Lavaca} / {Port O'Connor} / {Port O'Comb} / Anaqua R. / {Refugio} / {Rockport} / {Corpus Christi} / {Kingsville} / {Alice} / {Falfurrias} / Nueces R.

SAND BELT / Arroyo Colorado / {Brownsville}

{Laredo} / RIO GRANDE / {Reynosa} / R. Pesqueria / R. San Juan / Las Aldamas

TEXAS / MEXICO / SABINAS / Sierra de Cerralvo / R. Salinas / {Monterrey}

Pecos R. / DESERT OF COAHUILA / {Boquillas} / RIO (Sabinas) / Sierra del Carmen / Rio Nadadores / {Monclova}

PAISANO PASS / {Alpine} / {Presidio del Norte}

CABEZA DE VACA
IN TEXAS

{Based chiefly on map of
Davenport and Wells, Southwestern Historical Quarterly XXII 259}

▬▬▬▬ Route of Cabeza de Vaca
▬ ▬ ▬ Route of Dorantes
▬▬▬▬ Route of Enriquez
xxxxxxx Route of Narváez
ooooooo Route of Peñalosa and Tellez
▭▭▭▭▭ Route of Figueroa and Asturian Priest

the tatters of strange clothing, sat down uncertainly by the shore. Thus the emissaries returned to camp, to divide their dog and few small fishes among two score men.

It was not half an hour before the whole band of warriors was assembled, a hundred bowmen, "who if they were not large, our fears made giants of them." They stood a little way off from the fire, evidently at a loss between curiosity, hostility, and fear. Had hostility won their minds, it would have gone ill with the Spaniards; "one could hardly have found six among us who could rise from the ground." Cabeza de Vaca and Alonso de Solís, the quartermaster, called to them, with the universal symbols of welcome. Hesitatingly, they drew near. They were tall and well-formed men, brown and naked. Their faces had a queer grinning appearance, for each wore in his pierced lower lip a piece of cane a quarter of an inch in diameter. One or both of their nipples were perforated from side to side; through the holes were thrust reeds an inch thick and more than a foot long.

The treasurer, with smiles and bows, and the most courteous of inflections, put in the hands of the leaders some beads and little bells which fortunately remained. Beads and bells, for some reason, have always been the undoing of the Indian. Crowding together to hear the seductive metallic jingle and to admire the splendid colors of the beads, they submerged hostility under the emotions of curiosity and savage gratitude. Each of them put in Cabeza de Vaca's hand an arrow as a pledge of friendship, indicating by signs that they would return in the morning bringing food, as at the time they had nothing.

And indeed they kept their word. At sunrise a group of envoys appeared, bearing many fish and the edible roots of that country, which were about the size of walnuts, and which were dug under water with much trouble.[1] And in the evening they came again, with a second burden of food, and bringing for a treat, their wives, girdled with Spanish moss, their deerskin-skirted daughters, and the naked children. Their Indian camp had been abuzz with wonder during the day; it was now judged safe for the women and children to approach the sea-

---

[1] This was probably a kind of briar-root. "It contained a farina as palatable and wholesome as arrow-root. The Indians extract this starch by pounding the root and washing it in water." J. H. Kuykendall, in Tex. Hist. Assn. Quar., VII, 131.

born strangers. These had found a new mood of cordiality toward the natives. They who had been conquerors were now reduced to the state of fearful suppliants. They who had come storming through Florida, with death ready for any native who should show reluctance in aid or any grimace of hostility, were now brought to fawning on these dark wild creatures, for the gift of a mouthful of food. It was an important early lesson in their long education in humility.

Around their fire in the evening they recalled the stories of swaggering veterans of the island conquests. They remembered how the Spanish knights would wager that one could behead more dexterously than another, and how the rivals would set forth on horseback, each choosing a native and endeavoring to remove the head cleanly at a single stroke, and so persisting until one or the other had performed the feat and won the bet.[2] Or they would recall how the Spanish in New Granada would raise their dogs on human flesh to make them good man-hunters, and how one would say to a companion: "Give me a quarter of Indian for my dog, and I will give one to you when I kill." [3] The story would remind another of Ponce de León's great man-killing dog, Berecillo, who did such execution that he received a crossbowman's pay on the expedition's books. And then some would be moved to anger, some to despair, and some, even, to a searching of the heart for their sins and for the sins of their fellows.

For several days the Indians came daily with gifts of food. The castaways humbled their pride to cajole the women and amuse the children. "They went back rich with the bells and beads given them." Gradually the Spaniards brought together enough fish, roots, and water to continue on their journey. With bits of driftwood and oyster-shells they dug their boat from the sand. The craft was dragged from the beach through shoal water, with much heaving and many pauses, "we being in such a state that things very much lighter sufficed to make us great labor." To keep their precious rags dry during the launching, all stripped and stowed their possessions on board. When the water deepened sufficiently to float their weight, all climbed in, squatting unbidden on the rough, knotty bottom. They took the oars and headed

[2] Las Casas, "Relation des Voyages," 10.
[3] Las Casas, "Relation des Voyages," 139.

her into the surf. At two crossbow shots from the shore they ran into combers; the clumsy, sodden, overloaded scow rose heavily; the naked men, their hands benumbed under the freezing norther, pulled vainly at the ponderous oars. A wave came overside that doused every man with icy water. The boat turned broadside to the rollers, and the next wave took her and turned her over and shook all her occupants into the sea. The quartermaster, Alonso de Solís, and two others clung to their seats, thinking that this would be safety; therein they erred much, for the capsizing scow held them as under a bell. The others, thrashing in the surf, were taken by a great wave and rejected upon the shore. Following some dim physiological imperative, they crawled out of the sea's promise of oblivion back to the shore of Bad Luck Island.

We survivors escaped naked as we were born, with the loss of all we had; and although the whole was of little value, at that time it was worth much, as we were then in November, the cold was severe, and our bodies were so emaciated the bones might be counted with little difficulty, so that we looked like pictures of Death. For myself I can say that from the previous month of May I had eaten no other thing than toasted maize, and sometimes I found myself obliged to eat it raw; for although the horses were slaughtered while the boats were building, I could never eat their flesh, and I did not eat fish ten times. I state this to avoid giving excuses, and that every one may judge in what condition we were. Besides all these misfortunes, came a north wind upon us, from which we were nearer to death than life. Thanks be to our Lord that, looking among the brands we had used there, we found sparks from which we made great fires. And thus were we asking mercy of him and pardon for our transgressions, shedding many tears, and each regretting not his own fate alone, but that of his comrades about him.

As the sun was sinking, the Indians, still ignorant of the Spaniards' effort to escape, came with their evening gift of food. Seeing their friends naked and huddling about the fire in postures of despair, they turned back in alarm. At this Cabeza de Vaca roused to the necessity; he pursued them, calling, and they halted, although with a show of fear. The captain, by this time skilled in the sign language of those coasts, pictured the sinking of the bark and told of the three drowned companions. He elucidated his signs with a grisly illustration; at the sand's edge two bodies were rolling in the water, like restless sleepers.

65

At this sight the Indians returned, sat down among the castaways, and together set up woeful lamentations, continuing thus for over half an hour. "It was strange to see these men, wild and untaught, like brutes, howling over our misfortunes. It caused in me as in others an increase of feeling and a livelier sense of calamity."

These outcries of despair which so chilled the Spaniards' hearts were, in fact, a savage ritual and not merely a burst of spontaneous sympathy. These tribes were known as "weepers"; La Salle's men, who were in this region in 1685, named them so because, before presenting a request or complaint, they would weep bitterly for half an hour. "They utter their outcries indifferently for good and evil," says Simars de Belle-Isle of a neighboring tribe. Cabeza de Vaca reported, when he knew them better, that when they would meet or visit, they would sit speechless for half an hour, shedding mutual tears. "And, this over, he that is visited first rises and gives the other all he has, which is received, and after a little while he carries it away, and often goes without saying a word."

When the wild voices died away, Cabeza de Vaca made to his fellows a recapitulation of the facts, his grim treasurer's report. Everything was lost, everything, except their rickety bodies, housing their silly hearts, still solemnly pumping. They had come naked as at their birth to what could only be, by God's harmonious dispositions, their death. The deadly norther, growing hourly colder with the dropping of the sun, would have them all by morning. There was only one chance of life: to take shelter in the Indian village.

At this some of the men who had been in Mexico protested. The Indians would only sacrifice them to their gods, tearing out their hearts while the eyes still saw and the mind for a moment understood, rubbing their blood in the matted beards of filthy priests, devouring their arms and legs and other dainties, highly spiced with chile.

Cabeza de Vaca shrugged his shoulders; of two deaths it were best to choose the more remote. He made his request to the Indians; they signified that such a visit would do them great honor. Thirty braves loaded themselves with driftwood and set off; the others remained with the Spaniards until it was almost dark. Then the Indian elders gave the order to start. The tottering whites clasped the sturdy red men;

half carried, half dragged, they were hurried a little way over the ground to a fire the advance party had built. There they rested and recaptured a little warmth and strength. When they were able to proceed their friends brought them to another fire, so swiftly that their feet hardly were allowed to touch the ground. There were four or five such fires, and at the end the native village, where was a house prepared, with many fires. "An hour after our arrival, they began to dance and hold great rejoicing, which lasted all night, although for us there was no joy, festivity nor sleep, awaiting the hour they should make us victims. In the morning they again gave us fish and roots, showing us such hospitality that we were reassured, and lost somewhat the fear of sacrifice."

Food, shelter, the warmth of the new day's sun, the sense of kindness the Indians bestowed, and the realization that somehow they had come alive out of the black pit of their despair, brought a vague movement of hope. Cabeza de Vaca stirred about in the camp, asking questions with signs and grunts. In one Indian's hand he noticed a trinket which seemed familiar. And yet it had not been in the boat he captained; of that he was sure. "Whence?" he inquired, pointing to the trinket. The native understood. "From men like you!" he indicated. "Behind!" He pointed to the northeast.

Cabeza de Vaca chose the two stoutest of his men and two Indians and bade them begone to the northeast. They had no need to go far; only a little way outside the camp they met Andrés Dorantes, Alonso del Castillo Maldonado, and all their crew, coming in search of Cabeza de Vaca and his men. The newcomers were shocked indeed to see the state of their friends, regretting much that they could be of no aid, for they themselves possessed only the few clothes they wore.

Dorantes had a dismal tale to tell. He and his men were cast ashore northeastwardly on the same island, on November fifth, the day before Cabeza de Vaca's shipwreck. They saved their possessions and their lives. It was then decided that those who still retained sufficient strength should continue their journey by boat, while the weaker should remain on the island until they might make their way to Pánuco by land. This project—which may well be taken as a statement that the weak were to be abandoned by the strong—came to no good end. Their craft foundered when it was launched, and the strong were thrown on shore, to make common cause with the weak. All their gear was lost in the sea. One of their number died; the rest, hearing from the natives of other survivors, set forth in search of them.

The combined parties took counsel together. It seemed certainly vain to attempt a further journey in the winter weather. Naked as they were, without food or means of transport, they could not hope to swim the rivers and penetrate whatever jungles might lie between them and Mexico. Better to huddle on their island through the winter, gathering strength for a determined effort when spring should bring warmth and some provision of fruits and other food. In the meantime four of the strongest men and best swimmers were chosen to make their way, with God's help, to Pánuco. Who could tell? Perhaps the Spanish settlement lay in the lee of the next cape! Perhaps within a week a rescue ship might stand off Bad Luck Island!

The four men were Figueroa of Toledo, Astudillo of Zafra, Méndez, and Alvaro Fernández, a Portuguese sailor and carpenter. They took with them an Indian. He led them to the channel—now filled in—that separated Bad Luck Island from the mainland, just east of the mouth of Oyster Creek. There they said farewell, after such leave-takings and such prayers, flatteries, and soft words to the saints as one may well imagine. They came easily to the main, waved finally, and dwindled westward, walking resolutely.

The remaining Spaniards and their Indian hosts readily recognized that they could not all remain in one place. When the castaways' strength permitted, they were divided into groups and quartered upon the various Indian settlements along the island. As one reads the account of the natives' barely-won struggle to keep themselves alive, one honors them for their acceptance of this intolerable burden, eighty hungry, helpless, useless men. The weather turned so cold and stormy that the Indians could not fish nor pull their roots in the submerged fields. Hunger and cold assailed Christian and pagan; the pagan suffered, but without complaint; the Christian's hunger drove him mad. The Indians, coming to visit a refuge of five Spaniards at a little distance, discovered an evil sight. Five bodies lay there; and the flesh of four bodies had been eaten.

The Indians returned to the main camp, furious with anger. Their good-will changed to threats and blows. "Had they known it in season to have done so, doubtless they would have destroyed any survivor." Their indignation was due, probably, to the proof that the Spaniards had succumbed to a temptation which they were trained to resist till death. Hunger was the very condition of their lives. "So protracted was the hunger we there experienced, that many times I was three days without eating. The natives also endured as much; and it appeared to me a thing impossible that life could be so prolonged, although afterwards I found myself in greater hunger and necessity." After any spell of the bad luck familiar on Bad Luck Island there would be starved bodies to be lightly covered over with sand. A dim sense of social welfare forbade the natives to learn the taste of their fellows.

And yet these tribes were later known as cannibals. The island seems to have been the dividing line between two cultures, races, and languages, the Attácapas, occupying the coast to the east, and the Karánkawas, whose range extended southwardly to the Rio Grande. The very name Attacapa means man-eater. In 1719 a French gentleman, Simars de Belle-Isle, was abandoned with three companions on the shore of Galveston Bay. The companions died; Belle-Isle subsisted on shell-fish, boiled grass, and the maggots in rotten wood. *"Je trouvay cela bien bon."* Taken prisoner by the Attacapas, he was brutally mishandled. He was present when an enemy was captured, dismembered, and entirely devoured, while the women danced with joy, waving the gnawed bones.[4] The Karankawas bore a similar reputation among early explorers and settlers.[5] But as Cabeza de Vaca specifically states that he saw no native cannibalism in all his progress, one must conclude that the practice arose in later times.

A bitter winter descended upon the Spaniards. Disease came to aid in the work of hunger and cold. A native plague visited them, infecting the bowels. It was perhaps the cholera called matlazahuatl, which caused great mortality in Mexico in 1545.[6] It was not long before the survivors of the two boat-loads were reduced from eighty to fifteen.

[4] Margry, "Mémoires et Documents," VI, 339.
[5] Gatschet, "The Karankawa Indians," 27.
[6] Coopwood, in Texas Hist. Assn. Quar., III, 110.

The plague spread to the Indians, whereof half their number died. The savage mind, like any civilized mind, argued from the strange effect to the preceding strange occurrence as the cause. The assembled braves were of the belief that the Christians were sorcerers, and that their spell of death could only be exorcised by the sacrifice of the survivors. This opinion was contested by Cabeza de Vaca's master, who expounded the view that, if the white-faced men were sorcerers, they would certainly not have decimated their own numbers; and if they had the power to check the plague, they would first have saved their own kind. This logic nonplussed the assembly, and the decree of death was rescinded. "In the condition in which they were, it was more cruelty to the Spaniards to leave them alive and not to kill them, than thus pitifully to keep them in such suffering, hunger, and torture." [7]

Still the idea persisted that these strange sea-born men must possess the secrets of healing.

They wished to make us physicians without examinations or inquiring for diplomas. They cure by blowing upon the sick, and with that breath and the imposing of hands they cast out infirmity. They ordered that we also should do this, and be of use to them in some way. We laughed at what they did, telling them it was folly, that we knew not how to heal. In consequence, they withheld food from us until we should practise what they required. Seeing our persistence, an Indian told me I knew not what I uttered, in saying that what he knew availed nothing; for stones and other matters growing about in the fields have virtue and that he, passing a pebble along the stomach, could take away pain and restore health, and certainly then we who were extraordinary men must possess power and efficacy over other things.

At length their masters' threats forced them to undertake the risky trade of the healer. They learned the therapeutics of the island medicine men; these were simple enough, and similar to those of other neighboring tribes. The practitioner made some cuts where the pain was felt, and sucked the skin around the incisions. They also cauterized with fire, a method which Cabeza de Vaca himself found to be beneficial, probably in the arresting of infections. Afterwards they blew on the seat of the pain, and thus gave the patient to understand that his illness was healed.

[7] Oviedo, III, 591.

This means of cure was practised among far-distant races, among whom it had probably developed from the same impulsions and by the same simple reasoning. Jacques Le Moyne, who was among the Timu-cua Indians of Florida in 1564, describes the medicine man's procedure in gashing the patient's forehead, sucking the blood, and discharging it into a bowl as a tonic for women.[8] Le Page du Pratz, who went out to Louisiana in 1718, says that after he had suffered four months with sciatica, in spite of the best efforts of the French doctor, a Natchez medicine man cured him by gashing the seat of pain and sucking for a half-hour.[9]

Cabeza de Vaca's phrase, "I have tried cauteries myself, and had good success with them," makes clear that he and his companions used all practical means of healing with which they were acquainted. In spite of the low state of medical knowledge in Europe—it was not until 1537 that Ambroise Paré concluded that the treatment of gun-shot wounds with boiling oil was a mistake—the Spaniards must have brought with them some simple maxims, manipulations, and soldiers' first-aid devices, that would be useful in their island practice. How-ever, it was not to these that they trusted, but to the continuing aid and benevolence of their Lord and Master, to whom they paid the touching tribute of unwavering faith.

Our method was to bless the sick, breathing upon them, and recite a Pater-noster and an Ave Maria, praying with all earnestness to God our Lord that he would give health and influence them to make us some good return. In his clemency he willed that all those for whom we supplicated, should tell the others that they were sound and in health, directly after we made the sign of the blessed cross over them. For this the Indians treated us kindly; they deprived themselves of food that they might give to us, and they presented us with skins and some trifles.

The medicine-man, whose craft was considered a form of sorcery, was the most honored member of the tribe, for Cabeza de Vaca's captors had no chief and no priest. The medicine-man, or shaman, had special privileges; he was allowed two or three wives, who lived together in friendship and harmony. In case of a cure, the grateful

[8] Ningler, "Voyages en Virginie et Florida," 266.
[9] "Histoire de la Louisiane," I, 135.

patient would give the healer all his possessions, and also those that he could command from his relatives. Even in death the shaman did not share the lot of ordinary mortals. He was not buried but burned, and around his pyre the tribe danced and made high festivity until his bones became powder. And after a year his funeral honors were celebrated, and the dust of his bones was presented in water for his relatives to drink.

Thus, in their rôle as sorcerers, the surviving Spaniards came somehow through the winter of 1528-29. Their position of honor among the savages rendered their lives for the moment secure, and made them confident of a share in what food the hunters and fishers could find. This was little enough; only the mysterious truffle-like root, painfully extracted from under water, and fish, probably red-fish, sea-trout, flounders, sheep's head, Spanish mackerel and jew-fish. These were captured in cane weirs or traps, or by shooting with arrows from canoes. The skill of these coastal Indians with bow and arrow deeply impressed the settlers three hundred years later. They stood hip-deep in the water, motionless, with bow drawn, until the quarry, unsuspicious of those rock-like legs, swam within range. Their aim was unerring, and their success greater than that of white men with hook and line. It was said that they could feel the approach of fish through roiled water by the undulations beneath the surface.

Two tribes, the Capoques or Cahoques, and the Hans, of different language, dwelt on the island. The Cahoques are probably identical with the Cocos who occupied this region in 1778. These Cocos were Karankawas—tall, well-built, naked men, the most primitive of native races, blood-thirsty, brutish, hostile to the whites, and said on good authority to be cannibals.[10] Of the Hans we know no more than Cabeza de Vaca tells us; presumably they were the Attacapas of Simars de Belle-Isle's narrative.

Cabeza de Vaca recognized in his Karankawa hosts simple virtues of fidelity to which later settlers were blind. They were generous and affectionate; no people in the world could equal them in their love and gentleness toward their children. When a child died the whole village wept for him, at dawn, noon, and sunset, for a year. When that mourning

10 H. E. Bolton, "The Founding of Mission Rosario," Tex. State Hist. Quar., X, 115.

HEALING AMONG THE TIMUCUA INDIANS

At the left, a medicine man is sucking a cut he has made in the patient's forehead. He spits the blood in a bowl, to be drunk by mothers to purify their milk. At the right, a patient is having his head fumigated with a fire of herbs, to induce vomiting. In the rear, an Indian is smoking "tapaco," to dissolve the evil humors.

period was done, they performed the rites of the dead; then they washed and purified themselves of their charcoal paint. "They lament all the deceased in this manner, except the aged, for whom they show no regret, as they say that their season has passed, and they are no longer of any use, but rather they cumber the earth and take food from the young."

And there was another custom of these grieving and melancholy Indians, a disastrous custom indeed. When a son or brother died, all the occupants of his house remained in seclusion for a month, choosing rather to die of hunger than to go for food. The others of the tribe brought to their doors any surplus above their bare need. But in this time of plague there was a dead son in almost every lodge; the few who were permitted to fish could in no way cope with the universal hunger. February was coming to an end, and the truffle-like root, beginning to grow, was no longer edible. The tribal council, therefore, decided to leave the island, and to seek some means of survival upon the mainland.

Cabeza de Vaca accepted the decision with various emotions. His eyes were ever turning southward, whence some day help might come, a Spanish coaster with Figueroa or Méndez in the look-out. That little chance was nearly all that remained to spur him to the daily struggle with death. If some bright morning—it might be to-morrow—the sloop should anchor off shore, and Figueroa should identify the spot, and the Spaniards should land to find only the faint spoor of man with the sand drifting over, what would they do? They could only have their priest sing a requiem and make some few blind explorations and turn south again, forever. However, as death took the castaways one by one, as the days passed with no answer to hope, Cabeza de Vaca knew well in his heart that the messengers had never found their way through innumerable perils to Pánuco. Even if they were not dead, Cabeza de Vaca himself would soon be so, if he lingered on the island. Better to go inland with his masters, where food would be more plentiful. Better anything than these lancing pangs of hunger. Better resign oneself to God's will, and His inscrutable purpose, and His mysterious favor.

It would seem that by this time Cabeza de Vaca's period of honor as a physician was at an end. Probably the continuance of the plague

73

had turned his early triumphs to disgrace, aggravated by the disappointment of the savages' hopes. Stripped of his authority, he was set to the hardest labors of the community life. As he had no skill with bow and arrow, he was given the womanish task of pulling the submerged roots from among the sharp salt-marsh rushes. "From this employment I had my fingers so tender that at but a straw's touch they would bleed. Many of the canes were broken, so they often tore my flesh, and I had to go in the midst of them with only the clothing on I have mentioned."

It was very cold when the northers blew. Once hail and snow came down together. He had no clothes, or only the thinnest rags from the dead bodies of his friends.

But probably nothing mattered greatly now to Cabeza de Vaca. Weak, almost starved, light-headed, he could not think much nor feel much. He obeyed dully, perhaps only wondering a little at the ridiculous persistency of life.

CHAPTER VII

THE WILDERNESS

WITH the returning spring, Cabeza de Vaca's masters put their few possessions—weapons, utensils, mat lodges, and their slave —in their dug-outs, and ferried over to the mainland. The slave roused from the habitual torpor of hunger as he saw new shores rise while Bad Luck Island dwindled. Behind him lay his friends, and the dear cajoling hope of rescue. Behind him lay Spain, a recurring fantastic dream, and the memory of a proud and valiant gentleman, commanding obedient soldiers, and confident in his own wisdom of counsel. Wisdom, indeed! By what wisdom were Christians led from the estate God had indicated for them, to affront the wilderness, to violate those secret lands which God, with inscrutable purpose, chose to hold in darkness? Were these dark brutes, with canes jiggling at mouth and breast, sons of Adam, partakers of his sin? Had Christ's blood been shed to save them? Were they not rather demoniac creatures, to whom the Christians were delivered for their manifold sins and wickedness, and especially for their interference with God's designs? Cabeza de Vaca furtively crossed himself.

A year before, in the tropic warmth of February's end, the expedition had been setting forth from Cuba. Bad Luck had led them from that hour. Pride had been their sin and their undoing, pride and the lust of mundane vanities. They had forgotten that this world is but a short road to the next, that our pleasures here are brief, but our pains in hell eternal. God had taken from them first their presumptuous dreams of wealth; then he had stripped them of their weapons and fine armor and all their worldly goods; then he had treated them to the tortures of purgatory; and when the lesson was finished, he had put them one by one to death. If Cabeza de Vaca was yet alive, it could be only because his lesson was not yet completed. Still some scrap of pride persisted, still some protest. He could not die until he should withdraw his protest, and recognize that God's wisdom was infinitely good, until pride, self-will, and selfhood were dead in his heart. There were darker defiles yet to be traversed in the valley of the shadow; there was an ultimate despair reserved for his training in humility.

The canoes grounded on the marshy shore of Oyster Bay. The slave was put to work setting up the mat houses on shell mounds as a dry foundation, and digging the shell-fish which were to be his sole food for three months. The water was brackish, rousing rather than allaying thirst. Swarms of mosquitoes dwelt here, coming to hungry new life in the spring. (Simars de Belle-Isle, when stripped of his clothes and turned loose in this region, was obliged to spend the nights in water up to his neck. Among the Louisiana marsh-dwellers, the supreme vengeance was to stake down one's enemy, naked; the mosquitoes would kill him by morning. The Karankawa Indians in later times would protect themselves from the pests by anointments of shark oil, most offensive of smell.)

After about two or three months (the end of April, 1529) the tribe removed to the seashore, presumably near where Oyster Creek flows into the gulf. Here, among the red geraniums, the foragers found black dewberries and various herbs, sufficient to prolong life until the next stage in their round of wretchedness.

And here Cabeza de Vaca fell deathly sick, very likely with malaria, and while he was in his delirium a group of the surviving Spaniards came, and learned that he was doomed and helpless, and pushed on southward to the Christian land, leaving him behind.

When he returned to consciousness and found himself lying, too weak for movement but with comprehending mind, his masters told him, with a savage humor, of the coming and going of his friends. In witness thereof they brought forth the fine coat of marten skins, once the pride of the Creek chieftain of Pensacola Bay. This, the last possession of the Christians, had been given as a fee for ferriage of the party to the mainland.

As Cabeza de Vaca was later to learn, this band of survivors consisted of twelve men. In command was Andrés Dorantes, co-commander of one of the boats wrecked on Bad Luck Island. With him were his two cousins, Diego Dorantes and Pedro de Valdivieso, and his slave, Estebanico, a negro from Azamor, on the Atlantic coast of Morocco. The others were Captain Alonso del Castillo, Estrada, Tostado, Chaves, Gutiérrez, Diego de Huelva, Benítez, and an Asturian priest.

These had been quartered during the winter among various Indian groups, on the island and on the mainland. Estebanico the black and the Asturian cleric had spent that time on Galveston Island. Andrés Dorantes and Castillo, ever the stoutest of heart and body, set themselves in April to assembling all the survivors for a final southward effort. There is no sign of reluctance on the part of the Indians to lose the Christians, their clumsy and incompetent servants, idle mouths, weak and sickly, frighteners of fish and less than women at root-pulling. All gathered on Bad Luck Island and Andrés Dorantes mustered his little army of skeletons. Besides the twelve just mentioned two more answered to the roll. These were Jerónimo de Alañiz, the notary, and Lope de Oviedo, who had had the strength to climb a tree at the time of the first shipwreck. Fever and hunger had not only dried their muscles but had got into their brains, paralyzing desire. Alañiz could not move and Oviedo would not. Well then, let them stay and rot. This was no time for court manners. The twelve who could still feel the burning of hope would make their way together, and die, perhaps, but die with their faces to the south.

On the mainland they found another companion, Francisco de León. They learned also of Cabeza de Vaca, and of his state, but on receiving word of his desperate illness they passed on. He could not keep their pace; probably he would soon be dead.

But Cabeza de Vaca did not die. Understanding flowed gradually back into his mind, drowning the little spark of hope that still persisted. His companions had passed by, they had left him behind. The rescue-ship of which he had dreamed would never come, for if the survivors should win to Pánuco, they would report that they had left only three dying men. In fact, they would probably avoid criticism by presuming that the dying men were already dead. He had come to the uttermost despair; there was no more hope at all.

When the dewberry season was over, there were certain roots like onions to eat, perhaps mulberries also, and fish, when luck was in. If luck was out, the tribe ate "very large spiders" (tarantulas?), lizards, snakes, and rats. Occasionally a hunter would bring down a deer, probably one of the plains antelope. We have no mention of bison. There was no maize, for the Indians did not attempt to cultivate the soil. Only of hunger was there any surety.

When Cabeza de Vaca was fit to stand, he was put to work with a wooden hoe, digging roots under the earth and under water. Every day he brought loads of driftwood on his bare back to the camp-fire. When the tribe moved its camp, as it did every three or four days in search of food, the Treasurer of His Majesty the Emperor Charles V shouldered the mat lodges of his savage masters. He had descended from his pride to the most abject estate of any human creature. He who had turned away from the flesh of horses would now fall gustfully upon a rat or a lizard. There was no ease for his body anywhere, and no flickering of cheer in his mind save in the hope of death.

Here, in the extremest pitch of despair, he found the full meaning of humility. He never questioned his God's purpose nor doubted divine goodness. Chopping at the stubborn roots with his wooden hoe, he praised God for his mysterious bounty. Into his soul, purged of all pride and of every evil growth that feeds on spiritual ease, came God's gift of courage.

Cabeza de Vaca was never again to walk among the shadows of this time. Before him lay hunger more terrible than any he had yet endured, and labors, stripes, and pain, and every peril of the wilderness. The messengers of Satan were to buffet him, as of old they had buffeted Saint Paul. "And the Lord said unto me, My grace is sufficient for thee: for my strength is made perfect in weakness. Most gladly therefore will I rather glory in my infirmities, that the power of Christ may rest upon me. Therefore I take pleasure in infirmities, in reproaches, in necessities, in persecutions, in distresses for Christ's sake: for when I am weak, then I am strong." Whether or not he remembered the words of the apostle, he must have murmured such thoughts; for he was making the same pilgrimage to the peace of God.

A year went by. Some time in the course of it the tribe returned to Bad Luck Island. There Cabeza de Vaca found Lope de Oviedo alone, for Jerónimo de Alañiz, the notary, had died an un-notarial and undocumented death. Lope had ceased to protest; he had no thought but the chance of catching a fish which he might devour in secret. When Cabeza de Vaca eagerly talked of escape, Lope would not listen. He would go no farther. Death might come to him, and any day it might appear; why should he go to seek it? There was nothing in the world but sunshine and a full belly. Let Alvar Núñez do what he wished. He would not stir.

This was just the sort of talk to feed Cabeza de Vaca's purpose. Escape he would, with God to guide him. For an idea, a fantastic hope, was taking shape in his mind. As the tribe moved back and forth along the coast, they would meet occasionally groups of other friendly clans, with whom long haggling and bargaining was undertaken. At these assemblies the white man with the hairy face was always the center of curiosity. There were certain Indians from Charruco,[1] inhabiting the woods of the mainland, whom he had cautiously sounded out. Why yes, they would welcome him to their tribe, if he would bring, as he promised, a load of sea-shells, to be used as knives, and shell-beads and fish.

The escape to the men of Charruco took place after Cabeza de Vaca had passed more than a year in the hands of the Cahoques. We have no details; but it is fair to suppose that when, in February 1530, the tribe removed from the island to the mainland, Cabeza de Vaca found a means of absconding by night with a load of seashore articles of commerce.

The warmth of his reception left no doubt of its sincerity. Thereby he was emboldened to put into practice the first part of his scheme. As a neutral, he had trading privileges forbidden to tribal members, in the midst of the incessant feuds of the seaboard. As a physical freak, he could ingratiate himself and his wares according to the ancient devices of the peddler. By such a course he could seek the way to his salvation.

The plan fell out to his utmost satisfaction. With the assistance of the friendly Charrucos, he established a trading enterprise. From the coast he brought shells and cockles, for the making of beads, and large conchs used for knives, especially for cutting a bean-like fruit used

---

[1] Unidentifiable by any later records.

as medicine and in the ritual dances. These he bartered for deerskins, perhaps even buffalo hides, tassels of deer's hair, dyed red, red ochre for painting faces and dyeing hair, hard canes for arrow-shafts and flints for the heads, and glue to hold them together.

This occupation suited me well; for the travel allowed me to go where I wished, I was not obliged to work, and was not a slave. Wherever I went I received fair treatment, and the Indians gave me to eat out of regard to my commodities. My leading object, while journeying in this business, was to find out the way by which I should go forward, and I became well known. The inhabitants were pleased when they saw me, and I brought them what they wanted; and those who did not know me sought and desired the acquaintance, for my reputation. The hardships that I underwent in this were long to tell, as well of peril and privation as of storms and cold. Oftentimes they overtook me alone and in the open field; but I came forth from them all by the great mercy of God our Lord.

In the winter, when the natives withdrew to their huts, torpid, with life's fires banked against the spring, he retired from business and practised hibernation as well as he might. Then when the rains were over, and warm awakening breezes blew from the gulf, and the prairies turned suddenly green with an over-pattern of the early white flowers, he sought some stay for his raging hunger, and then prepared his peddler's pack. His friends the Indians greeted him as later they did La Salle, rubbing their hands on their own breasts, then on the breast of the visitor, and as a mark of special friendship, blowing in the honored guest's ear. The hawker told the winter's news, communicating partly by sign language, partly in the common phrases of the racial tongue, with utterance which sounded to Joutel, La Salle's lieutenant, like the clucking of a hen shepherding her chickens. Long arguments would follow concerning the worth of his wares. The interlocutors spoke with averted faces, with long interruptions of silence. Sometimes a flash of unbidden memory would reveal to the chafferer, warily testing a snake-skin, his former business dealings with kings and governors. Perhaps he smiled, when a reeking barbarian worsted in a bargain the Treasurer of His Majesty the Emperor Charles V.

He would be offered food, and would gravely accept, unwinking when his host put a bare foot on a piece of deer meat, to steady it while he cut off a titbit with a conch-shell knife. *"Il ne faudrait pas parmi eux des gens bien délicats,"* said Joutel, noting this item. Often he was present at the religious festivals, celebrated at the full of the moon, or after a very successful hunting or fishing expedition. The warriors gathered about a fire, on which was brewing their black drink, made of the leaves of the yaupon, an evergreen shrub. From time to time, the officiant stirred the bitter drink with a whisk to a yellowish froth. It was then solemnly drunk in large quantities by all the celebrants. "It never seemed to produce any visible effect on the Indians," says an eye-witness,[2] and that is strange, for the yaupon is known as *ilex vomitoria,* and the Creeks still use it for their ceremony of purification.

One tall Indian, probably a chief, stood within the circle and passed round and round the fire, chanting in a monotonous tone. He was a grotesque figure, being wrapped up to his head in skins, and his face concealed; his long, black hair streamed over his back, and he bent nearly double as he moved about, seldom raising himself to an erect posture. The chant rose and fell in a melancholy sort of cadence, and occasionally all the Indians joined in the chorus, which was *Há-i-yah, Há-i-yah; haí, haí-yah, haí-yah, haí-yah.* The first two words were shouted slowly, then a loud haí, then a succession of haí-yahs very rapidly uttered in chromatic ascending and descending tones, ending in an abrupt haí! very loud and far reaching. There were three instruments of music, upon which the Indians accompanied the chant. One, a large gourd filled with small stones, or shot, was frequently shaken;[3] another was a fluted piece of wood, which was held upon the knees of the player and over which a stick was quickly drawn, producing a droning noise; the third was a kind of rude flute, upon which no air was played, but which was softly blown in time to the chant.[4]

Cabeza de Vaca adds other interesting details in his account of the black drink. The yaupon leaves were toasted in an earthen pot; then the vessel was filled with water. When it had twice boiled, it was poured into halves of gourds for cooling, and whipped to froth, and then drunk as hot as it could be borne. From the time of the first decanting until it was drunk all shouted "Who wants to drink?" When the women heard these cries, they had to stop still, and if any one of

---

[2] Alice W. Oliver, in Gatschet: "The Karankawa Indians," 18.
[3] Cabeza de Vaca first saw these gourds farther south.
[4] Alice W. Oliver, *ut sup.*

them moved she was beaten with sticks, and the prepared liquor was poured out, and those who had drunk vomited it forth, which, according to Cabeza de Vaca, they did very easily and without any trouble. For, they said, if a woman stirred, an evil and death-bringing substance entered into the drink. Further, the drink had to be covered while boiling; if it were open and a woman passed by, custom required that the whole be poured away. In the three days of the festival the communicants ate nothing, but each drank daily six gallons of the black drink.

Not only in the festivals of peace, but in war as well was Cabeza de Vaca the companion of the wild men. Once when he was among the Doguenes, their tribal enemies the Quevenes surprised his hosts at midnight, killed three, wounded many, and drove the remainder into the open country. But when the pursuit ceased, the Doguenes rallied, returned to the camp to pick up the arrows that had been shot, and then stealthily made their way to the camp of their enemies. They attacked at dawn, killed five, left many wounded and captured a fine lot of bows as spoils of war. Shortly afterward a peace mission of the Quevenes appeared, in the form of a committee of women. A parley was held, and peace declared and for a time the two tribes became friends. "Sometimes, however, the women are the cause of war."

War, ranging from personal feuds to large tribal hostilities, was constantly in progress among these cruel and combative peoples. Individuals settled their disputes with their fists, fighting until they were exhausted. Sometimes the women parted them; the men never. After such a quarrel the disputants took their lodges and retired to the open country for some days, until their heat had subsided. Sometimes they joined neighboring peoples, even though hostile, and were well received by them. When time had purified the bad blood, they would return to their own, rich with gifts from their temporary hosts, and all animosity would be forgotten.

The inter-tribal wars bred in the natives great military ingenuity. "They have as much strategy for protecting themselves against enemies as they could have were they reared in the continual wars of Italy." When in the presence of danger, they encamped on the edge of a wood, the thickest they could find. They dug trenches at its skirt, covering them over with branches, with peep-holes arranged therein. In the trenches, securely hidden, the warriors slept. A narrow way was opened to the middle of the wood, where the women and children lay. Then deceptive fires were lit to lure the enemy, and if he took the bait the warriors sprang out from their trench ambush and did great slaughter. If there was no forest they dug trenches in the open prairie, similarly masked and with loop-holes for shooting arrows; and then they enticed their foes into the range of these nests.

They were the readiest people with their weapons of any in the world, testifies our author. In enemy country they lay awake the night through, with bow taut and a dozen arrows ready. They fought crouching, and while winging their shafts they talked and dodged about, avoiding the foemen's arrows. In general, reported Cabeza de Vaca, the Indians mock at the white man's crossbows and muskets; these are of most service in defiles and in swamps. Their chief fear is of horses, and by these they may be conquered.

Whosoever would fight them must be cautious to show no fear, or desire to have anything that is theirs; while war exists they must be treated with the utmost rigor; for if they discover any timidity or covetousness, they are a race that well discern the opportunities for vengeance, and gather strength from the weakness of their adversaries. I believe these people see and hear better, and have keener senses than any other in the world. They are great in hunger, thirst, and cold, as if they were made for the endurance of these more than other men, by habit and nature. Thus much I have wished to say, beyond the gratification of that desire men have to learn the customs and manners of each other, that those who hereafter at some time find themselves amongst these people, may have knowledge of their usages and artifices, the value of which they will not find inconsiderable in such event.

Among these peoples Cabeza de Vaca the trader lived, sharing their food and their hunger, speaking their tongues and learning the habits of their minds. He found the way to turn hostility to welcome, how to please the women and how to amuse the children. He could shout haí-yah to the shuffling dance, and drink the *ilex vomitoria* by the gallon. He traveled far into the interior, and forty or fifty leagues along the coast. And one cautious question was forever on his lips, one constant and undimming purpose in his mind. What lay to the south?

When could he start on that long journey from which he would not return?

Only one thing held him back. One Spaniard, Lope de Oviedo, still dwelt on Bad Luck Island. "To get him out from there, I went over to the island each year, and entreated him that we should go, in the best way we could contrive, in quest of Christians. He put me off each year, saying in that next coming we would start." The spring of all Oviedo's purpose was broken. Long starvation and the sight of such abundant death had brought him to a hopeless atony. He would not dream of Spain and its delights; he would make no effort, would dare no new dangers. As he could not swim, he was afraid of the rivers lying ahead. Rather he would drift heedless and unthinking to his death. Perhaps, as the text faintly suggests, he had mated with a native woman, stinking with fish-oil, and he would not leave without her.

When the needs of trade permitted, Cabeza de Vaca would go to Bad Luck Island. The two men embraced, and tasted the strange pleasure of talking in stumbling Spanish. Cabeza de Vaca broached his project, and Lope put forward his petty hangdog objections. Ever they would part in high anger, Cabeza de Vaca vowing to wait no more, but to set off on a solitary search for rescue. And then, bearing his pack through the wilderness, he found it impossible to abandon his futile companion on that ill-fated shore. Through all the slowly shifting torments of another year he remained faithful to his companion and steadfast to the honor of a Spanish gentleman.

It was apparently in the late summer of 1532 that Cabeza de Vaca's fire melted the numbed heart of Lope de Oviedo. He ferried that reluctant body to the mainland; if with the cognizance of the Malhado Indians, we are not told. The two made their way along the coast, by routes that Cabeza de Vaca had certainly charted in advance. They swam Oyster Creek, with Lope de Oviedo clinging to the shoulders of his tormenting savior. The Brazos River, with its strong current, they must have crossed by canoe or raft. It is not impossible that Cabeza de Vaca asked the favor of ferriage from some of his business friends. A few miles farther, they forded the San Bernard River, and, beyond that, they parted the green slime that covers Caney Creek. Thence for several days they plodded the fifty-mile length of Matagorda Peninsula,

84

that interminable sand-bar, dividing the sea from Matagorda Bay. Along the barren spit they had no food but shell-fish and a sort of sea-weed. At its tip, now Decros Point, they looked across Pass Cavallo to the sand-hills rising on Matagorda Island. Here the pilgrims found a settlement of Doguenes, whom Cabeza de Vaca had visited before, and among whom he had experienced the night attack from the Quevenes.

This was the limit of Cabeza de Vaca's previous journeyings. Now he must venture into strange lands and among unknown peoples. His friends the Doguenes transported the two across the pass, probably to the mainland near Port O'Connor. A band of Quevenes awaited them on the farther shore. They came boldly to land; the white men and "some women" disembarked; the obliging ferrymen shouted farewell and turned back across the gap.

A parley followed. The grinning Quevenes informed the newcomers that not far away, to the south, were two other white-faced men and one black-faced. "Who? What are their names?" cried Cabeza de Vaca. By dint of much questioning and trial of names it was determined that these three were Andrés Dorantes, Alonso del Castillo, and Estebanico. And the others? The Indians made a sign of ignorance. Dead of cold, of hunger, of despair. And the living, in what state were they? In very bad state indeed, replied the Quevenes, with an air of humorous delight. The men and boys kicked them, slapped their faces, and beat them with sticks all day, for fun. "Thus!" they explained, falling upon Lope and Cabeza de Vaca with their six-foot bows. So for several days they repeated their joke, which never lost its savor. "Many times they threw lumps of mud at us, and every day they put their arrows to our hearts, saying that they were inclined to kill us in the way they had destroyed our friends."

The jest was too much for Lope de Oviedo. As he had well foreseen and predicted, he had left the rude peace of Bad Luck Island only to run upon cruel straits and a horrid death. He turned on his companion, upbraiding him for the dreadful pass into which they had come. In vain Cabeza de Vaca urged constancy, and promised a near reunion with the other three survivors. No promise could compensate for the drawn bows at their breasts, the unfailing threat of a comical murder. Lope made his farewells, and with the Indian women he took his place in a canoe and paddled back across the inlet, back to Bad Luck Island and an unrecorded death.

Cabeza de Vaca, watching the canoe grow small, thought bitterly of more than two years lost in the wilderness, waiting to save a coward's soul. Was there still any obligation of honor that bound him to labor for Oviedo? No, he decided, his duty was done. He and the faint-heart could turn their backs upon each other.

So thinking, he employed the best of his blandishments upon the Indians. On one hard face he caught a little sign of sympathy. "Your friends have come," grunted this well-wisher two days later. "I am going to visit their masters. You run away. Hide at the point of a certain wood. My kinsmen and I will pass there. We will take you."

So it fell out. Cabeza de Vaca was brought to the strangers' camp on the River of Nuts, the Guadalupe. The stir of his arrival flooded into the mat lodge where Dorantes was working. Dorantes emerged to recognize the bearded, naked form of his fellow-captain, whom he had given up for dead three and a half years before. The two embraced, weeping, amid the croaking laughter of the spectators. By a common impulse the two fell on their knees and looked up to sob out their thanks to God, in Spanish.

"This was a day to us of the greatest pleasure we had enjoyed in life."

CHAPTER VIII

DORANTES'S STORY

THE Indians of the River of Nuts were the Mariames, of a different speech from those Cabeza de Vaca had just quitted. They came every second year to the pecan groves of the Guadalupe, to eat the nuts during the two months of their bearing. They ground the kernels with certain small grains or seeds, and this was all their food for that time.

Cabeza de Vaca was given as a slave to Dorantes's master, an Indian blind of one eye, as were his wife and son and a companion. Castillo was in the service of a neighboring tribe, the Iguaces. Before long, apparently, a reunion was permitted among the three, and with Estebanico, Dorantes's negro slave. The natives must have been delighted by the spectacle of Estebanico's exuberant joy, mingled with humility. A slave abasing himself to a slave! Indeed, it does not seem that Estebanico ever thought that release from civilization implied any emancipation from legal servitude. Service of the Indians was an abuse of justice; but Dorantes was his master, whom to serve was God's ordinance. Such are the groovings of habit in the brain.

As the two captains of the king bent over their work, pounding nuts in gourds with stumps of wood, they exchanged at long length the tales of their distress. Dorantes told his story thus:

"There were twelve of us when we crossed from Bad Luck Island to the mainland, giving the fine marten-skin coat to the Indians as a fee for our transport. We surrendered it willingly; it was too heavy to carry in the warm spring weather. We asked the Indians about you; they told us first that you were dying, and then that you were dead. The Asturian priest said prayers for your soul, and we envied you taking your ease in purgatory.

"We went only two leagues to the first of the rivers which were to be our torment. Though they certainly thin to a trifle in the summer, they were then in spate. Most of our party, including Castillo and Estebanico, could not swim. But by the aid of clumsy rafts we came across this river [Oyster Creek] with great difficulty. We went then three leagues to a very great river [the Brazos], very full and powerful, flowing with such fury that its fresh water was carried well out to sea. There we made two more rafts, and one of them with seven men crossed safely, but the other was borne by the current more than a league off shore. Two men saved themselves by swimming, and two men drowned. And one man clung to the raft until the current ceased to run seaward; then, as a shoreward wind was blowing, he stood up on the raft and made a sail of his person and was blown to shore on the far side of the river.

"Now there were ten of us left. But here we found Francisco de León, and he joined our party. We went on three or four leagues to another river [the San Bernard]. There, by its mouth, we saw, cast up on the sand, the remains of a boat. At a glance we knew it. It was one of the craft we had built with no tools but our hands and fury in Apalachee. By certain well-remembered marks we recognized it to be the ship of the inspector, Alonso Enríquez, and the cleric, Fray Juan Juárez. But there were no signs anywhere of our friends.

"We continued then five or six leagues to another great river [Caney Creek, then a main channel of the Colorado River], and there we found two encampments of Indians.[1] These fled from us across the river, and there awaited us. We hallooed to them, and some returned, signifying to us that they had seen others of our kind. It appeared that not one boat but two had come ashore near there. That of the inspector and Father Juan had been abandoned, and the survivors had made their way southward, some on foot and some in the remaining vessel, which we took to be that of our governor, Don Pánfilo de Narváez.

---

[1] The distances given, the spacing and characteristics of the rivers, as recorded in Oviedo, "Historia general," III, 593, identify beyond question the scene of these adventures. The Brazos, for instance, is the only river between the Mississippi and the Río Grande which empties directly into the gulf with sufficient force to carry a raft out to sea. This identification was first made by a gifted undergraduate of the University of Texas, Miss Brownie Ponton (and Bates H. McFarland) in Texas State Hist. Quarterly, I, 166 (Jan. 1898). The promise contained in Miss Ponton's brilliant deductions was cut off by her death a year or so later.

We knew that by the Indians' description of the wrathful one-eyed man.

"These Indians gave us a little fish, which was welcome indeed, for we had no food but the sand-crabs, all shell and no flesh, and a kind of *hierba pedrera,* which we use to make glass in Spain.[2]

"For three days we came on south along a narrow, barren, sandy spit [Matagorda Peninsula]. Two men died here of hunger and exhaustion, so now we were nine. We arrived then at that inlet [Pass Cavallo], a league in width, over which you were ferried by the Doguenes. But there were no Indians when we came there; and we looked with heavy hearts across the waters to the white sand-hills marking the entrance to the bay.

"Then by God's grace we found a broken and abandoned Indian canoe. This we repaired as best we might, and got safely across the pass. We had cheated the sharks, but of what a sorry feast! Though we could barely crawl with hunger our bodies were puffed up from the eating of seaweed. Thus we came to a small inlet, about twelve leagues onward [Cedar Bayou, dividing Matagorda Island from St. Joseph's Island]. Here we stopped, helpless. On the following day an Indian came to the opposite side, but though we called to him he went away. In the evening he returned, with a companion. And that companion was none other than Figueroa!"

"Figueroa? One of the four we sent forward from Bad Luck Island, at the beginning of our first winter?"

"Yes. He told us, shouting across the inlet, how they had pushed on this far; but in a freezing norther Astudillo of Zafra and Alvaro Fernández, and the Indian companion, died. He and Méndez were left alone. They were taken by the Indians, for indeed they could not have fought a child with a wooden sword. When their strength was somewhat restored, Méndez escaped, fleeing desperately southward toward Pánuco. But his masters pursued and killed him. So of those messengers only Figueroa remained, and no word had ever been carried to the Spaniards of the south."

[2] "Doubtless kelp. It was burned and from the product glass and soap were formerly manufactured. It is still a source of manufacture of carbonate of soda and iodine." Hodge, "Spanish Explorers," 60 n.

"Had he found any trace of the boats of the governor and the inspector?"

"Oh, had he not indeed! He had met one of that party, Hernando de Esquivel, of Badajoz. He was a slave in the hands of our own present masters, the Mariames."

"And what was Esquivel's story?"

"He was in the inspector's boat. He told how it was upset and stove in beyond repair on the shore [at the mouth of the San Bernard River]. Near there they joined forces with the governor, whose boat was still intact. The governor and his crew coasted along shore, helping the marchers over the rivers and the coves. They came to that wide pass which baffled us both [Pass Cavallo], and their whole party was easily ferried over.

"There the governor fell into one of his great fits of anger, which his weak body could hardly contain. He cursed and abused Enríquez the inspector, and formally withdrew his commission as lieutenant of the expedition. And he appointed in his stead Captain Pantoja. Enríquez only laughed; he was past caring. The governor, sulking, refused to spend the night on shore, but retired to his boat, with only a steersman and a sick page for company. In the night a norther rose, and when morning came the boat was gone. As they had only some stones for anchor, they must have been blown out to sea; having no food nor water, they may have died of privation; or, as the page was sick and Don Pánfilo was very feeble and full of leprosy, they may have been overwhelmed by the waves. At any rate, nothing was ever heard again of our commander.

"Esquivel continued telling Figueroa how the rest of the party, under the headship of Captain Pantoja, went on south along the coastal island, till starvation and lack of water determined them to make a cast for the mainland. They made rafts with much labor, and crossed to the main. As they approached a wooded point they descried a band of Indians, who, in alarm, put their houses in their canoes and departed. So the party disembarked at the Indian camp [somewhere near Rockport], and finding fresh water, fuel, crabs, and shell-fish, decided to stop there until winter should be past. But there, one by one, they died of cold and hunger. Pantoja, their commander, used them very hardly, which Sotomayor, the Cuban, resenting, they came to blows and Sotomayor struck Pantoja on the head with a club, killing him instantly. The others were pleased, for in their weakness they could think of no smaller punishment than death for one who caused annoyance. They cut off the best of his flesh and dried it; they had learned to relish the meat of their companions.

"They all died, one by one, and the living ate the dead. Sotomayor was the last to go; then Esquivel dried his meat and fed on him until about the first of March [1529]. He was ready to die, when an Indian appeared and carried him off as his slave.

"Figueroa said that Esquivel told him all this once when their two masters met. And Figueroa pleaded with him that they should escape together and make their way onward to Pánuco. But Esquivel refused, saying that the friars had maintained that they had already left Pánuco behind, and that they were on the middle coast of Mexico. So they parted, and Esquivel was carried off inland by his masters, and for all Figueroa knew, he was still alive.

"Such was the story Figueroa told us, shouting his words across the narrow inlet. And he invited us to come with him, and make one last effort to escape toward Pánuco. All of us would gladly have done so, but only the Asturian priest and one young man could swim. These two made a rendez-vous with Figueroa; but when they came to the opposite shore they were promptly taken by the Indians. The young swimmer escaped and returned to us, bringing a few fish. The priest remained, however, in the Indians' hands.

"So now we were eight. The next day a band of Indians arrived on the opposite bank [of Cedar Bayou]. Answering our entreaties, they came to us and transported us over, although with every sign of contempt and scorn. They took from us what few possessions were still ours, but they gave us fish, and led us with them to the regions where they went to eat blackberries.

"As we were of little service to our masters, they soon tired of feeding us. Five of our party were sent forward to other Indians by an inlet six leagues forward [Aransas Pass]. On the way the young swimmer and one other died; I myself, a few days later, saw their bodies on the beach.

"This, then, was our state in the spring after our shipwreck: Of the five boats that set forth from Ante Bay, four were accounted for. Only of the boat of Captains Peñalosa and Téllez has no word been had. Those who sailed with Governor Narváez and with Inspector Enríquez were all dead but Esquivel, and in his belly they had a sort of Christian burial. Most of the two boat-loads, yours and mine, that were wrecked on Bad Luck Island, died where they came ashore. Oviedo still remains there, and much joy may he get from the roots he grubs up like a pig. Of the exploring party we sent out only Figueroa survived. There were twelve of us who started forth together from the island when spring came in, and Francisco de León joined us on the way. We had lost, by drowning and hunger, Estrada, Tostado, Chaves, Gutiérrez, Benítez, and León. The Asturian priest was somewhere in the wilderness with Figueroa. That leaves six, who were divided in two groups of three. The forward group, the survivors of the five whom the Indians had sent on to the pass six leagues away, were my fellow-captain Alonso del Castillo, my cousin Pedro de Valdivieso, and Diego de Huelva. There remained with our first captors my cousin Diego Dorantes, my slave Estebanico, and myself.

"We three served our masters so ill that after a few days they drove us out, naked and starving. We turned blindly to the south, and came to the pass whither our three companions had been taken. There we found Valdivieso. He told us how Figueroa and the Asturian priest, the good swimmers, had passed through there. The Indians had stripped and beaten them and taken their few possessions, because they would not stay. I myself saw the rags of the priest's cassock, and his breviary and journal, which the Indians regarded as a great magic.[3] They had gone on unheeding, for they had sworn a great oath to stop for nothing until they should die, or until they should come to a land of Christians. And from the reports the Indians have given me, they have found no land of Christians, unless it be Heaven.

"So then, not counting Figueroa and the priest, but counting Esquivel somewhere in the woods, we were seven. Valdivieso, after giving

[3] La Salle's disastrous expedition, which settled on Matagorda Bay, was equipped with a fine library, most of which fell into the hands of the Indians who massacred the few survivors. A hint to border bibliophiles. (H. E. Bolton, "Spanish Exploration in the Southwest," 398.)

us this word, went back to his masters, and two days later he was killed for trying to escape. And then we were six. A little later they killed Diego de Huelva, because he passed from one lodge to another. Then we were five.

"There we remained for more than a year in slavery, treated more cruelly than the captives of any Moor. Naked and barefoot, we carried wood and water over those molten sands, and dragged the canoes through the shallows, where the sun burns as against polished steel. We had no food but a little fish, and no drink but brackish water, and even that was rare and precious. And as we carried this foul water on our backs for our masters and their neighbors—for all the natives ordered us about—we got only kicks and curses for gratitude. The boys pulled our beards constantly by way of pastime, and if we were at all careless they would pull our hair, with great laughter, the best pleased in the world. And they would forever be scratching us, so as to bring blood; their nails are very long, and sharpened to serve as knives for daily uses. The boys would also assail us with stones, or any other missile they found to hand. It was for them a new sort of hunting game, of great delight."

"And you, a hidalgo, did you never break out against them?"

"God gave us strength to be patient, as a payment on account against our sins, we knowing that we merited more than we received. Gladly would we have died, had that been his will; but as so strangely and unaccountably were we preserved, we knew that our life must be in his purpose.

"Fifteen months we stayed there, from May of 1529 until August of 1530. And then one day I was alone on the landward side of the island, where shallow waters two leagues wide separate it from the mainland. [The sand-flats, now nearly dry, dividing the south end of Mustang Island from the mainland at Flour Bluff.] Despair suddenly fell off from me, and I thought of God parting the waters of the Red Sea. So I commended my soul to God, and entered the shallows, and came safe to the other side, unperceived by my masters. Arriving at the mainland, I thanked God for his care, and then turned inland and walked as fast and as far as I could, with much fear. The next day I met some Indians, who received me willingly, because they had observed that

93

the Christians had become good servants. So they took me, and treated me as cruelly as had my former masters.

"Three months later Estebanico followed me, and we met, although we were not kept together. And after another year and a half Castillo came over, but did not find me, for by that time I had again escaped. But my poor cousin Diego, after two years of servitude, escaped only to the other world, with all the stain of unabsolved sin upon his soul.

"And then we were four.

"I had escaped, as I said. Because I remembered some Indians along our way who seemed kinder of heart, I turned back to find them. I arrived first among the Iguaces, with whom Castillo and Estebanico are now. After a few days I escaped again to our present masters, the Mariames. The first thing I learned from them was that they had had Esquivel among them. But a woman dreamed that her son would kill him. And since they do anything at all to fulfil dreams, even killing their own children,[4] Esquivel attempted to escape. They followed after, and slew him. They showed me his sword, and rosary, and mass-book.

"Then we were three. Now at last you have come, as an augury of turn of fortune. If we make a final census, we may say that we four are all that remain of the great Narváez expedition. For Lope de Oviedo will cower until he dies on Bad Luck Island, and a true-seeming rumor tells that Figueroa and the Asturian priest are dead."

"You forget the boatload of Peñalosa and Téllez."

"True. They may indeed, by the best of fortune and God's grace, have come to Pánuco. But I think that had they done so, we would have seen a rescue ship along the shore. There remains no hope but our own courage."

"Tell me about our masters."

"They are of a different race and language from the coast tribes.[5]

---

[4] A similar habit existed among the Coahuiltecan Indians. See Alonso de León, "Historia de Nuevo León," 48–9.

[5] The description of the Mariames and Iguaces Indians, as reported in Cabeza de Vaca and in the Oviedo narrative, would identify them with the Jaranames and the Anaquas, who were Tónkawa Indians, distinct from the coast-dwelling Karankawas. See the references given by Davenport and Wells, Southwestern Historical Quarterly, XXII, 139 n. For a horrible tale of Tónkawa humorous torture, see R. I. Dodge, "Plains of the Great West," 418.

They are cruel enough, and yet somehow not so devilishly evil as the men of the seaboard. My chief fear is that some woman will dream a bit of nonsense, for which they will put me to death, the way that Esquivel went. Whenever, as I dig at my roots, I see an Indian approaching, I quake until he passes by. Especially since their best joke is to put an arrowhead at my breast or other vital and pull the nock to the ear, scowling fearfully; and then they laugh and say, 'Were you frightened?'

"Because we are now eating these fine nuts, do not think that you have come to a land of plenty. When winter comes we shall dig roots with much labor, and for dainties we shall eat snakes, lizards, mice, insects, frogs, and any reptile we can find. When, in the spring, the rivers overflow, we shall catch some floundering fish, but as there is no salt, we cannot preserve them for our later need. Then at the end of May we shall go to eat the prickly pear, and snails for garnishing, the best food of all the year. And perhaps we shall take some deer. Our method of hunting is strange indeed; we round up a herd of them and drive them into the sea, and hold them there all day until they are drowned.

"But all this and more you will learn for yourself, before we shall have a chance for escape."

Indeed there was time enough. Cabeza de Vaca describes the Mariames with more fullness than any other of the tribes to whom he was subject. And since I fear by paraphrase to lose his sharp accent of veridicity, I shall transcribe his words, in Buckingham Smith's sounding translation, with some emendations in favor of accuracy.

"In obedience to their custom they take life, destroying even their children on account of dreams. They cast away their daughters at birth, and cause them to be eaten by dogs. The reason of their doing this, as they state, is because all the nations of the country are their foes; and as they have unceasing war with them, if they were to marry away their daughters, they would so greatly multiply their enemies that they must be overcome and made slaves; thus they prefer to destroy the girls, rather than that from them should come a single enemy. We asked why they did not themselves marry them; and they

95

said it would be a disgustful thing to marry among relatives, and far better to kill than to give them either to their kindred or to their foes.

"This is likewise the practice of their neighbors the Iguaces, but of no other people of that country. When the men would marry, they buy the women of their enemies: the price paid for a wife is a bow, the best that can be got, with two arrows: if it happens that the suitor should have no bow, then a net a fathom in length and another in breadth. They kill their own children [daughters?] and buy those of strangers. The marriage state continues no longer than while the parties are satisfied, and they separate for the slightest cause.

"Their support is principally roots, of two or three kinds, and they look for them over the face of all the country. The food is poor and puffs up the persons who eat it. The roots require roasting two days: many are very bitter, and withal difficult to be dug. They are sought the distance of two or three leagues, and so great is the want these people experience, that they cannot get through the year without them. Occasionally they kill deer, and at times take fish; but the quantity is so small and the famine so great, that they eat spiders and the eggs of ants, worms, lizards, snakes, and vipers that kill whom they strike [rattlesnakes]; and they eat earth and wood, and all that there is, the dung of deer and other things that I omit to mention; and I honestly believe that were there stones in that land they would eat them. They preserve the bones of the fishes they consume, of snakes and other animals, that they may afterwards beat them together and eat the powder. The men bear no burthens, nor carry anything of weight; such are borne by women and old men who are of the least esteem. They have not so great love for their children as those we have before spoken of. Some among them are accustomed to sin against nature. The women work very hard, and do a great deal; of the twenty-four hours they have only six of repose; the rest of the night they pass in stirring the fires to dry those roots they eat. At daybreak they begin to dig them, to bring wood and water to their houses and get in readiness other things that may be necessary. The majority of the people are great thieves; for though they freely divide with each other, if one turns his head, his son or his father will take what he can. They are great liars, and also great drunkards, which they become from the use of a certain liquor.[6]

"These Indians are so accustomed to running, that without rest or fatigue they follow a deer from morning to night. In this way they kill many. They pursue them until they tire them out, and sometimes catch them alive. Their houses are of matting, placed upon four hoops. They carry them on the back, and remove every two or three days in search of food. Nothing is planted which might be of use. They are a merry people; notwithstanding the hunger they suffer, they do not cease to observe their festivities and dances. To them the happiest part of the year is the season of eating prickly pears; they have hunger then no longer, pass all the time in dancing, and eat day and night. While these 'tunas' last, they squeeze out the juice, open and set them to dry, and when dry they are put in baskets like figs. These they keep to eat on the way back. The peel is beaten to powder.[7]

"It occurred to us many times while we were among this people, and there was no food, to be three or four days without eating, when they, to revive our spirits, would tell us not to be sad, that soon there would be prickly pears, when we should eat a plenty and drink of the juice, when our bellies would be very big and we should be content and joyful, having no hunger. From the time they first told us this, to that at which the earliest were ripe enough to be eaten, was an interval of five or six months; so having tarried until the lapse of this period, and the season had come, we went to eat the fruit.

"We found mosquitoes of three sorts, and all of them abundant in every part of the country. They are very bad and troublesome, and during the greater part of the summer they gave us great annoyance. As a protection we made fires, encircling the people with them, burning rotten and wet wood to produce smoke without flame. The remedy brought another trouble, and the night long we did little else than shed tears from the smoke that came into our eyes, besides feeling intense heat from the many fires, and if at any time we went out

[6] F. W. Hodge suggests ("Spanish Explorers," 66 n.) that this is the peyote, or mescal button.
[7] One of La Salle's soldiers died from eating prickly pears without removing the prickles. Margry, III, 211.

for relief to the shore and fell asleep, we were reminded with blows to make up the fires. The Indians of the interior have a different method, as intolerable, and worse even than the one I have spoken of, which is to go with brands in the hand firing the plains and forests within their reach, that the mosquitoes may fly away, and at the same time to drive out lizards and other like things from the earth for them to eat.

"They are accustomed also to kill deer by encircling them with fires. The pasturage is taken from the beasts by burning, that necessity may drive them to seek it in places where it is desired they should go. They encamp only where there are wood and water; and sometimes all carry loads of these when they go to hunt deer, which are usually found where neither is to be got. On the day of their arrival, they kill the deer and other animals which they can, and consume all the water and all the wood in cooking and on the fires they make to relieve of mosquitoes. They remain the next day to get something to sustain them on their return; and when they go, such is their state from those insects that they appear to have the leprosy of holy Lazarus. In this way do they appease their hunger, two or three times in the year, at the cost I have mentioned. From my own experience, I can state there is no torment in this world that can equal it.

"Inland are many deer, birds, and beasts other than those I have spoken of. Cattle [8] come as far as here. Three times have I seen them and eaten of their meat. I think they are about the size of those of Spain. They have small horns like the cows of Morocco; the hair is very long and woolly like a rug. Some are tawny, others black. To my judgment the flesh is finer and fatter than those from here [Spain]. Of the smaller hides the Indians make blankets, and of the larger they make shoes and bucklers. They come as far as the seacoast of Florida, from a northerly direction, ranging through a tract of more than four hundred leagues; and throughout the whole region over which they run, the people who inhabit near, descend and live upon them, distributing a vast many hides into the interior country."

[8] This is the first printed reference to the bison; "hunch-backed cows" he calls them in another passage of the narrative. They were apparently more familiar along the coast in La Salle's time. At one time they were common along the Río Grande, and were occasionally seen in Mexico. See Coopwood, in Texas State Hist. Quarterly III, 231, *et sqq.* and Bandelier, "Contributions to History of the Southwest," 28 n.

CHAPTER IX

THE FIRST STAGE OF THE GREAT JOURNEY

ABOUT midsummer, said Dorantes, the happy season of the prickly pears would come round again. Then the whole tribe would migrate thirty leagues south to the cactus country, and all would feast in good-fellowship, making their bellies big and their hearts glad. To this prickly pear region would come all the tribes from miles around, and for a time all hatreds would be forgotten in the bliss of gluttony. The Iguaces, masters of Castillo and Estebanico, would be present, under the Truce of the Tuna. With any good fortune, the four could concert a flight and flee southward. Their masters would not abandon their tunas to go slave-hunting over the sands.

The half-year of delay was, for Cabeza de Vaca, a period of relative happiness. True, his normal state was one of cruel hunger, only to be appeased by loathly foods; yet his body had been trained to Indian ataraxy by his wilderness schooling. The plaints of his empty belly could be stilled by long conversations with his dear friend Andrés Dorantes, in the sober and measured speech of the Spanish hidalgo. Cabeza de Vaca had not spoken his native tongue for three years, except during his brief reunions with Lope de Oviedo.

Andrés Dorantes de Carranza was a native of Béjar del Castañar, in Old Castile, south of Salamanca. He was of ancient and noble lineage on both sides, and was a kinsman of the Marqués Dávila Fuente, still a great name in Spain. Seeking his fortune, he went to Seville, where fortunes were to be had by the ambitious and well-connected. He was a guest in the household of the Duke of Béjar, Don Alvaro de Zuñiga the Good, Lord of Plasencia and Arévalo: through the influence of that grandee commissions were found in Narváez's expedition for Don Andrés and his cousins, Diego Dorantes and Pedro de Valdivieso. Don Andrés took with him his personal slave, Estebanico of Azamor in Morocco (who may have been enslaved in the expedition against that city in 1513, in the course of which Ferdinand Magellan was lamed for life).

All dead now, all those proud riders who thought to conquer the Indies, all dead and carried quick to hell by their unshriven sins. All dead, and yet he lived by God's mysterious mercy, the same mercy which condemned the band of gentlemen and spared a negro Moor. If Dorantes was inclined, in fever and the hallucinations of hunger, to doubt the wisdom of God's strange purposes, he must have been supported by the faith of Cabeza de Vaca. To him it was clear that the four had been preserved alive for some important divine intention, as yet unrevealed.

Such were the strengthenings of faith exchanged by the dying camp-fires when the masters were asleep. And in other waiting hours, in the sluggish moments of the camp's routine, Dorantes and Cabeza de Vaca tasted the delicious pleasures of sharing memory. Dorantes would recall, with gathering detail, the small incidents of life in his bleak and austere highland town. He would tell of the visits of the balulú, the strolling comedian, performing his dramatic loas in the market-corner, with the village priest passing the hat. Or Cabeza de Vaca would dwell on the luxury of the famous baths of Seville, inherited from the Moors; the wide halls, the spouts of hot and cold water and of perfumes, the masseurs and their miraculous healing unguent.[1] And into these minds, from which all but the urgent sense of the moment's need had long been burned away, would return memories of old songs, of gallant banter under the cool awnings of the patios, of peace and courtly ease. Perhaps they would sing; Dorantes would patch together a mountain ballad, a serrana or serranilla, or a long romance of the Reconquest. Singing, he would remember the market-day minstrels, who hang on a house wall a sheet with each incident of the ballad clumsily drawn, in the manner of a transept window, indicating, as they unfold their tale, the proper scene with a pointer. Then Alvar Núñez would take his turn, singing the strange Oriental *coplas* of the south, quavering interminably on a single note, recounting a story of love or despair in two phrases of

[1] A. María Fabié, "Viajes por España," 447.

ejaculation. Or one of those furious dancing-songs, telling with casta-
nets of Christ's Nativity or the Deposition from the Cross.[2] Or, sweet-
est to the homesick Andalusian, old songs of longing for Seville and
its golden river:

> Río de Sevilla
> de barcos lleno,
> a pasarlo el alma
> no pasa el cuerpo.

Or the great heartbreaking ballads with their sobbing refrains:

> Fonte frida, fonte frida,
> fonte frida y con amor.

Many of them telling tales of the singer's own glittering country:

> Mi padre era de Ronda
> y mi madre de Antequera,
> cativáronme los moros
> entre la paz y la guerra
> y lleváronme a vender
> a Jerez de la Frontera.

Curious songs to rise in the Texas prairies, but in their melodies was
balm and comfort. "*Quien canta sus males espanta,*" says the old saw.
"The man who sings scares off all evil things." [3]

Even the customs of the natives gained an interest when two could
discuss their strangeness, and supply gaps in one another's observa-
tion. Quaint indeed was some of the savages' behavior. The children
were suckled until about the age of twelve. This was no mere oddity
but a measure against the constant attacks of starvation. The tender

---

[2] Such as "churumbé con la churumbela"; see J. Cejador y Frauca, "La Verdadera
Poesía castellana" (Madrid, 1921) II, 42.

[3] To the Spaniard, song, dance, and religion were all one. Pfandl ("Spanische Kultur
und Sitte," 152) quotes a strange old song:

> Pues hubo quien
> Dijo que el día de Dios
> Era cada cascabel
> De un danzante silogismo
> Contra el apostata infiel.

Or: "There was one who said that on God's day every knee-bell of a dancer is a syllogism
against the infidel apostate."

children had not yet hardened themselves to bear three or four days without food, while the mothers had learned to make milk from air and sand.

If any one chance to fall sick in the desert, and cannot keep up with the rest, the Indians leave him to perish, unless it be a son or brother; him they will assist, even to carrying on their back. It is common among them all to leave their wives when there is no conformity, and directly they connect themselves with whom they please. This is the course of the young men; those who have children remain with their wives and never abandon them. . . . When the women have their indisposition, they seek food only for themselves, as no one else will eat of what they bring. In the time I was thus among these people, I witnessed a diabolical practice; a man living with another, one of those who are emasculate and impotent. These go habited like women, and perform their duties, use the bow, and carry heavy loads. Among the Indians we saw many such. They are more muscular than other men, and taller: they bear very weighty burthens.[4]

The Indians roamed through a pleasant country-side of broad savannas, well grown with grass. "I think it would be a very fruitful region were it worked and inhabited by civilized men." Its drawback was the lack of fresh water.

When at last the summer of 1533 came, and the long-promised

[4] A similar custom was prevalent among the Timucua Indians of Florida. De Bry thus describes them, elucidating his curious drawing: "There are in that country numerous hermaphrodites, sharing the characteristics of both sexes and born of the Indians themselves. As they are robust and strong, they are used to carry burdens in place of pack animals. When the kings go forth to war, the hermaphrodites carry the food. They carry the Indians dead of wounds or illness on a litter." (Ningler, "Voyages en Virginie et en Floride," 261.)

Laudonnière also mentions them in his account of his settlement in Florida in 1564. Father Marquette was troubled to find among the Illinois and the Nadouessians certain men who took women's dress in youth and wore it throughout their lives. "There is a mystery about it; for they never marry, and count it their glory to abase themselves to do all that women do. Yet they go to war, though they may use only the war-club. Bow and arrow are reserved to the men. They are present at all the jongleries and the solemn dances held in honor of the calumet; they sing thereat but may not dance. They are called to the councils, where nothing can be decided without their opinion. In short by the profession they make of an extraordinary life, they pass for manitous, that is to say, for genii or persons of consequence." ("Voyages du Père Marquette," Lenox reprints 52–53.)

The cinaedi among the Choctaws, much scorned, were obliged to wear women's clothes (Romans, "Natural History of East & West Florida," 83). A similar custom existed among the Coahuiltecan Indians, whom Cabeza de Vaca came to know well. Certain men wore women's clothes, did their work and bore the *huacal*, or basket, without incurring social displeasure (Alonso de León, "Historia de Nuevo León," 54). Also the narrative of Hernando Alarcón, in Hakluyt, "Navigations," IX, 308.

journey to the prickly-pear country was to be fulfilled, the tribe gathered its possessions together, loaded them on the backs of the women and burden-bearers, and set off on the annual southward trek. The masters were happy, grinning and rubbing their bellies with anticipation of the annual distention; and the slaves were happy, dreaming of escape.

The line of march took them about thirty leagues south and ten leagues west. They must have passed along a road crossing the sweet-watered rivers where they join the salty bays; and somewhere about Corpus Christi or a little south they turned inland for about ten leagues. They were in the heart of the prickly-pear region. The fruit, still common thereabouts, was more plentiful than it is to-day. Even within the memory of old Texas settlers, it has diminished mightily, owing to cultivation, root rot, the great freeze of February 1899, and the appearance in recent years of barbed wire and the spread of mesquite and huisache.[5]

Here assembled tribes from all the littoral (though not, apparently, the Karankawas, the island fisherman) to glut themselves with food under the Truce of the Tuna. There could be no reluctance shown; the prickly pear was all their meat and drink, as indeed it now is through certain seasons in parts of Sicily. At best they could vary the diet with snails, and perhaps an occasional deer. The sweetness of the tuna roused active thirst; this, for lack of water, could only be quenched by draughts of tuna juice, which was collected in holes in the earth. "There are many kinds of prickly pears, among them some very good, although they all appeared to me to be so, hunger never having given me leisure to choose, nor to reflect upon which were the best."

News came to Cabeza de Vaca and Dorantes in this meeting-ground. "We have seen others like you, hairy-faced men," said some strangers. "They appeared out of the sea in a boat. They came to land in the country of our shoreward neighbors, the Camones. They were very weak and sick. Our neighbors killed those that did not die, for their sharp glittering knives and their well-sewn garments. You may see some knives and garments which we took from the Camones."

[5] Davenport and Wells, in S. W. Hist. Q. XXII, 209. The existence of this tuna region is an important aid in identifying Cabeza de Vaca's route.

The wanderers recognized the garments and the knives. They had belonged to passengers in the boat of Captains Peñalosa and Téllez.

Thus the fifth and last craft of the armada that had left the Bay of Horses was accounted for. The toll was complete. The survivors of Narváez's expedition of conquest were four. It remained only for them to meet, to pray together, and to take the great oath of Figueroa and the Asturian priest, never to stop until they should come to the land of Christians or to the kind arms of death.

Questioning revealed the whereabouts of Castillo and Estebanico. Cabeza de Vaca and Dorantes decided that at the first fair chance they would steal away and attempt to unite with their friends.

And one night a great uproar arose in the tuna fields. Two braves began to fight about a woman; relatives and friends took a hand. There was much savage warring with hard fists and feet, much bloodying of heads with sticks. [Yet we are told that weapons were forbidden by custom.] Anger took hold of the camp. When all were exhausted, the different factions quickly packed their lodges and set off for their home ranges. The white slaves, under their heavy loads, plodded under the Texas sun a hundred miles northward. Their opportunity had passed, untaken.

A dreadful year followed, from about September of 1533 to the summer of 1534. Cabeza de Vaca tells us little about it; he was tired of remembering those days of hunger and pain. Apparently he had lost his one-eyed master, who seems to have treated him well. He was separated, therefore, from Dorantes. He says only: "Three times I was obliged to run from my masters, and each time they went in pursuit and endeavored to slay me; but God our Lord in His mercy chose to protect and preserve me; and when the season of prickly pears returned, we came together in the same place."

As the Indians roamed the tuna fields, one of the Spaniards met another and the second contrived to pass the word to the other two. The message was that at the September full of the moon, the four should meet at a certain recognizable spot in the tuna country. And, said Cabeza de Vaca, if one is hindered, or if all are hindered, I shall go on by myself alone.

There was no thought in his mind of failure. Failure was impossible. Another year of slavery was impossible.

The September moon appeared, pure and slender in the western sky, like God's first thought of light. Day by day it grew like His dream, troubling the waning sun, and by night smiling in front of all the importance of the universe. Soon it was a great enormous creature, occupying the sky.

It was the thirteenth day of the moon.

On that night Dorantes and Estebanico brazenly appeared in Cabeza de Vaca's camp. Dorantes said that he had fled from his previous masters, and had fallen into the hands of the Anagados. Word of this came to Estebanico and Castillo; they followed him and the three assembled there. Now the Anagados were enemies of the Mariames, but they were planning a rapprochement and in a day or two would meet to smoke the pipe of peace. This indeed was done; and in the festivities the four Christians were reunited.

"And all three praised our Lord," says Oviedo (for the praises of Estebanico, the negro slave, were not taken into account).

And they resolved to do their duty as Christians, and as hidalgos, which each one of them was, and not to live this life, so savage and so divorced from the service of God and all good reason. And with this good resolution, like determined men of good birth, they went; and so Jesus Christ guided them and worked with his infinite mercy upon them, and opened roads to them in a land where there were none. And God moved the hearts of savages and untamed men to be humbled before them and to obey them, as will be told further on. And thus they went that day without being heard, and without knowing where they were going, but confiding in divine mercy, and seeking those tunas that there were in the land, although it was already time for them to be over, for it was in October.[6] And it pleased the Mother of God that that day at sunset they met some Indians, which was what they desired, because they were very gentle and had some knowledge of the Christians, though little, because they did not know how badly the others had treated them (which was a very fine thing for those sinners).

The Mother of God must at last have heard the sound of Latin salutations in the pagan wilderness. The pilgrims caught sight of smoke

---

[6] Such small disagreements with Cabeza de Vaca's story are by no means infrequent.

rising, and an Indian running. They sent Estebanico in chase; the Indian, seeing only one pursuer, halted. Parleying, he offered to bring the Christians to his tribe, the Avavares. And this was done; and the four were well received, Dorantes and Estebanico being honorably lodged with a medicine-man. That night their thanks arose to the gratified ear of God's Mother, for these gentle Indians had come from the south, where lay Pánuco, to eat the tunas, and they were about to return to their homes.

Cabeza de Vaca had seen the Avavares before, for they were dealers in bows, and had visited the Mariames in the course of trade. Thus they spoke the Mariame tongue, although they were of a separate stock and language. They are now identified as Coahuiltecans, a race long extinct. Something in their character or tradition made them kind.

They said that south along the coast, among the People of the Figs (perhaps near the mouth of the Río Grande), they had seen two white men. These were Figueroa and the Asturian priest, who had set forth, vowing never to stop except for death or the homes of Christians. This is the last that any one has heard of those valiant men.

As, that evening, Cabeza de Vaca and Castillo squatted with their hosts, gravely discussing food and climate, a little deputation of tribesmen drew near. The spokesman addressed Castillo, who was, perhaps, the more striking figure of the pair. He explained that he suffered from a great pain in his head, which the medicine man could not drive away; would not the white shaman exercise a magic?

At a prompting from Cabeza de Vaca, Castillo knelt and commended his spirit to God. *In nomine Patris, Filii et Spiritus Sancti.* In accord with the Indian tradition, he blew upon the seat of the pain. Then, to lure the power of God's mercy, he traced upon the aching brain the sign of the Cross, the memory of Christ's agony, the oblation and satisfaction of the sins and pains of the world. And he called upon the Lord to aid him, in the official tongue of Heaven. *Famulis tuis Domine subveni, quos pretioso sanguine redemisti.* Most ardently of all he spoke to God's Mother, in words of supplication that came readily to his lips. *Ad te clamamus, exsules filii Hevae; ad te suspiramus, gementes et flentes, in hac lacrymarum valle. Eia ergo advocata nostra, illos tuos misericordes oculos ad nos converte.*

The Indian rubbed his head and grinned. No more pain! Pain all gone! With signs of gratitude he retreated from the new magician, to return in a moment with a handful of prickly pears and a piece of venison, "a thing to us little known."

All that night the sick of the village besieged the wonder-worker, with many whose pains were suddenly remembered only for the excitement of submitting to the novel magic. Each brought a piece of venison for fee, "until the quantity became so great that we knew not where to dispose it." Every sufferer went away smiling and shouting, crying out that his pain had been charmed away. A great festivity was suddenly ordered; all that night and for three days after the Indians danced and sang and leaped with praise. And while the camp resounded with these discordant testimonies to divine power, the four Christians knelt on the sand and rendered thanks for God's compassion and his gifts.

When the festivities were finished by exhaustion, it became clear that, for lack of food, the tribe could no longer remain in the tuna country, but must return to its home ranges. These lay to the south, five days' journey through a cruel desert. The Indians would be glad of the society of their new friends; and the Christians were no less glad to make this stage of their progress in company.

From their station, somewhere in the neighborhood of what is now Alice, in Jim Wells County, Texas, they turned southeast across the Great Sand Belt of Brooks and Willacy Counties. After five thirsty and hungry days they reached a watercourse, presumably the Arroyo Colorado. Here they found a few late-blooming tunas, and trees bearing a fruit like peas. These are securely identified (by Judge Bethel Coopwood),[7] as the ebony-tree. Its pods, called maguacatas, are palatable when boiled or roasted. They are now used by the Mexicans of this region as a coffee substitute.

Here all the party scattered to seek this welcome food. Cabeza de Vaca, ranging far, found himself lost with the descending night.

Thank God I found a burning tree, and in the warmth of it I passed the cold of that night. In the morning, loading myself with sticks, and taking two brands with me, I returned to seek them. In this manner I wandered five days, ever with my fire and load; for if the wood had failed me where

[7] Tex. State Hist. Qu., III, 129.

none could be found (as many parts are without any), though I might have sought sticks elsewhere, there would have been no fire to kindle them. This was all the protection I had against cold, while walking naked as I was born.

For the nights I took this measure: going to the brush by the riverside woods, I would stop there before sunset. I would make a hole in the ground and throw in branches which the trees abundantly afforded, collected in good quantity from those that were fallen and dry. About the hole I would make four fires, in the form of a cross, which I watched and made up from time to time. I also gathered some bundles of the coarse straw that there abounds, with which I covered myself in the hole. In this way I was sheltered at night from cold. On one occasion while I slept, the fire fell upon the straw, when it began to blaze so rapidly that notwithstanding the haste I made to get out of it, I carried some marks on my hair of the danger to which I was exposed.

All this while I tasted not a mouthful, nor did I find anything I could eat. My feet were bare and bled a good deal. Through the mercy of God, the wind did not blow from the north in all this time, otherwise I should have died. At the end of the fifth day I arrived on the margin of a river, where I found the Indians, who with the Christians had considered me dead, supposing that I had been stung by a viper. All were rejoiced to see me, and most so were my companions. They said that up to that time they had struggled with great hunger, which was the cause of their not having sought me. At night, all gave me of their prickly pears, and the next morning we set out for a place where they were in large quantity; with which we satisfied our great craving, the Christians rendering thanks to our Lord that he had ever given us his aid.

The next day some emissaries arrived from another tribe, bringing five companions with a kind of paralysis. They fell down before Castillo, whose fame was spreading through that country. Each patient offered his bow and arrows for pay, and Castillo accepted them. "At sunset he blessed them, commending them to God our Lord; and we all prayed to him the best we could to send health; for that he knew there was no other means, than through him, by which this people would aid us, so we could come forth from this unhappy existence. He bestowed it so mercifully that, the morning having come, all got up well and sound, and were as strong as though they never had a disorder. It caused great admiration, and inclined us to render many thanks to God our Lord, that we might more completely know his goodness and hope that he would liberate and bring us to where we might serve him. For myself I can say that I ever had trust in his providence that he would lead me out from that captivity, and thus I always spoke of it to my companions."

The hearts of men of great faith, we know, are seldom occupied by faith alone. Worldly shrewdness for godly purpose often lives with the pure fire of the spirit. The preachers of crusades studied elocution like any lawyer; in every monastery the Brother Steward can drive a hard bargain for the greater glory of God. There was in the heart of Cabeza de Vaca at this moment true ardor and faith, and the spiritual strength gained by six years of unfaltering purpose concentrated on one end, with the steadfast refusal of the one easy solution—death. If the human soul can ever, through solitary exercise, accumulate a high potential, to be discharged in great crackling sparks into the souls of others, the soul of Cabeza de Vaca should have possessed that power. If divinity ever does its work with human instruments, it could have found none more cleansed of pride by adversity, none that had reached a more perfect faith through a more abject humility.

And yet Cabeza de Vaca knew that the cunning and quickness of wit that had so often saved him alive was compatible with trust in God's providences. He was exasperated with Castillo's procedure in healing. The man would hang back, and show uncertainty; he had not profited by the arts of the medicine-man, as Cabeza de Vaca had himself, years before. "Castillo was a timid practitioner," say the memoirs, "most so in serious and dangerous cases, believing that his sins would weigh, and some day hinder him in performing cures."

Envoys from a neighboring tribe appeared, begging Castillo to come and cure some wounded and sick, especially one who was very near his end. Cabeza de Vaca, by his side, felt Castillo shrink. Anger rose in him, the anger of faith. He knew that Castillo would fail from lack of conviction, and failure would undo all their new prestige. He stepped forward and offered himself as healer, to Castillo's sigh of relief.

Cabeza de Vaca, Dorantes, and Estebanico accompanied the envoys to their camp. Coming near, they saw an ominous sign. The patient's hut was thrown down; around it sat his friends and kin, uttering the keen of death.

When I arrived I found his eyes rolled up, and the pulse gone, he having all the appearances of death, as they seemed to me and as Dorantes said. I removed a mat with which he was covered, and supplicated our Lord as fervently as I could, that He would be pleased to give health to him, and to the rest that might need it. After he had been blessed and breathed upon many times, they brought me his bow, and gave me a basket of pounded prickly pears. The natives took me to many others who were sick of a stupor, and presented me two more baskets of prickly pears, which I gave to the Indians who accompanied us. We then went back to our lodgings. Those to whom we gave the fruit tarried, and returned at night to their houses, reporting that he who had been dead and for whom I wrought before them, had got up whole and walked, had eaten and spoken with them and that all to whom I ministered were well and much pleased. This caused great wonder and fear, and throughout the land the people talked of nothing else. All to whom the fame of it reached came to seek us that we should cure them and bless their children.

When the visiting tribes departed, they pressed upon the Christians all their prickly pears, saving none for themselves. They gave also their precious flint knives, a palm and a half in length. Mostly they asked the wonder-workers to remember them, and to pray to God that they would always be well. On receiving the desired promise "they left, the most satisfied beings in the world, having given us the best of all they had."

The four looked soberly upon each other that evening. Had a miracle been performed, so quietly, with no blinding light from heaven?

"About a hundred years ago," said Castillo, "St. Vincent Ferrer, in Valencia, often brought the dead to life, as he gave sight to the blind and feet to the stump-legged. I have heard further that he preached his sermons in the Valencian tongue to great audiences, including French, English, and Italians, all of whom understood perfectly."

"When I was staying in Seville in the house of the Duke of Béjar," said Dorantes, "I heard tell that Don Juan de Zuñiga, Master of Alcantara, and present Archbishop of Seville, who is the son of the old Duke of Béjar, died when a child, and was raised from the dead by the miraculous intervention of blessed St. Vincent Ferrer." [8]

[8] Ortiz de Zuñiga, "Anales eclesiásticos," 422.

"St. Vincent Ferrer was a saint of the church," replied Cabeza de Vaca somberly. "And I am not a saint, nor even a holy priest, nor even a lay brother. I am only a soldier and a miserable sinner. *Ay, ¡pecador de mí!* Is it not most likely that the dead man was only in a trance, and my breathings and rubbings chafed back the life into his heart?"

"If it is so, it is still God's will," said Dorantes. "In my opinion, it would be best, if we ever come alive to Christian lands, to tell the circumstances exactly as they were, and to let the doctors of the church interpret them as they will. But I think that Holy Church looks askance at the miraculous deeds of laymen." [9]

"It would be best," murmured Estebanico, "to eat our fill of the tribute of prickly pears, for the season is almost at an end, and I see no other food in all this barren land. It may be that we shall need another miracle to keep life in our bodies through this winter."

The meeting became a council of expediency. The kindness of the Avavares, the esteem in which the four were held, the failing food, and the gathering cold made them decide to go into winter quarters with their hosts. They needed hides for covering, and these were reported to be unobtainable to the south.

So all that winter and through the spring of 1535 they remained there, waiting for the tuna season and returning plenty. In the mean-

[9] Caspar Plautus, in his "Nova Typis Transacta Navigatio" (1621), p. 91, blames Cabeza de Vaca, a *"scelestus miles,"* for usurping the clerical privilege of miracle. He is ardently defended by Antonio Ardoíno, in his "Examen apologético," prefixed to the 1736 edition of Cabeza de Vaca's "Naufragios."

The Rev. Samuel Purchas makes a delightful comment in his "Purchas His Pilgrimes" (XVII, 482): "Cures very wonderfull, yet true. Benzo (which travelled fourteene yeeres in the Indies with the Spaniards from 1541) [as a matter of fact, it was 1614—M. B.], saith that of six hundred of Narvaez his company scarsly ten returned, which at Mexico reported that they had by breathing on them cured the sicke, raised to life three dead men, etc. But, saith hee, Let their holines pardon me, I will easier beleeve that they killed foure living men then that they raised halfe one dead man to life. Ben. *l. 2. c.* 13. I permit some of these relations, more for knowledge of the Countrey, then for credit of Spanish cures in the Indies, which you shal find in Casas of another nature. These here challenge no Divine end to convert people to God, and therefore are not like to have any divine beginning, but are either falsly told, or falsly done, or falsly intended by the Father of falshood. And why may they not be ascribed to the Devill, either as lies, if never done; or if done, as devillish Arts to maintaine rapine and superstition, which are here mentioned the effects thereof? Acosta tells of a great miracle-worker in the Indies, a vicious man, and hanged for knaveries. This Cowes-Head the Author is also by Schmidel before, recorded for a bad man in his acts at the River of Plate. I will conclude with S. Aug. de unit. Ecc. *c.* 16. *Removeantur ista, vel sigmenta mendacium ominum vel portenta fallacium spirituum, etc.*"

W. Gleeson (History of Catholic Church in California, San Francisco, 1872, pp. 45–64) inclines to the belief that genuine miracles were performed.

time the fame of their cures spread widely and the sick came and were healed and proclaimed that the white men were truly children of the sun. Dorantes and Estebanico timidly tried their hand at curing, and found that God's grace was manifest in them as in their two teachers. They developed a technique, blowing upon the wounds in the manner of the saludadores, or faith-healing charlatans, of Castile. "I was the most extreme in being venturous and bold to attempt the performance of any cure," wrote Cabeza de Vaca, with the pride which came to him in security and which was destined to be his undoing. "No one whom we treated, but told us he was left well; and so great was the confidence that they would become healed if we ministered to them, they even believed that whilst we remained none of them could die."

Before long hunger, the old enemy, appeared. These Indians had no fish; probably they were barred from the sea by the fierce coastal Karankawas. Nor had they nuts or acorns, but only the roots painfully wrenched from the soil. Men and women forgot kindness in the hunt for food. The boys and girls went about so weak and swollen that they looked to the Spaniards like toads. Hunger obliterated such luxurious emotions as respect for one's neighbor. When a grateful patient would pay his doctor with a precious bit of deer-meat, the physician would gobble it raw; "for if we had put it on to roast, the first native that should have come along would have taken it off and devoured it; and it appeared to us not well to expose it to this risk; besides we were in such condition it would have given us pain to eat it roasted, and we could not have digested it so well as raw."

These gentlemen whose hands had once been too proud to touch any tool but a sword had found, in the wilderness, a craftsman's deftness. They made combs, bows, arrows, nets, and matting, which they bartered with the Indians for food.

Sometimes the Indians would set me to scraping and softening skins; and the days of my greatest prosperity there were those in which they gave me skins to dress. I would scrape them very deep and eat the scraps, which would sustain me two or three days. . . . I have already stated that throughout all this country we went naked, and as we were unaccustomed to being so, twice a year we cast our skins like serpents. The sun and air produced great sores on our breasts and shoulders, giving us sharp pain;

and the large loads we had, being very heavy, caused the cords to cut into our arms. The country is so broken and thickset, that often after getting our wood in the forests, the blood flowed from us in many places, caused by the obstruction of thorns and shrubs that tore our flesh wherever we went. At times, when my turn came to get wood, after it had cost me much blood, I could not bring it out either on my back or by dragging. In these labors my only solace and relief were in thinking of the sufferings of our Redeemer, Jesus Christ, and in the blood he shed for me, in considering how much greater must have been the torment he sustained from the thorns, than that I there received.

And yet, through all the body's woe, the heart burned bright with the new hope. In place of the old blind endurance now dwelt a definite purpose. The refugees dreamed forward and not alone backward. Most of all were they supported by the belief that somewhere in heaven there was a saint whose ear had caught their prayers.

Also, their Indian hosts, though sometimes heavy-handed with starvation, wished them well. Squatting about the camp-fires, on an equality with the braves, the exiles could feel almost the sense of comradeship. Perhaps they ventured to astound the ears of their friends with tales of castled Spain. Certainly they told of heaven's courts of bliss and the compassion of the sweet saints. The Indians responded with the marvels of their own folk. Cabeza de Vaca preserved in his book the strange story of Badthing. This, they said, had happened fifteen or sixteen years before.

They said that a man wandered through the country whom they called Badthing; he was small of body and wore a beard, and they never distinctly saw his features. When he came to the house where they lived, their hair stood up and they trembled. Presently a blazing torch shone at the door, when he entered and seized whom he chose, and giving him three great gashes in the side with a very sharp flint, the width of the hand and two palms in length; he put his hand in the gashes and drew forth the entrails, from one of which he would cut off a portion more or less the width of a palm, and throw it on the embers. Then he would give three gashes to an arm, the second gash being on the inside of an elbow, and would dislocate the limb. A little after this, he would set it again, and putting his hands on the wounds, these would instantly be healed. They said that frequently in the dance he appeared among them, sometimes in the dress of a woman, at others in that of a man; that when it pleased him he would take a buhío, or house, and lifting it high, after a little he would come down with it in a heavy fall. They also said that many times they offered him victuals, but that he never ate: they asked him whence he came and where was his abiding place, and he showed them a fissure in the earth and said that his house was there below. These things they told us of, we much laughed at and ridiculed; and they seeing our incredulity, brought to us many of those they said he had seized; and we saw the marks of the gashes made in the places according to the manner they had described. We told them he was a demon, and in the best way we could, gave them to understand, that if they would believe in God our Lord, and become Christians like us, they need have no fear of him, nor would he dare to come and inflict those injuries, and they might be certain he would not venture to appear while we remained in the land. At this they were delighted and lost much of their dread.

Somehow, day by day, the hungry winter passed. Spring came in, softening the hard heart of the wilderness. Guarded by the fierce spines of the cactus the sweet fruits took their form, and as they swelled the purpose of the Christians grew toward ripeness. About mid-May of 1535 the word was given; they were ready to make another start forward on their great journey.

CHAPTER X

THE GREAT JOURNEY

O<small>NE</small> day in the spring of 1535 Cabeza de Vaca found himself alone with Estebanico at some distance from the camp of their hosts, the Avavares. Was not this their moment for a forward stride? Seizing the impulse and the opportunity, the two walked the seven leagues separating them from the friendly tribe of the Maliacones. Their cordial reception encouraged them to believe that their action was sealed with heavenly approval. Three days later Estebanico returned to the Avavares, with plausible excuses for the savages' ears, and a private summons for Castillo and Dorantes. The three departed unobtrusively, carrying their little wealth of deerskins and weapons, and rejoined Cabeza de Vaca among the Maliacones. Though indeed they felt regret to quit so informally the kind barbarians, they well recognized that the affections of a host might prove as embarrassing as the rigors of a master.

The Maliacones were bound for a camping ground where mesquite and ebony beans would be found. On the way they were joined by the Arbadaos, amazingly weak, gaunt, and puff-bellied with hunger. Finding the promised food not yet ripe, the Maliacones proposed to return; they were indeed astonished when the four refused to accompany them. Instead, the Christians went into the plain beside the camp of the sickly Arbadaos, and there waited unspeaking, according to the etiquette of which they were now masters. They could see the Indians discussing together, with the sluggish interest of starving brains. At length several emissaries came forth from the encampment; one took each of the Spaniards by the hand, and led him to his lodging. He proffered friendship and shelter, but, alas, no food.

Here the pilgrims remained a week, eating the leaves of the prickly pear, baked, and, in desperation, the green pears themselves, filled with burning milky juice. This method of stilling the belly's cries served only to alter the form of suffering. The fire of the green tunas called for quenching with water, of which in that country there was none.

In this extremity the Christians could feel their strength ebbing day by day. They dared not venture forward, for fear that weakness would bring them down before they could find food and water. They dared not remain, lest they die, between starvation and the rebellion of the bowels against cactus leaves and the needled fruit.

Succor came in the form of two small dogs, the property of one of the Indians. The Christians bargained for these, and obtained them in return for most of the rewards of their winter's healing, nets, deer hides, and other things.

The blood and flesh of the dogs, which must have been more gaunt and bloodless than their Indian masters, brought a lift of strength to the Spaniards' bodies and a gush of courage to their minds. Commending their souls to God, and asking his special guidance, they bade farewell to their Arbadaos hosts. These, caring little if their guests came or went, pointed the way to a friendly tribe near by that spoke their language. So once more the quaking pilgrims girded themselves to follow their one clear purpose.

Rain fell heavily that day, slaking their thirst but chilling their fevered frames. They lost their way, and came to a wide forest, where they camped for the night, first plucking many leaves of the tuna. These they buried in the earth, to soften their harshness; in the morning they baked them well, until, with great good will, one could call them edible.

After breakfast, the travelers prayed long and urgently, confiding themselves most specially to the almighty's care. Emerging from the wood about mid-day, they encountered two women and some boys. The apparition of three white-skinned men and a black, uttering imperious cries, frightened the shy Indians into the forest. But the wanderers had learned how to decoy their game, and how to lure the natives' simple impulses. They remained at the wood's edge unmoving. After an hour they could hear the faintest of stirrings behind the trees. Stolidly, the hunters acted the part of the hunted, allowing the hidden savages time to observe them at length, letting their strangeness descend a little toward the commonplace. Their patience outlasted that of the

Indians, who finally ventured timidly forth, poised for flight or assault. Then with the practised air of welcome the Christians made the signs of peace and amity. The Indians, reassured, stepped forward, passed their hands over the Christians' faces and bodies, and then similarly smoothed their own.

The strangers would be welcome, they said, to their poor lodgings, which lay a few hours' journey distant. So the troop set forth, and came at nightfall to a settlement of fifty huts.

It is evident from this account and from the tone of our two sources that by this time the Christians had learned to trust that sense of guidance, which identified their own purposes with God's. No longer did they cringe like slaves when they saw an unknown red man. To fear had succeeded a calm courage, born of their belief that God or some kindly saint had chosen to save them alive for deep purposes, manifest in the current of healing that went out from their fingers into wasted and fevered bodies. They spoke to strange bands of natives with no betraying under-accent of apprehension, but with the authority of those who have received the certainty of God's grace.

In the morning these Indians, the Cuchendados, brought the sick to be healed. The four prayed, and put the cross on the maladies, and blew upon the wounds. The patients professed themselves much relieved, and offerings were made of food, only the odious, harsh buried leaves of the tuna, and the green fruit roasted. There the travelers remained a fortnight, recovering a little their strength as the prickly pear came to ripeness. When they dared press forward, they passed to a tribe two leagues farther to the southwest, leaving the Cuchendados inconsolable and all weeping.

By this new people they were likewise well received. The children were brought forward, to touch the strangers' hands and gain good fortune. An offering was made of a great quantity of the flour of mezquiquez, or mesquite. This mesquite-bean, now scorned by all but the most abject peon, made a welcome delicacy for the palates of the hidalgos.

The fruit while hanging on the tree, is very bitter and like unto the carob; when eaten with earth it is sweet and palatable. The method they have of preparing it is this: they make a hole of requisite depth in the ground, and throwing in the fruit, pound it with a club the thickness of the leg, a fathom and a half in length, until it is well mashed. Besides the earth that comes from the hole, they bring and add some handfuls, then returning to beat it a little while longer. Afterward it is thrown into a basket-shaped jar, upon which water is poured until it rises above and covers the mixture. He that beats it tastes it, and if it appears to him not sweet, he asks for earth to stir in, which is added until he finds it sweet. Then all sit around, and each putting in a hand, takes out as much as he can. The pits and hulls are thrown upon a skin, whence they are taken by him who does the pounding, and put into the jar. Thereon water is poured as at first, and when the froth and juice have been squeezed out, the pits and husks are thrown upon the skin. This they do three or four times to each pounding. Those present, for whom this is a great banquet, have their stomachs greatly distended by the earth and water they swallow.

The Spaniards, guests of honor at such a feast, felt the blessed distention of their stomachs. A great dance followed the banquet; the Indians, men and women, leaped and caprioled, unretarded by their earthy ballast. With their faces painted with red ochre and minium, they circled about the fire, to the rhythmic scraping of grooved sticks. They kept their feet together, their elbows out, their shoulders hunched; and thus they hopped round and round, belly to rump, for the space of six hours, without ever ceasing their circular progress or their lamentable cries. If any, overcome by weariness and the drugging of the peyote, fell unconscious, they were scratched from shoulder to ankle with rake-like tools armed with fish-teeth.[1]

The Spaniards gazed in solemn boredom until the dancers halted with exhaustion. Then each was led to a separate hut, before which six Indians stood guard, permitting no one to enter until daybreak. And during the following days the natives went hunting deer, solely for their guests. Thus once again they were strengthened for the great enterprise.

One day some women came, as emissaries from a tribe "further on," or to the southwest. They offered to carry the possessions, probably deerskins, of the great Magicians, if only they would come to confer their healing presence. At this word the old impatience seized the Spaniards so irresistibly that they would not wait for any en-

[1] Alonso de León, "Historia de Nuevo León," 44-45.

treaty of the Indians, not even until the women ambassadors should be enough rested to guide them on their way. The four set out once more, amid the howling lamentations of all the village.

Before they had gone four leagues they found themselves lost, and their directions at fault. Having recognized this mild correction of impetuosity, they were permitted to meet at a spring the women who were following them. They now submitted to these guides, and were led by them to a great swift river, as wide as the Guadalquivir at Seville. This they forded, with the water first to the knee, then to the thigh, then for more than two lances' length to the breast.

This great river was the Río Grande, and the point of the crossing was probably near Penitas and Cosner, in what is now Hidalgo County, Texas, and Reynosa Viejo, Mexico.[2]

They were now in the midst of tribes of whose life and habits we have an excellent description written only a century later. Captain Alonso de León, one of the earliest explorers of this region, found the inhabitants untouched by the high near-by civilizations of Spaniard and Aztec. Many of his observations serve to corroborate and elucidate the statements of Cabeza de Vaca.[3]

Though, according to the captain, they were a handsome race, tall and very fleet, they were a filthy, base, and ignorant people; cruel, vengeful, nursing their grievances, slow-witted, treasonable, sexually promiscuous, inclined to theft, mendacious, abhorrent of all labor.

They do not sow, or cultivate the land. They live freely and in idleness, which is the root of all the bad in which they are swallowed up. . . . They are gluttons, epicureans, sloths, and vagabonds. Their women are the ones who by day and by night seek the food and prepare it. In the meantime they sleep or move about. An Indian is accustomed to have a clump of tunas by his pillow when they are in season, in bulk like a hundredweight measure, of any sort whatsoever, and at night, without raising his head, he greedily eats

[2] Davenport and Wells, in S. W. H. Q., XXII, 232–236.

[3] It is much credit to the captain's sagacity that he states that Cabeza de Vaca must have passed through Cerralvo, in Nuevo León (p. 30). This village lies only thirty miles north of the line of march authoritatively laid down by Davenport and Wells (Southwestern Historical Quarterly, XXII). Yet all other investigators (except Bethel Coopwood, in Texas State Historical Quarterly, III, 134; and C. W. Raines, in Bibliography of Texas) went innumerable miles astray, taking the wanderers through mid-Texas and even northern New Mexico.

everything. And at dawn he is still so hungry as to collect the peels he has thrown away.[4]

The Indian women are not different from the men, in the very small lines [of body decoration] or in the rest of it. They cover their shameful parts with hay or grass, or some twine which they make of a certain herb like flax, and over this they wear loosely, if they have them, a deer hide behind and one before, like a skirt. The one before is shorter, and descends to the shins. The one behind drags a hand's breadth on the ground, clustered with beads, beans, or small hard fruits, or a kind of snails, or the teeth of animals, which rattle as they move about, and this they hold very pleasing. They usually wear another hide over the shoulder, like a cloak. Other nations wear, both men and women, mantles of rabbit skin, twisted in such a manner that each skin makes one thread, and many of these are woven together and thrown over the shoulder, in the manner of St. John the Baptist.[5]

In each rancho, or hut, live eight or ten or more persons, men, women, and children. . . . They live in bell-shaped huts of grass or cane, no larger than one of our silk tents. The doors are low, so they are obliged to enter stooping. In the middle they ordinarily have a fire, not so much that it may force them to leave the hut, nor so little that they may be cold in winter. They have it rather according to custom, than from any need of light, since they would rather be in the dark than filled with smoke. They sleep on the ground, with some hay or grass for a pillow, and some on bad deer hides, if they have any.

They are a very filthy people; they do not clean house, and all the filthiness remains, inside the hut as well as outside; and it is a shameful thing, and causes nausea and abhorrence to enter a settlement, by reason of the uncleanliness and stink that is there, inasmuch as a man can hardly find a place to put his feet. They do not wash their hands; and in case they bathe, it is rather for refreshment than for cleanliness. They use any part of the body for a napkin.

They had no morality, and their lusts knew no check, whether of age, sex, or kinship. Virginity was never preserved beyond the age of ten. Thus, in Alonso de León's time, all shared in common every

---

[4] Translation by Davenport and Wells (with corrections) in S. W. H. Q., XXII, 292–4 n.

[5] Cf. Bandelier, "Southwestern Historical Contributions," 141: "Even at the present time, the Moquis of Arizona manufacture blankets out of the fur of the jack-rabbit and the cony. The fur is cut into narrow strips, which are afterwards wound around a core of yucca fibre so as to form a cord, and out of such cords the blankets are plaited or tressed rather than woven. The garment is extremely warm and quite heavy." See the fine specimen in The American Museum of Natural History, New York.

venereal affliction. They were cannibals, eating the flesh of friends and enemies, grinding the bones to flavor their horrid drink, the peyote, and to strengthen their mezquitamal, or mesquite bread.

Some deduction may be made from Captain de León's estimate of a hostile, heathen race, predestined to servitude for the benefit of their souls. Nevertheless, he was a close and accurate observer, who spoke the native tongue and lived among the indigenes for many years. His picture may be taken as essentially accurate. If Cabeza de Vaca makes no mention of the loathly details, it is only because his nostrils were by this time accustomed to ever-present stenches and his eyes to the sight of bestiality.[6]

The four travelers, then, with their Indian women for guides, forded the Río Grande and came out on the shore of present Mexico. By nightfall they reached a village of a hundred *ranchos,* or lodgings. They were met outside the settlement by all the inhabitants, posted in expectation of the shamans' coming. The reception was loud and joyful; all leaped and shouted terrifically, slapping their hands with violence against the thighs.

They brought us gourds bored with holes and having pebbles in them, an instrument for the most important occasions, produced only at the dance or to effect cures, and which none dare touch but those who own them. They say there is virtue in them, and because they do not grow in that country, they come from heaven; nor do they know where they are to be found, only that the rivers bring them in their floods.[7]

In a fury of enthusiasm the natives flung themselves upon the holy visitors, only to touch them and be healed, "so that they lacked little of killing us." Then with the instinctive symbolism of all enthusiasts, they took the objects of their honor, hoisted them high, and carried them on heads and shoulders into the village. There they crowded so close, thrusting forward their diseased for healing, that the

---

[6] Anyway, our nice nostrils are a modern luxury. In the time of Ferdinand and Isabella, the narrow, swarming streets of Seville were swept of their accumulated filth and garbage every two weeks. Public latrines were established by the simple device of painting a cross on the wall, and clerics complained of the crosses at every external angle of their churches. (F. Rodríguez Marín, "Rinconete y Cortadillo," 62.)

[7] Alonso de León describes these gourds (p. 44). See the many examples, richly decorated, in the American Museum of Natural History.

Christians retired in dudgeon into the huts prepared for them. "On no account would we consent that they should rejoice over us any more that night." Thus they had learned to command, to subdue the purposes of a whole tribe to their comfort. For a time they had shrewdly adapted their ways to the habits of the wild men; now their authority could force the savages to obedience. That night they could hear, afar in the desert, the howled music and the rattle of the gourds of the Indians banished from their own village.

Next day, in solemn ceremonial, the Christians touched and blessed the sick. The Indians dismissed with a gift of arrows the women guides. Then the pilgrims turned again southwestward, accompanied by all the population of the village. They came soon to another settlement, where they were richly fed with tunas and deer meat, and were presented with twenty-eight loaves of mesquite meal.

The abundance of ripe tunas indicates that the midsummer of 1535 had arrived.

Here the four were surprised to witness a new custom. Their conductors acted as managers of the traveling faith-healers; when a man came to be treated, they would take from him his bow and arrows, shoes, and beads, and only then admit him to the presence.

After being attended to, he would go away highly pleased, saying that he was well. So we parted from these Indians, and went to others by whom we were welcomed. They brought us their sick, which, we having blessed, they declared were sound; he who was not healed, yet believed we could cure him; and with what the others to whom we had administered would relate, they made great rejoicing and dancing, so that they left us no sleep.

At the next village the Indians organized on a large scale the system of requiring the payment for the cures wrought by their illustrious companions. The inhabitants had gathered together the best of their possessions as propitiatory offerings to the magicians; but as these had no desire of any burdens and no need but for a little food, the accompanying guard of honor from the rearward village took all the gifts. And as the distinction between free-will offerings and loot seemed too fine for the Indian mind, the native escort entered the lodges of the village, ransacked them utterly, and carried off all

they found within. To the inhabitants they explained that this procedure was an ordinance of the healers, laid down in heaven, and
applied on earth by their express command. The hint was further
dropped that this custom would inevitably be enforced upon the next
village along the way.

To witness this unjust procedure gave us great concern, inflicted too
on those who received us hospitably; we feared also that it might provoke
offense, and be the cause of some tumult between them; but as we were
in no condition to make it better, or to dare chastise such conduct, for the
present we had to bear with it, until a time when we might have greater
authority among them. They, also, who lost their effects, attempted to
console us by saying that we should not be grieved on this account, as
they were so gratified at having seen us, that they held their properties to
be well bestowed, and that farther on they would be repaid by others who
were very rich.

The troubles of godhood were now evident. These simple barbarians
were hardly less exigent as suppliants than they had once been as
slave-holders. Three hours of blessing were required before the faithful companions would return to their own village and permit the four
to resume their progress.

Journeying still to the southwest, they found a race of handsome
men and women, tall and whiter than any yet seen. Many of them
were entirely blind, and many more were troubled by cataracts. These
Indians are identified with a race later known as Blancos or Pintos
(spotted), whose descendants along the lower Río Grande are still
noticeably lighter colored than is the common case. Cabeza de Vaca
makes no claim to have given sight to these blind, and the Oviedo
narrative merely avers: "though the Christians did not heal them all,
the Indians believed that they would heal them."

Here, in the clairvoyant air of morning, they discerned mountains
rising, bounding the way to southeast, south, and west. These, the
Sierra Pamoranes, perhaps the Sierra Madre Oriental, and the Mountains of Cerralvo, were the first interruptions to the green and brown
levels which they had seen from Florida forward. And these Spaniards
were hill-born men, whose boyhood vision had been bounded by
somber burning peaks. Cabeza de Vaca remembered the Sierras east

of Jerez, standing blue on a glassy base of heat, and he felt the hope that lies in all familiar things.

From the village of the blind Indians the course turned somewhat westward, for their hosts wished to introduce the healers to some kinsmen. The ritual looting of the kinsfolk proceeded according to the now established custom; yet the yield was small. The villagers had concealed their chiefest treasures. Thus the devout commonly accept their Lord, with a privilege of minor peculations against him. In the midst of the high festivities and rejoicings, the faithful repented their petty larcenies from Deity, and brought forth gifts of beads, ochre, and little bags of pearls.[8] These the four presented to their escort from the village of the blind. The dances and festivities were resumed, louder and more frantic.

The settlement where they now paused was on a river at the foot of a mountain. It stood probably near Los Aldamas in Nuevo León, on the Río San Juan, just below its junction with the Río Pesquería. Here, as the wild music of the dance throbbed about them, the four took counsel together and came to an important decision.

The tribesmen were urging them to turn again eastward toward the coast, for there dwelt rich people, the loot of whose villages would bring wealth, to cap the miraculous health now rewarding piety. Certainly, admitted the Spaniards, that would be the shortest route to Pánuco and their salvation. But the coast! How well they remembered the thirsty islands bounding the shallow sounds, peopled by the tall, fierce Karankawas! They shuddered, smelling again on a gust of memory those rank fishy bodies, enduring again the cuffs of those horny hands, feeling anew the welts on back and shoulders from the loads of wood and water and mat houses, submitting once more to the bloody jokes and witty tortures. No, better any circuitous way among these docile and adoring creatures than ever to fall again into such savage hands.

To the south, then? But to the south rose the high wall of the Sierra Madre mountains. Best to mount the bed of the river, the Río Pesquería, which flowed down from the west, and hope, in good

---

[8] Perhaps mica, or foliated gypsum (Bandelier *ed.* of "Journey of Cabeza de Vaca," 134 n.).

time, to turn southward to the land of Christians. Although the Indians persisted that no men dwelt toward the sunset, except far away, it would be better to go that way, and even north of west, making a circuit of the barren lands, rather than to venture again along the evil coast. Had they not, among the friendly people, gained near as many miles in four months as in the seven years before?

There was another reason for the election of the inland course. "Moreover, we chose this course because in traversing the country we should learn many particulars of it, so that should God our Lord be pleased to take any of us thence, and lead us to the land of Christians, we might carry that information and news of it." This reason may nevertheless have been an afterthought, which came to the writer when he was setting down his story for the king's ear and for his own worldly advantage. I think that at this time the pilgrims' thought was not of mundane wealth, but of saving the treasure of their souls and bodies.

So they turned westward, on a journey that was to take them two thousand miles before they should see a white face. Had they chosen to head directly southward, against the noon-day sun, they would have found Spanish settlements within about three hundred miles, and news of them long ere that.

Westward, then, they went, along the plain near the river, with a large escort and with women to carry water, "and so great was our authority that no one dared drink of it without our permission." But as they found no dwellers here, the Indians, who had lost their all and saw no means of reimbursing themselves, fell into deep discouragement. After vain attempts to persuade the wonder-workers to return toward the rich country, they dropped their loads and said farewell, weeping bitterly. The Christians watched them go. Could this be the end of a brief glory? Were the guiding saints speaking perhaps with the voices of the Indians, not with the counsels they heard in their hearts? What lay to the west, among the bare mountains, along the dwindling river?

They kneeled in prayer, took up the abandoned burdens, and marched again westward. For all they knew, nothing lay before them but the sunset.

As they plodded forward, somber, beside the stream twining through the narrow valley, they had a sign. Far ahead, something stirred among the cottonwoods by the waterside. Trudging toward them, out of the unknown, baleful west, came two women, carrying heavy packs. These two advanced, and offered the Spaniards a tribute; it was corn-meal. The travelers thanked the Lord for this evidence of good will. They had seen no sign of maize since they had left Florida, seven years before. The women said that higher up the river would be found dwellings, plenty of that corn-meal, and prickly pears. They shouldered their loads and slogged off down-stream, and the Christians set their backs to those retreating backs.

About sunset they arrived at a settlement, and were received with no joy, but with weeping and great sorrow, for the inhabitants had already heard tales of the pillaging that accompanied the saints on their way. Their sorrow turned to gladness when they saw the travelers alone, and again to sorrow in the following dawn, when the laggard escort from the previous village appeared, having received good tidings from the women transporting corn-meal.

As they came upon the occupants unprepared and in supposed safety, having no place in which to conceal anything, all they possessed was taken from them, for which they wept much. In consolation the plunderers told them that we were children of the sun and that we had power to heal the sick and to destroy; and other lies even greater than these, which none knew how to tell better than they when they find it convenient. They bade them conduct us with great respect, advised that they should be careful to offend us in nothing, give us all they might possess, and endeavor to take us where people were numerous; and that wheresoever they arrived with us, they should rob and pillage the people of what they have, since this was customary.

At these instructions awe and reverence succeeded to sullen looks. Eagerly the tribesmen proposed a forward march. And indeed, if the pilgrims had sought for some subtle means of hastening their onward journey, they could have devised nothing more effective than this method of successive recompense from the tribes that lay before. Three days they went up river, to a large settlement; an advance party from their escort ran ahead to inform the villagers of the custom inaugurated by the children of the sun. New details were added to the growing legend, "for these people are all very fond of romance, and are great liars, particularly where they have any interest."

In this village an important ceremony occurred. Two medicine-men presented to the strange wonder-workers two ceremonial rattles, painted gourds filled with seeds or pebbles, fitted with handles and dangling feathers. Such rattles are sacred objects to all Indians, from Alaska to the gulf, the mace of the ruler, the wand of the magician, the crucifix of the priest. The precious symbols were thankfully received. Estebanico especially rattled the gourds with incessant joy, unwitting that one of them was one day to bring about his death.

So still westward, up the Río Pesquería, up the Río Salinas, while those streams went dry, till finally there were no more whitened stones to mark the course of the spring freshets. To-day, the traveler from Laredo to Mexico City, waking in the early morning, raises the window-shade of his Pullman berth to look down from a steel bridge to the Salinas river-bed, along which the pilgrim band once made its way.

When the river failed, they went "inland," apparently north of west, along the slopes of the Sierra Madre, for an estimated fifty leagues. At a certain settlement they found men of a different nation and tongue. These gave the Christians two marvelous gifts, to Dorantes a great copper rattle, with a human face rudely represented on it, and to the others shawls of cotton. Cotton was amazing enough; but the sight of copper acted with magic, to draw every old memory out of the nearly forgotten past. The four suddenly ceased to be refugees, desperately hunting for their safe home; they remembered that all their old purpose had been Gold.

Now, in their evening colloquies and during midday rests, their thoughts played with the fancy of emerging from their trials with the clue to that Gran Copal, the mountain reliably asserted to shine so bright with diamonds that travelers must approach it by night, or to the Eldorado northwest of Mexico where the fishermen used gold nuggets for sinkers. In the midst of heaven's great mercies they dreamed of wealth, governorships, and worldly pride; and this, as any churchman would have told them, was an offense against the Grace of God.

Whence came this copper? The Indians, closely questioned, pointed to the north, and said that there, among strange peoples, the metal was plentiful.[9] The cotton probably came from the land of the Pueblos, in present New Mexico.

Next day the pilgrims climbed the ridge of mountains, bestrewn with iron-filled lava, and descended into a green valley by a beautiful river. The stream must have been one of the branches of the Nadadores, which still flow between fine groves of cypress, pecan, and walnut. As the travelers approached a populous village, the happy inhabitants came forth to meet them, carrying their children on their backs. The Christians received many gifts, bags of pearls, and, for the first time, buffalo hides. Thus they were verging north to the southern limit of the buffalo range. Here also they had their first acquaintance with piñones, the delicious pine nuts of the southwest.

In that country are small pine-trees, the cones like little eggs; but the nuts are better than those of Castile, as its husk is very thin, and while green is beaten and made into balls, to be thus eaten. When the nut is dry, it is pounded with the husks, and consumed in the form of flour.

Here Cabeza de Vaca performed a notable surgical feat. A man was brought to him who had been wounded long before by an arrow; the head, he said, was lodged above his heart, wherefor he was always sick. The healer, after proper prayers, felt and palped the region, and found the arrow-head had passed through the cartilage.

With a knife I carried [of flint or obsidian?], I opened the breast to the place, and saw the point was aslant and troublesome to take out. I continued to cut, and, putting in the point of the knife, at last with great difficulty I drew the head forth. It was very long. With the bone of a deer, and by my knowledge of surgery, I made two stitches. That done, as he was bleeding copiously, with the hair of a skin I stanched the flow. They asked me for the arrow-head after I had taken it out, which I gave, when the whole town came to look at it. They sent it into the back country that the people there might view it. In consequence of this operation they had many of their customary dances and festivities. The next day I cut

9 As a matter of fact, it was extremely rare. But when Coronado, in 1541, reached Quivira, probably near Great Bend, Kansas, he found the chief wearing a copper plate about his neck. "Spanish Explorers in the Southern United States," 337, n.

the two stitches and the Indian was well. The wound I made appeared only like a seam in the palm of the hand. He said he felt no pain or sensitiveness in it whatsoever. This cure gave us control throughout the country.

So great, indeed, was the white men's mastery, that two thousand grateful people accompanied them on the next stage of their progress. The way now led northward, for to the west rose the stern and waterless bulk of the Sierra del Carmen. But the lower slopes were populous and abounding in game. The Indians displayed amazing skill as hunters. Each carried a curved stick like a boomerang, about a foot and a half in length (the rabbit sticks of the Pueblos). These they would throw with sportsmen's humor, cutting off a rabbit's retreat, driving the crazed creature from one hunter to another, and finally into the hand of the complimented guest; "so that, according to my thinking, it is the most pleasing sport which can be imagined." Meanwhile, up on the ridges, the archers would be hunting deer; at night they would return with five or six for each Christian, beside quail and other game. "Indeed, whatever they either killed or found, was put before us, without themselves daring to take anything until we had blessed it, though they should be expiring of hunger, they having so established the rule, since marching with us."

As night drew down, the Indians would lead the way to a suitable camp. The women burden-bearers set up the mat lodges they carried, one for each of the saints, with a space before for his guard of honor. The game was cleaned and set to roast in certain ovens, quickly constructed. The best bits were laid before the masters; then the Indians, in endless file, knelt in turn for the sign of the cross to sanctify their meat.

Frequently we were accompanied by three or four thousand persons, and as we had to breathe upon and sanctify the food and drink for each, and grant permission to do the many things they would come to ask, it may be seen how great was the annoyance. The women first brought us prickly pears, spiders, worms, and whatever else they could gather; for even were they famishing, they would eat nothing unless we gave it them.

By such progress, traveling northward, they came to a river flowing from the north. This we may take to be the Sabinas. They had been following the present route of the Mexican International Railroad from Monclova.

From here forward the indications of the route are fewer and less exact. Cabeza de Vaca, tiring of his record of the daily routine of travel, says: "We traveled through so many sorts of people, of such diverse languages, the memory fails to recall them." The itinerary states that they traversed thirty leagues of plain and fifty of barren, rugged, thirsty mountains, where they found little game and much hunger, and at the end a very large river, which they forded with the water to the breast. Evidently then they had turned northwestward from the Río Sabinas, and soon had left the watered plains for the grim ranges of the Desert of Coahuila. The very large river was unquestionably the Río Grande; they had this second sight of it perhaps at Boquillas, perhaps down-stream to the northeast. Davenport and Wells suggest the mouth of Sanderson Creek. The stream was low and fordable, because two years of drought had gone before.

Faith dwelt in the mountains and deserts, as in all history it has. The tribesmen to whom the travelers came did not merely suffer themselves to be plundered; rather they brought forth all their goods as a free-will offering. To this they were encouraged by the escort from the village next before, who had marched empty to go back full.

They would tell those among whom we came, to be careful and make no concealment, as nothing could be done without our knowledge, and we might cause them to die, as the sun revealed everything to us. So great was their fear that during the first days they were with us, they continually trembled, without daring even to speak, or raise their eyes to the heavens.

When the procession descended into the Río Grande Valley, the four may well have felt twinges of unfaith. Here the great river cuts its way through solid rock for many a long mile, dividing the mountains in the enormous semicircle of the Big Bend. The old axiom, that a waterway is man's way also, that beside the river runs the path, is here proved false. In many a gorge and defile, the walls rise vertically from the rushing water a thousand feet. There was no chance for the pilgrims to take their way westward. Their only escape was to climb northward up one of the lateral ravines that break the river's wall, and thus reach the plateau, whereon they might again shape their course toward the Christian land.

They must have ascended thus, perhaps up one of the trails by which the Comanches in later years would annually raid south into Mexico, returning with thousands of cattle across the fords and up into the trackless mountains. At any rate, the relentless four came to a plain beyond mountains, with many of their companions undone by exhaustion and privation. Not improbably they were in the neighborhood of Alpine. Here they found people who had come from afar to meet them, with rich gifts, twice as many as the escort could carry. "I told those who gave, to resume the goods that they might not lie.there and be lost; but they answered that they could in no wise do so, as it was not their custom after they had bestowed a thing to take it back; so they were left to perish." Thus the catchword of the "Indian giver" is belied.

These new friends demurred when the Christians ordered a continuance of the journey toward the setting sun. The Indians said the next people were far away, and that with them they were at war. But the Christians spoke again, mercifully explaining that their words were sacred and their commands could not be countered by any worldly circumstance. The Children of the Sun had spoken; they must be taken to the Sun, in the land where he comes down to earth. Reluctantly, the Indians sent forward two women as ambassadors, "for the women can negotiate even though there be a war." One was a captive from the hostile nation, who went as interpreter; the other was a native of the mountain tribe. The Christians followed toward the appointed place where the answer from the embassy was to be brought.

They were following, most likely, the old Salt Trail that ran from the Pecos River past the Comanche Springs, over Paisano Pass, and down to the Río Grande at its confluent with the Conchos. This was the highway to the great salt deposits, and the road to the land of the buffalo; it was the course of the early Spanish explorers; in the nineteenth century it was the Chihuahua Trail, over which Mexican treasure made its twelve-month journey to St. Louis; and now one may ride the length of it in a railroad train.

Coming to the rendezvous, they found no sign of the women ambassadors. The Indians descended into a gloom more doleful even than before. The women, they vowed, had sought in vain a settlement; they were captured; they were dead. The Children of the Sun should not go forward.

The Children of the Sun were much offended. Cabeza de Vaca, when food was proffered him, refused it, and stalked out of camp to spend the night in the solitary open. "But directly they came to where I was, and remained all night without sleep, talking to me in great fear, telling me how terrified they were, beseeching us to be no longer angry, and said that they would lead us in the direction it was our wish to go, though they knew they should die on the way."

In the midst of the masters' displeasure, a number of the Indians fell ill, and on the next day eight men died. Then through all the country "there was such dread that it seemed as if the inhabitants would die of fear at sight of us. They besought us not to remain angered, nor require that more of them should die. They believed we caused their death by only willing it, when in truth it gave us so much pain that it could not be greater; for, beside the distress of their death, we feared that they might all die, or abandon us of fright, and that other people henceforward would do the same, seeing what had come to these. We prayed to God, our Lord, for help; and from that time the sick began to get better."

No one could have been more tender with suffering than these Indians; yet after the death of a wife or brother they remained stoical and dry-eyed. Any revelation of emotion was shameful. The travelers, in their fortnight's stay among them, never saw an infant smile; once only was a child observed in tears. Quick punishment was wreaked for that show of sensibility; "with the sharp teeth of a rat they scratched him from the shoulders down nearly to the end of the legs. Seeing this cruelty, and offended at it, I asked why they did so: they said for chastisement, because the child had wept in my presence."

Though stern and impatient of weakness, these Indians of the Big Bend Mountains were the most obedient that the travelers had seen. They were a handsome people and of fine stature. Ethnologists have not surely identified their race.

Three days after the arrival at the rendezvous, the women sent as envoys returned. The news was not good. Only a few men were left in the region ahead, for nearly all had gone buffalo-hunting in the north country. And little food or wealth was to be found there, too little to support a pillaging army.

At this word great lamentation sounded in the camp. The Indians complained that they were all sick and hungry and far from home; let the Children of the Sun go north to the buffalo country, not southwest to that barren, hostile land.

The Christians had learned to speak as masters, nay as gods walking the earth for some celestial whim. The sick, they decreed, might remain behind, but a guard of honor of twenty or thirty braves must accompany them to the enemy's city to the southwest.

Here, in the text, is a suggestion of the shrewdness with which the prestige of the four was supported. The two women were the first voices annunciatory of Deity. (Ordinarily four braves, one to represent each of the heavenly envoys, performed this service.) Then, as the main body approached the town, the women guides went ahead with Castillo and Estebanico, a white man and a black, the proofs of miracle. The two organized the reception; they led all the population, bearing gifts: beans, squashes, gourds, and buffalo hides, on the back trail to a meeting with the wonder-workers. Now these Indians were filled with awe at the fulfilment of the annunciation, hope for the cure of their ills, and delight at the interruption to life's boredom. The guard of honor was dismissed; the four, with well-practised deific majesty, paced down the trail to the village.

To their delight, this settlement was built of permanent houses, the first the wanderers had seen. The inhabitants, the finest, strongest, and most intelligent encountered on the whole journey, had some seed-corn and understood its cultivation. Fields of maize would have been growing green in the valley, had not a two years' drought parched all the plains. Notwithstanding the natives' advancement, they had no pottery. They boiled food by dropping red-hot stones in a gourd with the food. "Thus it may be seen and remarked how curious and diversified are the contrivances and ingenuity of the human family."

These Indians were later known as Jumanos; the meeting-place was the present Presidio del Norte, at the junction of the Río Grande and the Conchos. This identification is one of the most securely fixed points of the journey.

Forty-seven years later, in the autumn of 1582, Antonio de Espejo, a god-fearing citizen of western Mexico, fitted out an expedition to rescue some Franciscan monks who were lost in the present New Mexico. His party descended the Conchos to its union with the Río Grande. There he found five pueblos, built of substantial flat-roofed houses, accommodating ten thousand people, tall men, with streaked faces, cultivating corn, gourds, and beans.

These people are all clothed, and seemed to have some light of our holy faith; for they made signes of God, looking up towards heaven, and call him in their language Apalito, and acknowledge him for their Lord, from whose bountifull hand and mercy they confesse that they have received their life and being, and these worldly goods. Many of them with their wives and children came unto the frier (which the captaine and souldiers brought with them) that hee might crosse and blesse them. Who demanding of them, from whom they had received that knowledge of God, they answered, from three Christians, & one Negro which passed that way, and remained certaine dayes among them, who by the signes which they made, were Alvaro Nunnez Cabeça de Vaca, and Dorantes, and Castillo Maldonado, and a Negro; all of which escaped of the company which Pamphilo de Narvaez landed in Florida; who after they had bene many dayes captives and slaves, escaped and came to these townes, by whom God shewed many miracles, and healed onely by the touching of their hands many sicke persons, by reason whereof they became very famous in all that countrey.[10]

So in that quiet valley, where life flows as steadily as the passing river, and the only pulse of time is the flood season and the drought season, the memory of the four godlike men out of the mountains was preserved. Others besides Espejo crossed the trail of the forlorn

10 "Colección de Documentos inéditos . . . de América," XV, 107. Translation from Hakluyt: Navigations, IX, 191.

Narváez expeditionaries. Soto's men, after months of the wilderness, had found the marks of their boat-building, the bones of their horses, on the shore of Florida. A year later, Soto saw the dagger of Theodoro the Greek, somewhere in the interior of Alabama. Nor is this all. When Coronado and his conquerors were ranging the Staked Plains, five hundred miles to the north, in 1541, they met an old blind Teya Indian who said that he had seen men like them many days before, but far to the south toward Mexico.[11] In a near-by valley the explorers found a village through which, as they understood it, Cabeza de Vaca and Dorantes had passed. The inhabitants had piled all their tanned buffalo hides and other possessions together, in the expectation that the white men would bless them and pass on. But the Spanish general and his men would follow no such precedent, and all together made a rush, "and in less than a quarter of an hour nothing was left but the empty ground. The natives who happened to see this also took a hand in it. The women and some others were left crying, because they thought that the strangers were not going to take anything, but would bless them, as Cabeza de Vaca and Dorantes had done when they passed through there."

Coronado's men must have misunderstood the natives, for it is impossible to reconcile such a northern course with the other indications of our pilgrims' route. No doubt the fact was that the natives had heard the stories of their magical doings in the south. The tale may have been brought to the plains by Río Grande Indians who had come north hunting buffalo. Later missionary records show an intimate relation between the Teyas and the Jumanos.[12]

Thus in the enormous waste of our continent the passage of four strong men was marked and remembered. A voice crying in the wilderness ripples with increasing sound until all the world and all time can hear it. The words spoken by these lost creatures in horrid solitudes are still reverberating, and perhaps the courage they drew

[11] So in the Jaramillo narrative. See George P. Winship, "The Coronado Expedition," in Fourteenth Annual Report of Bureau of Ethnology, I, 588.
[12] "Spanish Explorers in the Southern United States," 332; James N. Baskett in Texas Hist. Ass. Q., X, 322. Garcilaso the Inca, in his somewhat romanced account of Soto's expedition, says that the explorers in the Province of Guacane (perhaps eastern Texas) saw wooden crosses on the houses, because the natives had heard of Cabeza de Vaca's miracles and cures. This is certainly impossible.

from suffering may even to-day bring, by example, some strength to present weakness.

The four halted, then, among these cordial, intelligent, field-tilling, well-traveled people, to take counsel. It was apparently about the first of December, 1535. Time was hurrying past, and the long journey seemed to bring the wanderers no nearer to their bourn. To the south the wall of the Río Grande was broken by the Conchos River; yet the Indians would not counsel the ascent of that tributary. If the Children of the Sun would not turn back to the northeast, where the hunch-backed cows roamed and where food was plentiful, they might indeed proceed northwest along the Río Grande. By that route they would come, after many days, to a land of corn; on the way they would find many people of the Jumanos tongue, though hostile to the speakers; but, because of the long drought, they would find little food. They would be forced to eat *chacan,* a kind of fruit ground between stones, so coarse and dry that the Children of the Sun would think it quite uneatable. In proof of this they laid some chacan before the Spaniards, and indeed it did repel even the humility of their stomachs.

In spite of all, the Río Grande route seemed the best. So they followed up the east bank, through a hungry region. No doubt they were given some maguey to eat, the roasted leaf bases and trunks of various species of agave. But they refused the chacan, and supported their strength with a handful of deer-fat daily, specially preserved for such an emergency. The inhabitants of this country, calmly starving through the long drought, offered willing gifts of buffalo-hides, but they had nothing else to bestow. Their fashion of receiving the strangers was somewhat changed from the familiar custom. They would not issue forth to meet the visitors, but would remain within their common houses, all sitting with faces to the wall, their heads bowed and the hair pulled over their eyes. All their property stood in a heap in the middle of the house, for the strangers to take as they would. Every night of this journey the wanderers slept in houses.

With all their hunger, the four made their way with arduous haste. The level valley floor, the unambiguous road of the river, the cool of the cottonwood shade, tempted them onward with utmost strides to their goal. The seventeen days the Indians allowed to the ford where they must leave the watercourse for the desert trail were covered in fifteen. So they crossed the Río Grande, probably at San Elizario, twenty miles down-stream from El Paso, and bade a last farewell to that friendly river.

Then westward for seventeen days. Undoubtedly they passed by way of Samalayuca, a green oasis in the desert, thirty-two miles by rail south of El Paso. West again through the Médanos, the shining hills of soft blowing white sand, which embraced the wagons of the Forty-Niners and held them there for leisured looting by the Apaches. The desert trails never change; they lie now, as in Cabeza de Vaca's time, from water-hole to water-hole. Thirty miles west of Samalayuca is the first gleam of water, the salt lake of the Salado, beside which stand some sweet water pools.[13] The trail continued over sands barren of any growth, among fantastic mountains, red and golden cones and cylinders, geometrical toys forgotten in the gods' sand-pile. Thus to the watercourse of the Santa María, a river that flows two hundred miles to an ignominious grave in the desert. Thence through mountain defiles to Correlitos, a region of more cheer, and a soil from which some sort of life can spring. Perhaps it was here that they found a people who for a third of the year ate nothing but powdered straw, which had of necessity to be the travelers' food. Over the great back of the Sierra Madre then, and down into a village of permanent houses (perhaps Babisbe, on the Yaqui River, in Sonora[14]), where they were joyfully received, and presented with much corn, corn-meal, squashes, beans, and cotton shawls. These, having been blessed, were bestowed upon the guides, who returned to their own people, the happiest creatures on earth. "We gave thanks to God, our Lord, for having brought us where we had found so much food."

They would have offered even more earnest thanks had they known that this was the last of their great hunger. Henceforward they found villages of settled races, dwelling in adobe houses or mat huts, sowing corn, beans, and squash. The women were modestly dressed in cotton aprons with bodices of deerskin, and these, marvel of marvels, they

---

[13] John R. Bartlett, "Explorations and Incidents," II, 371.
[14] Davenport, in S. W. H. Q., XXVIII, 149.

would launder with the soap-like root of the yucca. The women were treated with more honor than among any tribe yet seen. The good will and piety of these people matched their high culture.

The procession ascended southward the narrow valley of the Yaqui to Guasavas, and there turned southwest, climbing the ridges by a trail later to be well known, which led to Batuco on the Rio Oposura and thence to Ures in the Sonora Valley.[15] And what a procession! First the guides; then the gaunt white men, breech-clouted, long-bearded, ardent-eyed, wearing clumsy wooden crucifixes, and empty-handed except for their ceremonial rattling gourds; and Estebanico the black, the officious major-domo of the heaven-born, and needing constant correction by them, for he was all too prone to abuse his privilege of godhood with the wives of man.

While traveling, we went without food all day until night, and we ate so little as to astonish them. We never felt exhaustion, neither were we in fact at all weary, so inured were we to hardship. We possessed great influence and authority: to preserve both, we seldom talked with them. The negro was in constant conversation; he informed himself about the ways we wished to take, of the towns there were, and the matters we desired to know.

Following along the trail came the crowd of the faithful, more than three thousand often, including the sick and the afflicted, walking with a strength not their own. Women in labor would fall out of the procession, and would appear an hour later with a new human being to be blessed. Mothers would bring tiny babies, taught to hold three kernels in their fists; for they believed that if the white men would accept this gift of corn, the baby making the present would never be sick.

The pilgrims found in this country people speaking many and dissimilar tongues, to which their knowledge of six Indian languages gave no clue. But communication was sure and instant, for they possessed a thorough acquaintance with the universal tongueless medium, the sign language.

Throughout all these countries the people who were at war immediately made friends, that they might come to meet us, and bring what they pos-

[15] Davenport, in S. W. H. Q., XXVIII, 150.

sessed. In this way we left all the land at peace, and we taught all the inhabitants by signs, which they understood, that in heaven was a Man we
called God, who had created the sky and the earth; him we worshipped
and had for our master; that we did what he commanded and from his
hand came all good; and would they do as we did, all would be well with
them. So ready of apprehension we found them that, could we have had
the use of language by which to make ourselves perfectly understood, we
should have left them all Christians. Thus much we gave them to understand the best we could. And afterward, when the sun rose, they opened
their hands together with loud shouting towards the heavens, and then
drew them down all over their bodies. They did the same again when the
sun went down.

They would bathe their bodies with their hands full of light, says
Las Casas, beautifully. The saintly historian recalls that the Galicians
adore the Holy Sacrament with the same gesture.[16]

So finally this army came down into the valley of the Sonora,
where the river emerges from its gorges into the coastal plain. They
found here three pueblos, a thriving settlement in an irrigated valley.
It was the site of the present Ures. The inhabitants made a special
offering to Dorantes of six hundred hearts of deer, opened; and for
this reason the travelers named the town Pueblo de los Corazones.
There were other gifts: cotton shawls, beads of South Sea coral, and
turquoises from the north. And, to their great amazement, five
emeralds (perhaps malachite?) made into arrowheads, used in the
ceremonial dances. "Whence do these come?" asked Cabeza de Vaca.
"From the high mountains to the north, where are great populous
cities and tall houses; those people sell us these emeralds in return
for the feathers of the Guacamayo, our green parrot."

These words were one of those little sentences, out of the multi-
tudinous voices of the world, that grow and grow evilly until they
become in themselves almost a demon, leading souls to ambush by
promises. The Indians of the Pueblo de los Corazones were telling,
in all honesty, of the high adobe pueblos of the poor and simple Zuñis
of New Mexico. But when the story was reported in Mexico and
Spain, greedy adventurers could imagine the emerald town only as
another Mexico, richer in gold and jewels, the more radiant for its

[16] "Apologética Historia," 448.

forbidding isolation. The phrase of the humble Indian of the Sonora mountains was one of the oracles that sent Coronado over desert and mountain as far as Kansas, and that led Soto to his grave in Mississippi mud.

Though greed may have stirred in the hearts of the four, it was not strong enough to turn them from their homesick passion. Coming down the western slopes of the Sierra Madre, with South Sea corals in their hands, they had the sense that they were drawing near to their own kind. Even gold now meant little to these homing men. Throughout the mountains they found what they took to be clear traces of gold, lead, iron, and copper, and yet they would not pause. By playing the part of gods, they had taken on some of the attributes of deity—imperiousness, scorn of base material concerns, and even the sacred jealousy of Jehovah.

At Ures the travelers had definite reports of the South Sea (the Gulf of California), which lies, in fact, a hundred miles to the west. On the coast, they were told, lived a timid and dejected people, without maize, feeding on fish and powdered foxtail grass and straw. They were a quick, nimble race, the Indians said, though very corpulent; they protected their naked bodies from rain in an unusual way. Having rapidly tied together a bundle of long straws or stalks, each seated himself, put his individual thatch roof on his head, and so sat for as many hours as the rain lasted.

Probably because of the nearness of the sea and the poor promise of food along its shores, it seemed best to the wanderers to turn southeast. Thus, paralleling the coast, they could not fail to strike the Spanish settlements of Mexico. After three days in Ures, they journeyed, therefore, by way of Matape to the Yaqui River. This they found in spate with the great rains, and they were obliged to wait a fortnight for it to subside.

It was here that Castillo noticed an Indian with a curious necklace. Idly, he went close to inspect it. He uttered a sudden great shout. The necklace ornament was the buckle of a sword-belt, and from the buckle dangled a horse-shoe nail.

"Where did you get this?" the white men asked with eager signs. The native pointed solemnly upward; from heaven. Ay, but what messenger had brought heaven's treasure to earth? White-faced gods, came the answer, with beards and shining clothes, with glittering sharp shafts in their hands and deadly lances. Some of them sat on enormous dragons. They had come to that river, and had killed two Indians with their lances.

In a manner of the utmost indifference we could feign, we asked them what had become of those men. They answered us that they had gone to sea, putting their lances beneath the water; afterwards they were seen on the surface going toward the sunset. For this we gave many thanks to God our Lord. We had before despaired of ever hearing more of Christians.

Who were these Christians? There is no record of precedent exploration by sea so far north in the Gulf of California. Perhaps they were the men of Hurtado de Mendoza, who sailed this way in 1532 and was eventually shipwrecked. He and all his men were killed on the Río Fuerte, a hundred miles south; only the boasts of the Indians brought the news to the historians.

In the midst of our travelers' new hope there dwelt a lurking fear. It was still possible that the landing-party on the coast were themselves lost creatures, driven thousands of miles from their course by the mysterious agents of the South Sea. Perhaps the four were still many a league from Mexico.

But as they hastened south with impatient feet this fear vanished, to be replaced by another fear. There came plenty of word of the Christians, and soon the wanderers learned this news with sinking hearts, and anger, and forebodings of their own misfortune. For all the news was in the form of smoking villages, and skeletons hung to trees by Spanish ropes, and buzzard-clusters startled by the wayside. The Spaniards were abroad through that country, hunting slaves. I can make no paraphrase to equal the eye-witness actuality of Cabeza de Vaca's story.

We passed through many territories and found them vacant: their inhabitants wandered fleeing among the mountains, without daring to have houses or till the earth for fear of Christians. The sight was one of infinite pain to us, a land very fertile and beautiful, abounding in springs and streams, the hamlets deserted and burned, the people thin and weak, all fleeing or in concealment. As they did not plant, they appeased their keen hunger by eating roots and the bark of trees. We bore a share in the famine along the whole way; for poorly could these unfortunates provide for us, themselves being so reduced they looked as though they would willingly die.

They brought shawls of those they had concealed because of the Christians, presenting them to us; and they related how the Christians at other times had come through the land, destroying and burning the towns, carrying away half the men, and all the women and children, while those who had been able to escape were wandering about fugitives. We found them so alarmed they dared not remain anywhere. They would not nor could they till the earth, but preferred to die rather than live in dread of such cruel usage as they received. Although these showed themselves greatly delighted with us, we feared that on our arrival among those who held the frontier, and fought against the Christians, they would treat us badly, and revenge upon us the conduct of their enemies; but, when God our Lord was pleased to bring us there, they began to dread and respect us as the others had done, and even somewhat more, at which we no little wondered. Thence it may at once be seen that, to bring all these people to be Christians and to the obedience of the Imperial Majesty, they must be won by kindness, which is a way certain, and no other is.

They took us to a town on the edge of a range of mountains, to which the ascent is over difficult crags. We found many people there collected out of fear of the Christians. They received us well, and presented us all they had. They gave us more than two thousand back-loads of maize, which we gave to the distressed and hungered beings who guided us to that place. The next day we despatched four messengers through the country, as we were accustomed to do, that they should call together all the Indians they could reach at a town distant three days' march. We set out the day after with all the people. The tracks of the Christians and marks where they slept were continually seen. At midday we met our messengers, who told us they had found no Indians, that they were roving and hiding in the forests, fleeing that the Christians might not kill nor make them slaves; the night before they had observed the Christians from behind trees, and watched what they were about, carrying away many people in chains.

Those who came with us were alarmed at this intelligence; some returned to spread the news over the land that the Christians were coming; and many more would have followed, had we not forbidden it and told them to cast aside their fear, when they reassured themselves and were well content. At the time we had Indians with us belonging a hundred leagues behind, and we could not persuade them to return to their homes. To reassure them, we stayed there that night; the day after we marched and slept on the road. The following day those whom we had sent forward as messengers guided us to the place where they had seen Christians. We arrived in the afternoon, and saw at once that they told the truth. We perceived that there were mounted men among them, by the stakes to which the horses had been tied.

The joy in Cabeza de Vaca's heart was strangely mingled with disquiet, even with something like regret. For a year he and his companions had been visited with God's special favor. They had been led through the wilderness, and through every danger of death by hunger, thirst, sunstroke, and sickness, and especially the danger from evil beasts and reptiles and still more evil man. They had healed thousands of pain and fever, by their hands and voices but not by their power. God had delivered them alone out of Narváez's four hundred. And for what purpose? Only as a reward?

No, such was not God's way. Cabeza de Vaca knew well that God expects reward for reward. He condemns those who lay away His Grace in a napkin. The just steward gives his labors to his Lord in payment. The fact of duty is manifest; the only puzzle lies in the understanding of God's will.

For once God chose to be specific. His command was revealed in the bitterness gathering in Cabeza de Vaca's heart. To struggle for eight dreadful years to rejoin the Christians and then to find them laying waste this peaceful land, killing, ravishing, burning, and carrying off the simple natives in chain-gangs to their prompt destruction! Almost he wished that by death in the desert he had been spared such a home-coming. What! These shy and happy creatures, who so eagerly welcomed his clumsy preaching of Christ's passion and Mary's mercy, were they to serve only to scrape gold out of the death-haunted mines? But these were immortal souls, begging to learn the blessed mysteries, that so they might dwell in everlasting light!

God spoke with no pompous oracles but with stern and clear command. Cabeza de Vaca must save his Indian companions from the hand of the spoiler. The adoration in their eyes was not for him, he was convinced, but for the God of whom he was the agent and symbol. He must save his Indian companions, and afterwards he must continue to save others, to save as many as his strength could compass, to save all the hunted wild men from devilish mankind, to save them for Christ.

The next day he took Estebanico and eleven Indians and set off in pursuit of the Spaniards. Dorantes and Castillo, though younger men, had not the strength for this rapid chase. The day after, he emerged from the bush to confront four men on horseback. These stood staring and dumbfounded, helpless to raise a crossbow, seeing a white man and a black, vastly bearded, wearing only girdles, but clothed in a kind of majesty. The white man stepped forward and spoke in Spanish; and the Indians fell on their knees in awe to see the armored men-monsters slip from their horses and embrace the Child of the Sun, who clung to them, weeping bitterly.

They were beside the River Sinaloa. It was early in March, 1536.

CHAPTER XI

MEXICO

FOR an hour, perhaps for a day, the joy in Cabeza de Vaca's breast was unmixed. Then gradually his vision cleared; he began to perceive the Spaniards, not as symbols of rescue, of home-coming, of the happy issue out of all affliction, but as human individuals with qualities of their own. The bright light of bliss faded, and out of the dazzle emerged mental topographies which the wanderer could recognize only too well. During the long captivity, he had dreamed of the white men as all kind, all virtuous; he had dreamed away their pettiness and cruelty. Now, as memory stirred, he remembered the old outlines of the pitiless, heavy-handed conquistador. He remembered, even, himself.

He was conscious, too, that his joy, religious in essence, made up of gratitude to his kind Savior, was met only by surprise, which changed gradually to the satisfaction of heartless self-interest. The captain, Diego de Alcaraz,[1] soon disclosed that all the wonder of Cabeza de Vaca's great journey was nothing to him beside the failure of his slave-hunting foray. And a certain greedy smile showed the forming of his sordid purpose, to use the Child of the Sun as a slave-decoy.

His expedition, which had begun with success, was now in a sorry state. Not only had the natives fled their villages to take refuge in the mountains; they had destroyed or hidden their crops of corn and beans. The Spaniards, too inexpert to live off the country, found themselves wandering through a hungry solitude.

From this pass they were relieved by the arrival of Dorantes and Castillo and six hundred Indian followers, "men and women, some with nursing babies in their arms, and with their mouths besmeared

---

[1] "A man unfitted to have people under his command," Castañeda, "Expedition of Coronado," in "Spanish Explorers in the Southern U. S." 303.

with corn pudding." [2] "Since you are so powerful," said Alcaraz, "send forth word to all the natives of this region to return to their villages. Tell the pigs we won't touch them. And tell them to bring food."

"This last was unnecessary," says Cabeza de Vaca's record, "the Indians being ever diligent to bring us all they could. Directly we sent our messengers to call them, when there came six hundred souls, bringing us all the maize in their possession. They fetched it in certain pots, closed with clay, which they had concealed in the earth. They brought us whatever else they had; but we, wishing only to have the provision, gave the rest to the Christians, that they might divide among themselves. After this we had many high words with them; for they wished to make slaves of the Indians we brought."

It was a conflict of irreconcilable minds. Captain Diego de Alcaraz was a familiar type of colonial subjugator, and a worthy subordinate of the infamous Nuño de Guzmán, governor of Nueva Galicia, who had inaugurated the export of natives to the Antillean gold-mines, Indian graves. It was Governor Nuño de Guzmán who caused several natives to be hung for failing to sweep the roads before him. Although, to be sure, the enslavement of Indians was illegal, interest found definitions which permitted the fact of slavery under improved names. The encomienda system, by which each settler was rendered responsible for "the spiritual welfare" of even hundreds of natives, flourished in Mexico. By the carrier system, officials could impress any needed number of Indians to act as burden-bearers. With such legal resources, an unscrupulous governor, like Nuño de Guzmán, and his fortune-hunters in the far northwest could laugh at the pious regulations of the authorities in the City of Mexico.

A curious feature of the formal code of gentlemanliness is that the obligations of honor are enforced toward gentlemen alone. To Diego de Alcaraz the capture of slaves by false promises was a warlike stratagem, as justifiable toward Indians as toward the Moors of Spain. Cabeza de Vaca had learned, in his wanderings, so many codes that he had a little forgotten, perhaps, the old formula of the gentlemen. So high words followed, and much anger, with no possibility of compromise. The Indians stood by, gaping; they understood no

[2] Oviedo, III, 612.

words, but they comprehended well that the Children of the Sun were very angry with the bad white men who carried off their wives and brothers.

Cabeza de Vaca turned to his followers, and in their own tongue bade them begone to their homes. At this they protested.

They were willing to do nothing until they had gone with us and delivered us into the hands of other Indians, as had been the custom; for, if they returned without doing so, they were afraid they should die, and, going with us, they feared neither Christians nor lances. Our countrymen became jealous at this, and caused their interpreter to tell the Indians that we were of them, and for a long time we had been lost; that they were the lords of the land who must be obeyed and served, while we were persons of mean condition and small force. The Indians cared little or nothing for what was told them; and conversing among themselves said the Christians lied: that we had come whence the sun rises, and they whence it goes down; we healed the sick, they killed the sound; that we had come naked and barefooted, while they had arrived in clothing and on horses with lances; that we were not covetous of anything, but all that was given to us we directly turned to give, remaining with nothing; that the others had the only purpose to rob whomsoever they found, bestowing nothing on any one.

Cabeza de Vaca spoke to his Indians, these comely and kindly people, as he calls them, and told them that they must obey and not question; that the Children of the Sun had come to the end of their journey, and their work was done; that the faithful servants of the Children of the Sun must now leave their masters and return home in peace and till their fields. For the Children of the Sun too were going to their home. And once there, they would not forget their friends, but would think of them often, and bless them, and pray for them, as they too had learned to pray. So he would bless them now, in the name of the Father, and the Son, and the Holy Ghost. . . .

He drew the sign of the cross in the air; the Indians, as they had been taught, spread their arms wide, to make of their bodies the holy crucifix.

The Indians, at taking their leave, told us they would do what we commanded, and would settle in their towns, if the Christians would suffer them; and this I say and affirm most positively, that, if they have not done so, it is the fault of the Christians.

Alcaraz and his men seemed strangely quieted and polite. They were impressed, perhaps, by the moving scene of leave-taking. Alcaraz detailed a lieutenant, Cebreros, and a guard of honor, to lead the four on the back trail south to the frontier outpost of Culiacan. The way was curiously difficult, mountainous, and solitary. No Indian was encountered in that desert. They were lost; they could find no stream, no waterhole. They passed two days in the burning country, without water. Seven men died. The steadfast reached at last a village of friendly Indians, near Culiacan, the present capital of Sinaloa.

There the four learned that they had been brought south by a crazy roundabout mountain route, only in order that they should meet no tale-bearing native. And in that time gained, Alcaraz had fallen upon the six hundred Indian companions and had taken them for slaves.

Perhaps it was at this moment that Cabeza de Vaca, sick with man's treachery, undoing God's blessing, vowed to make reparation for the enslaved six hundred, and for all the misery of the subject race. In the midst of anger, grief, and bewildered prayer, he may now have sworn to spend his life in the service of these simple people, to act as a mediator between the strong and the weak. For this, he felt, the Lord had given him his experience of the most abject weakness. "Who is weak, and I am not weak? Who is offended, and I burn not?"

He was aware of evil, drowning in it. He knew that he must not sink gently in that sea, and sinking exclaim that evil had disappeared, because it was universal. If he should breathe in that universal evil his soul would die.

Through some such spiritual passion Las Casas had passed when, a priest in Cuba, he found for his Pentecost sermon of 1514 the text of Ecclesiasticus: "The bread of the needy is their life; he that defraudeth him thereof is a man of blood. He that taketh away his neighbor's living slayeth him; and he that defraudeth the laborer of his hire is a shedder of blood." From that day of revelation until his death in 1566 Las Casas had no other purpose but to comfort and succor the desolate millions of the new world.

In the face of Cabeza de Vaca's anger, Cebreros fled by night to put his case before Melchior Díaz, the alcalde mayor in charge of the garrison and at the same time the vice-governor of the district. Unfortunately for Cebreros and Alcaraz, fortunately for Cabeza de Vaca, Melchior Díaz was an honorable man, with bowels of mercy.[3] He came in all haste to the village where the four Christians lay. "He wept with us, giving praises to God our Lord for having extended over us so great care. He comforted and entertained us hospitably. In behalf of the governor, Nuño de Guzmán, and himself, he tendered all that he had, and the service in his power. He showed much regret for the seizure, and the injustice we had received from Alcaraz and others. We were sure, had he been present, what was done to the Indians and to us would never have occurred."

Melchior Díaz could ease somewhat Cabeza de Vaca's dismal apprehensions as to the lot of the natives. The slave-hunters were acting on very questionable orders. The second Mexican Audiencia, in 1530, had issued stringent regulations against slavery, which, though much disregarded, could be enforced by a willing vice-governor. Don Diego Fernández de Proaño, Melchior Díaz's predecessor at Culiacan, had about two years before been tried, and condemned to death—though later pardoned—for branding, chaining, and selling gangs of Indians. But just recently, in the current year of 1536, Governor Nuño de Guzmán in Compostela had sanctioned the enslavement of rebels, conspirators, and disturbers of the peace. This was taken by his agents as a license for general slave-taking. Well, the conscienceless govenor's provincial decree could not invalidate the king's laws for all of Mexico. In fact, as the event proved, Nuño de Guzmán paid dear for his greedy temerity. "There was so much cruelty in making these slaves," says a chronicler, "that the clamor of the innocent reached the pious and Christian ears of the King our Lord, who provided an efficient remedy," to wit, a judicial examination of Nuño de Guzmán, resulting in degradation, imprisonment, and confiscation of property.[4]

---

[3] He was destined to die grotesquely, while with Coronado's expedition in 1541. Riding at a gallop, he cast his lance at a marauding dog. The lance bounded, caught with butt in earth, and pierced him through the body, rupturing his bladder. Castañeda, in "Spanish Explorers in the Southern United States," 325.

[4] Tello, "Nueva Galicia," *apud* Coopwood, in T. S. H. Q., III, 257.

Melchior Díaz, a newcomer to the province, recognized all too well the results of Governor Guzmán's countenancing of slave-making. Count pity and humanity but womanish weakness; still it must be recognized that an uninhabited country is valueless to any conqueror. The only salvation of the land lay in the suppression of slavery and the tempting back of the people from their mountain refuges.

The alcalde mayor besought us to tarry there, since by so doing we could be of eminent service to God and your Majesty; the deserted land was without tillage and everywhere badly wasted, the Indians were fleeing and concealing themselves in the thickets, unwilling to occupy their towns; we were to send and call them, commanding them in behalf of God and the king, to return to live in the vales and cultivate the soil.

Cabeza de Vaca, Dorantes, and Castillo shook their heads doubtfully. All their escort had been dismissed, and with the escort had vanished, perhaps, the tradition of miracle and authority. These Indians spoke an unfamiliar language. But still—the purpose of Díaz was their own. They had succeeded already in many a more unlikely venture.

They chose two native captives who had accompanied them as carriers and who had seen the arrival of the six hundred faithful from the north. They had heard of the god-like origin of the Children of the Sun, and had had direct testimony of wonders worked, of ailments cured, and of the kind bounties of the strangers. These two had their fetters struck off; they were ordered to go, with others of the town, to the hostile tribes in the mountains, and to bring summons from the men of God. The tribesmen must come to the feet of the men of God, who wished to speak with them. The messengers bore, as a symbol and as a guarantee, one of the holy orbs of the Children of the Sun, a rattling gourd filled with stones, carried reverently in the white men's hands from the lower Río Grande.

For seven days no word came, and the Christians were turning to the belief that the envoys, having once found safety, had chosen to preserve it. But on the eighth day they returned, with three chiefs and fifteen retainers, bearing gifts of beads, turquoises, and feathers.

The messengers said they had not found the people of the river where we appeared [the Sinaloa], the Christians having again made them run away into the mountains. Melchior Díaz told the interpreter to speak to the natives for us; to say to them we came in the name of the Lord, who is in heaven; that we had traveled about the world many years, telling all the people we found that they should believe in God and serve him; for he was the Master of all things on the earth, benefiting and rewarding the virtuous, and to the bad giving perpetual punishment of fire; that, when the good die, he takes them to heaven, where none ever die, nor feel cold, nor hunger, nor thirst, nor any inconvenience whatsoever, but the greatest enjoyment possible to conceive; that those who will not believe in him, nor obey his commands, he casts beneath the earth into the company of demons, and into a great fire which is never to go out, but always torment; that, over this, if they desired to be Christians and serve God in the way we required, the Christians would cherish them as brothers and behave toward them very kindly; that we would command they give no offense nor take them from their territories, but be their great friends. If the Indians did not do this, the Christians would treat them very hardly, carrying them away as slaves into other lands.

They answered through the interpreter that they would be true Christians and serve God. Being asked to whom they sacrifice and offer worship, from whom they ask rain for their corn-fields and health for themselves, they answered of a man that is in heaven. We inquired of them his name, and they told us Aguar; and they believe he created the whole world, and the things in it. We returned to question them as to how they knew this; they answered their fathers and grandfathers had told them, that from distant time had come their knowledge, and they knew the rain and all good things were sent to them by him. We told them that the name of him of whom they spoke we called Dios; and if they would call him so, and would worship him as we directed, they would find their welfare. They responded that they well understood, and would do as we said. We ordered them to come down from the mountains in confidence and peace, inhabit the whole country and construct their houses: among these they should build one for God, at its entrance place a cross like that which we had there present; and, when Christians came among them, they should go out to receive them with crosses in their dwellings, giving of what they have to eat, and the Christians would do them no injury, but be their friends; and the Indians told us they would do as we had commanded.

The captain having given them shawls and entertained them, they returned, taking the two captives who had been used as emissaries. This occurrence took place before the notary, in the presence of many witnesses.

The power of the white man's revelation had not diminished. The natives came flooding into the village, fearless and eager, with gifts of beads and feathers. They promised to build churches and put crosses on them. The priest baptized the tribal chiefs and the children. And Captain Melchior Díaz "made a covenant with God, not to invade nor consent to invasion, nor to enslave any of that country and people, to whom we had guaranteed safety."

When, therefore, Cabeza de Vaca could feel that his friends had found some sort of safety for their bodies in this world and their souls in the next, he was willing to take another step toward his own happiness. He and his companions went the little distance to Culiacan. They arrived there on April 1, 1536, and were obliged to remain until May 15. They dared not advance southward without a considerable guard, for all this country was wasted and in rebellion, only because of Spanish slave-hunts.

During the long delay, good news came from the north. Diego de Alcaraz returned, much mystified. He had received peremptory orders from Melchior Díaz to release his captives; and he had seen, throughout that country, the natives coming down, fearless, from the hills, each with a cross in his hand. In return for the Spaniards' lashes, they brought food; in return for banishment from their homes to the unkindly mountains, they invited the Spaniards to sleep as honored guests in their villages. "The Christians had slept among them over night. They were surprised at a thing so novel; but as the natives said they had been assured of safety, it was ordered that they should not be harmed, and the Christians took friendly leave of them."

The six hundred Indians who had accompanied the four from the north, and who had been so treacherously captured by Alcaraz, were settled on the Rio Fuerte. They were Pima Indians, probably from Ures, the village of the deer hearts. And still to-day, in their village of La Concepción de Bamoa, their descendants speak the Pima tongue in their linguistic island.[5]

On the fifteenth of May, a guard of twenty mounted men being assembled, the four set off for the subjugated regions to the south. On the way they were joined by six Christians with five hundred slaves. It seemed vain to persuade the six Christians to part with all their wealth; but as the procession advanced, the groans of the cap-

[5] Bandelier, "Southwestern Historical Contributions," 650.

tives, their bewildered misery, the whipping of the sick to keep up the step in the long chain, the halts to unfetter a laggard to die by the wayside,[6] left unhealing wounds in Cabeza de Vaca's mind. And gradually a bold purpose formed within him, as he walked. When he should come to the Court of King Charles, he would ask the privilege of returning as governor to the land of his slavery, and there give an example of rule by honor and justice. It was a pretty dream, which dispossessed little by little the familiar dreams of beds with sheets, of Spanish hams, of the wines of Jerez.

At the end of a hundred leagues of travel, the convoy arrived at Compostela, hard by the present Tepic. The three hidalgos were most graciously received by Governor Nuño de Guzmán himself. All testimonies concur in recognition of the governor's charming manners and evident culture. It was no doubt with humorous grace that he had personally supervised the burning of his interpreters' feet until the toes dropped off, and had dragged King Tangaxoan at the tail of a horse before burning him at the stake.[7] The govenor's politeness toward the wanderers was due not alone to his gentlemanly instincts. He recognized that, after having witnessed the operations of his slave-gatherers, they were on their way to the court of Mexico, and perhaps to the presence of His Majesty himself. He put his own clothing on the refugees' backs, and showed them to soft and downy beds. This was agony! The persistent softness of cotton tickled their hard bodies, and woolen shirts bit them like insects. For some time, Cabeza de Vaca confesses, he could sleep nowhere but on the ground.

All Nuño de Guzmán's winning courtesy could not distract the merciful conquistador from his purpose. Secretly, Cabeza de Vaca obtained from a notary a *testimonio,* or certified copy of Nuño de Guzmán's protocol, authorizing his agents to take slaves. Having this safe, he dared to remonstrate with the governor, telling him "that he had let his hand slip." [8] All the governor's courtesy fell away; fearing, no doubt, to resort to violence, he sent the four on their way, after forwarding to the viceroy the best proofs he could contrive of their sun-crazed irresponsibility.

[6] Bancroft, "History of Mexico," II, 332.
[7] Bancroft, "History of Mexico," II, 345–6.
[8] Coopwood, in T. S. H. Q., III, 261.

The journey along the old Camino Real, up over the mountains to Mexico, took the form of a triumph. "Many came out on the roads to gaze at us, giving thanks to God for saving us from so many calamities." Arriving in Mexico on July 23, they were most handsomely received by the viceroy Antonio de Mendoza, and by Hernán Cortés, Marqués del Valle, who was leading an irritable existence as subordinate in the land he had conquered. The viceregal wardrobe was put at the gentlemen's disposal; they sighed and shuddered as they donned gold-laced brocades, but a Spanish hidalgo might not walk the streets of Mexico in a breech-clout. However, Spanish foods and wines made a happy change from Aztec diet, the everlasting tamales and tortillas, with such delicacies as frog spawn and stewed ants peppered with chile. On St. James's Day, July 25, a bull-fight and a joust with canes was held in the newcomers' honor. Meanwhile Estebanico swaggered among the Spanish negroes who filled the capital.[9]

At the first opportunity Cabeza de Vaca sought a private interview with Viceroy Antonio de Mendoza. This gentleman, commonly referred to as "el bueno," was an honest and intelligent administrator. Austere and ascetic in physical habit and in character, he had been chosen to suppress the abuses of the colony. After the conqueror, fearless and bold, and also lawless, thievish, brutal, and reckless of any permanent good, comes the organizer, the legalist. Mendoza received grimly the news from the northwest. He noted down a reprimand for Captains Alcaraz and Cebreros.[10] He accepted Cabeza's *testimonio* and added it to a bulging dossier marked "Nuño de Guzmán." "Have no fear on that score," he said. "I have just had word from Spain that His Majesty is sending out a special judge to investigate and try his case, and I warrant you there shall be no slackness." He was indeed imprisoned, tried, and condemned about the end of the year.

Mendoza showed particular interest in the travelers' tales of the north country which, the first of any Christians, they had explored. How much gold had they seen? Only traces and indications, they

---

[9] The number of negroes was regarded as a menace as early as 1523, and their numbers were restricted. In 1537 a negro plot to massacre the Spanish and seize the country was bloodily suppressed. Bancroft, "History of Mexico," II, 384-5.

[10] Bandelier, "Southwestern Historical Contributions," 75.

admitted, but there were circumstantial stories of great cities to the north, beyond a desert. They had received a gift of emeralds, with a veracious account of their origin. Don Antonio's eyes gleamed with satisfaction. This news fitted with another report, each certified the other. Had they heard of the Isle of the Amazons, where the fierce, rich, man-hating women dwelt? No, to be sure; but as they had traveled south in the lee of the western mountains they had heard that the coast of the South Sea abounded with pearls and riches. It was not conclusive, but there was enough in the story to tempt further exploration. He ordered the refugees to make a map of their wanderings, and this they did.

If some researcher will discover that map in the Archives of Mexico or Spain, he will settle many a dispute.

Cabeza de Vaca had, in his turn, a diffident question to ask. Had news come from Spain of the grant to any man of the rights once issued to Narváez—the right to explore and colonize "Florida," the present Florida and all the gulf region to Pánuco? No, said Mendoza; since the disappearance of Narváez none had shown any desire to visit those ill-omened shores. The field was free; Cabeza de Vaca could ask the privilege as well as another.

That summer and autumn of 1536 and the following winter were spent in Mexico. Cabeza de Vaca was eager to return to Spain; but a ship in which he spoke for passage in October foundered; and all through the winter no vessels braved the winter gales. Time passed agreeably in the diversions of the capital. And a task which provided the three gentlemen with much occupation was the redaction of a report on the great journey. When finished, it was forwarded to the Audiencia of Hispaniola, which was the General Headquarters of the Spanish colonies. Although the report itself has disappeared, Oviedo, the contemporary historian, consulted it, and made an ample summary in his History of the Indies. Dorantes's share in the work is evident; the episodes of the long captivity on the Texas coast are told from his point of view. Oviedo's abstract enlightens many difficult passages of Cabeza de Vaca's personal narrative.

During the winter in Mexico, Don Antonio the viceroy sought to persuade the three gentlemen to remain with him. With all secrecy, for fear of his ambitious rival Cortés, he outlined a scheme of exploration and conquest to the seven golden cities of Cíbola, beyond the northern deserts. It was notorious that Nuño de Guzmán owned a Tejos (Texas) Indian who was the son of a trader, long deceased, whose business had been the transport of feathered plumes for head dresses. These he had carried across the desert to beautiful cities, and bartered for great weight of gold and silver, base metals of that country.

This Tejos slave, when a boy, said the viceroy, had once or twice accompanied his father, and he had seen with his own eyes cities as large as Mexico and its suburbs. There were seven of these cities, and in them whole rows of streets inhabited by gold and silver workers. To reach them it was necessary to cross a desert for forty days, barren of any growth except a dry grass five inches high. What other proof was needed than the emeralds that Cabeza and his companions had brought home from the north? Very well; let them remember that in the eighth century, when the Arabs invaded Portugal, the Bishop of Lisbon took his flock and sailed west into the ocean until he came to a land he called Antillia, and there he founded seven noble cities, perhaps in the same region as the lost continent of Atlantis. Some of the first discoverers thought they had found this country, wherefor the islands are still called the Antilles. Clearly they were mistaken; the old story must point to the Seven Cities of Cíbola.

Now, continued the viceroy, would not the gentlemen remain and lead an expedition which he would raise and equip? With their knowledge of the country and their prestige among the natives they could find their way where all others would fail. They would be well rewarded; as a guarantee, in case of failure or success, he would marry then to certain rich widows and give them fine estates and large encomiendas of docile natives. And in case of success the rewards would be illimitable and unimaginable!

Cabeza de Vaca resolutely put away the temptation. He had other purposes, the first of which was to see His Majesty the King and Emperor. Whatever power he might win must come from the fountainhead itself. He would be the agent of no subordinate, not even a viceroy. He had his own plans of government, which might prove most unacceptable to a viceroy, Mendoza or his successor; he could not risk the checkmating of all his purpose by a peremptory order from his superior. Probably also he regarded the dreams of golden cities as mere chimeras. What tangible proof had he seen of these legends? Only a copper rattle with a crudely indicated face, and a handful of emeralds; perhaps not genuine emeralds at all!

Dorantes, as well as Cabeza de Vaca, refused the bait. Dorantes had had his bellyful of adventure; his chief desire was to see again his home in Béjar and the serene patios beside the Seville streets. He made only one concession to Mendoza's purpose; he gave or sold to him his Estebanico, who, no longer Deity's steward, had unquestioningly resumed his status, under civilization, as a slave. Alonso del Castillo, who seems never to have deeply impressed his superiors, remained in Mexico, but to him no captaincies were offered.

Dorantes and Cabeza de Vaca went to Vera Cruz in Lent of 1537, to take ship for home. Three vessels lay in harbor, waiting a fair wind. The two veterans boarded one of the craft; while idling at anchor Cabeza de Vaca was alarmed by the constant rattle of the pumps. Although Dorantes ridiculed his fears, Cabeza de Vaca insisted on transferring to another ship. Dorantes vowed that no peril of the sea could affright one who had cruised the length of the Gulf of Mexico in a crazy barge calked with palmetto fibre; the two would race to Spain. But prudent Cabeza de Vaca would not be robbed of his home-coming for lack of a little care.

The three ships left port on the tenth of April, and sailed together for a hundred and fifty leagues. One morning Cabeza de Vaca looked in vain for his companions. As he afterward learned, the two vessels leaked so badly that the captains turned back in apprehension to Mexico.

Let us return to Mexico with Andrés Dorantes. When Mendoza heard of his return to Vera Cruz, he bade him return to Mexico City. There the viceroy repeated his suggestion of a northern reconnoissance. Dorantes acceded, perhaps fearing further adventures on the sea, perhaps tempted by the prospect of sole command. Mendoza raised some troops, with accompanying clerics, forty or fifty horses, and a baggage train of Indians. He set aside the considerable sum of 3,500 or 4,000 pesos for expenses. "I spent much money for the expedition," he reported to the king,[11] "but I don't know how it happened that the matter came to nothing."

Dorantes continued in official favor. Mendoza married him to a rich widow, María de la Torre, the owner of the wealthy towns of Asala and Jalazintzo, and bestowed another wealthy widow, as the most perfect recompense for long adversity, upon Alonso del Castillo. Sufferings in the wilderness had not sapped Dorantes's stamina. He served gallantly in the subjection of Jalisco and other regions, and begat eleven children, whose line, no doubt, still flourishes in the Republic of Mexico. Castillo's children were all girls; Andrés Dorantes's son was unable to trace them.[12]

Estebanico was destined for a more spectacular end. In 1539 the viceroy, disappointed by the failure of his military expedition to the north, proposed to the Order of St. Francis that they send some monks on an exploring journey in the interests of religion and His Majesty. Brother Marcos of Nice, vice-commissioner of the order, and a companion, answered the call. The governor instructed them to push northward as far as possible, and to reassure the Indians along the way, promising them that they should not be enslaved, "that therefore they shall lose all fear." The monks should take Estebanico as a guide, "and I command him to obey you in all and everything you order him to do, as if you were my own self; and in case of disobedience he will be severely punished, according to the penalties imposed upon those who disobey persons holding from His Majesty power to command them." [13]

The little band left Culiacan on March 7, 1539, and proceeded northwest through country which Estebanico remembered well, as far as Matape, forty miles south of Ures, the village of the deer hearts. Along the way Indians came humbly forth to greet him, recalling old acquaintance, begging for the healing touch of his hands. Arrogantly he swaggered before his Franciscan masters; he alone knew the road; he bore a magic rattling gourd in hand; he alone could speak and understand, and if words failed he possessed the Esperanto of the

[11] Winship, "The Coronado Expedition," 349 n.
[12] Dorantes de Carranza, "Sumaria Relación," 265.
[13] Bandelier, S. W. H. C., 110.

wilderness, the rich idiom of the sign manual. His authority, by which he could king it over the Indians and loftily belittle a vice-commissioner of the Franciscan order, induced him to the misdeeds of intolerable pride.

At Matape, Fray Marcos despatched Estebanico on a reconnoitering journey. The negro's instructions were to proceed north forty or fifty leagues, and if he found any knowledge of any rich and peopled country to go no further but to return in person, or to send Indian messengers with a token, which should be "a white cross of one handful long; and if it were any great matter, one of two handfuls long; and if it were a country greater and better than Nueva España [Mexico], he should send me a great cross. So the said Stephen departed from me on Passion Sunday after dinner; and within four days the messengers of Stephen returned unto me with a great cross as high as a man." [14] The messengers reported that Fray Marcos must come at once to join Estebanico, for he had learned that it was only thirty days' journey to the city of Cíbola.

He affirmed also that there are seven great cities in this province, all under one Lord, the houses whereof are made of lime and stone, and are very great, and the least of them with one loft above head, and some of two and of three lofts, and the house of the Lord of the Province of four, and that all of them join one onto the other in good order, and that in the gates of the principal houses there are many turquoise-stones cunningly wrought, whereof he saith they have there a great plenty; also that the people of this city go very well apparelled; and that beyond this there are other provinces, all of which (he saith) are much greater than these seven cities.

No more was necessary to send Fray Marcos—his brother-monk had fallen sick—hastening after Estebanico, tense with excitement. But his forerunner would not wait. He enjoyed his sole authority; he had a taste for Indian women, and not content with accepting their hospitality for the night he would carry away with him those who especially pleased him. He was also making a collection of turquoises. He feared, certainly, the Franciscan's interference with these godlike impositions on the simple people.

[14] Hakluyt, "Navigations," IX, 128.

Estebanico, the bearded negro Moor from Azamor, felt himself dangerously akin to Deity. In his hand he carried with majesty the sacred gourd. He wore feathers on his arms and legs, and belled anklets and bracelets that chimed nobly with his holy rattle. At his heels followed two adoring Spanish greyhounds. He carried green dinner plates for the proper service of his food.[15]

Estebanico passed through Ures, the village of the deer hearts. There his course diverged from the way he had previously followed. Instead of taking the mountain path to the northeast he headed directly up the valley of the Sonora. Every day he would send back word to Fray Marcos, or would leave a large cross planted on a hillock; but he took good care not to be overtaken. Emerging from the Sonora Valley, he crossed the uninhabited height of land and was guided to the northward-flowing San Pedro. He descended the river, near Tombstone, perhaps as far as its junction with the Gila. He then turned northeast across the desert, hurrying toward the pueblo of Zuñi. He was careful to mark his passage; Fray Marcos found shelters constructed for his nightly rest.

Coming within a day's journey of Zuñi, Estebanico halted, with his three hundred companions from the south. He then sent messengers to the lord of the place, carrying as a holy symbol of authority the master's great gourd, hung with bells and feathers; the envoys announced that a Child of the Sun was at hand, bringing good fortune and offering to heal the sick. The style of Cabeza de Vaca is easily to be recognized. In this circumstance, however, was some confusion of the symbols. The lord of the place took the gourd in his hands, and threw it angrily on the floor, crying: "I know these people, for these rattles are not the make of our own! Tell them to return at once, else not one of them will remain alive!"

When the trembling ambassadors brought this word to Estebanico, he only laughed, saying that they need not fear, for those who gave him evil words at the outset always received him most devoutly in the end. He led his band forward to the city; but when he reached the walls, uttering promises and threats, he found no entry. Some

---

[15] Hernando de Alarcón heard these stories in the following year, as far away as the mouth of the Colorado. (Hakluyt, "Navigations," IX, 300, 305.)

citizens met him, and showed the troop courteously enough to an outlying house.

That night, as Castañeda, the recorder of Coronado's expedition, was informed by the Zuñis, the elders met in council. They were offended by Estebanico's demand that they surrender to him their treasure and their women, and alarmed at his proclamation that he foreran two white men, sent by a mighty prince to teach them a better religion. What chiefly distressed and disturbed them was that a black man should come as agent and annunciator of a people whom he asserted, and they knew, to be white! Might this not be a demon's masquerade? They puzzled long over this baffling problem, and finally concluded that the wisest judgment was death.

In the morning, when the sun rose a lance-length high, Estebanico stood forth in the manner of Joshua and called on the city to surrender. He was answered only by a shower of arrows and a sudden sortie. Estebanico's companions turned to flee, and after a moment he joined them, all his godhood dropping away. He fell pierced by an arrow; all the Indian escort were killed but three, who escaped to bring the news to Fray Marcos. Estebanico's body was cut in pieces and distributed to various chiefs as a proof of death and as an interesting curiosity. The chief of Cíbola kept his dogs and the four green dinner plates.

Toward the end of the last century, Mr. Frank H. Cushing went to live among the Zuñi Indians for anthropological purposes. One of the ancient legends he recorded tells how, before the first coming of the Mexicans, a black stranger appeared at the village of Kia-ki-ma. He was very greedy, voracious, and bold, and so they killed him. After his death the Mexicans appeared in great numbers, finally subduing the Zuñis.[16]

Time, at its graveyard work, moves slow in those still altitudes. It has not yet interred the memory of a solitary black slave's death, by the arrows of savages, in the desert.

When the refugees brought to Fray Marcos word of the calamity, he was hard put to it to restrain his escort from immediate flight. He was a hardy friar, and having come so close to his goal, he would not

[16] Bandelier, S. W. H. C., 154.

yet turn back. He undid the bundle of presents prepared for the Lord of Cíbola, and offered them to any willing guide. At last two "principal men" offered to take him to a spot whence he might see Cíbola from afar. They made their way cautiously to a summit, from which he looked down on the populous town, and imagined the riches of gold and silver, "for they have no other metal," behind the adobe walls. "I was tempted to go thither, because I knew I could but hazard my life, and that I had offered unto God the first day that I began my journey; in the end I began to be afraid, considering in what danger I should put myself, and that if I should die, the knowledge of this country should be lost, which in my judgment is the greatest and the best that hitherto hath been discovered." Having then looked on Canaan from his Nebo, he turned about and fled back to Mexico, "with much more fear than victuals," bringing news that was to send Coronado and his men hunting gold over all the plains of the west.

Let us now return to Cabeza de Vaca, beating across the Gulf of Mexico on his voyage to Spain. Leaving Vera Cruz on April 10, 1537, he reached Havana on May 4, a two days' journey to-day. Entering the harbor, he crossed his outward track. He set sail again on June 2, much in fear of French corsairs. "Having arrived near the island of Bermuda, we were struck by one of those storms that overtake those who pass there, according to what they state who sail thither." Twenty-nine days out from Havana, they were off Corvo in the Azores, the spectrum-bright cloud-pedestal that New York-Mediterranean liners pass, for their passengers' delight. Here a French corsair, with an accompanying prize, gave chase. By dusk he was only a cannon-shot distant. All that night the Spanish captain tried to give his pursuer the slip, and all night the Frenchman foiled the maneuvers, and hung close, firing an occasional shot, and waiting for morning.

What were their contrary emotions when, with the dawn, the three ships were found to be close to nine other sail, Portuguese men-of-war! The French captain was a man of ready wit. He brought up from his ship's prison the master and the pilot of his prize, a Portuguese slaver with a cargo of negroes, and informed them that his quarry, the Spanish freighter, was in fact a French companion. The master and the pilot believed the tale. The Frenchman then put the two in a boat to join the Portuguese men-of-war, and thrusting sixty oars overside, fled away with oar and sail, "moving so fast it was hardly credible." The slaver informed the fleet that the Spaniard was a French corsair, and Cabeza de Vaca and his mates came near to being sunk on suspicion. The admiral asked their name and freight; the Spanish captain answered simply that they were loaded with silver and gold. "And how much silver and gold might that be?" "Three thousand pounds." The commander's reply Cabeza de Vaca humorously transcribes in Portuguese: "In honest truth you come very rich, although you bring a very sorry ship and a still poorer artillery. By God, that renegade whoreson French bastard has lost a good mouthful! *¡o fi de puta! can, a renegado frances, y ¡que bon bocado perdio, vota Deus!*"

The Frenchman got clean away; the Spanish treasure ship joined the Portuguese fleet, which was convoying three spice-ships from the Orient. They waited two weeks at Terceira in the Azores for a strayed Indian spice-carrier, then left with the whole armada for Lisbon, arriving there on August 9, four months out from Vera Cruz.

Alvar Núñez Cabeza de Vaca, writing the report of his adventures, here came to his conclusion. He attested all he had written by his name and his honor as a gentleman. "That what I have stated in my foregoing narrative is true, I subscribe with my name. Cabeza de Vaca." Thereto he added the symbol of his arms.

This was the end of half his life. By the fortitude of his great heart, by readiness of wit and strength of body, and by the grace of God, he had emerged whole out of the deepest pit of disaster. But these did not preserve him in a later day of success.

PART II

SOUTH AMERICA

CONTENTS

PART II

CHAPTER I

SPAIN

WHEN, on that August day of 1537, the fleet of Indiamen stood off the Tagus bar, a band of lateen-rigged pilot-boats danced out to meet them. Dangerous sand-bars guide the sweet waters into the salt, and the floor of the sea here is carpeted with the bones of men and ships. The pilots, well used to the curiosity of seafaring men after years of absence, were prepared with a budget of news from Portugal and Spain and Europe.

The Emperor Charles V was warring with the French, to teach those dogs at last a lesson they would remember for all future ages. Seventy thousand gallant Spaniards were in Provence on this errand. The emperor was purging Spain of heresy, vigorously pursuing Lutheran sectaries and the Moriscos, who were notoriously practising the rites of Mahmoud in secret. Barbarossa's pirates, the allies of France, infested the Mediterranean coast, even though Charles himself had smoked them out of Tunis the year before. Of the Indies, all the news was of Peru, the golden kingdom. Francisco Pizarro, the Estremaduran swineherd, had conquered with 320 good fellows that country whose streets were cobbled with gold. One of his companions, a certain Hernando de Soto, brother-in-law of that Balboa who discovered the South Sea, had returned from Peru with more ducats than a man could count in a year. He was living in Seville in such high and mighty style as to make the king jealous. Indeed, King Charles, Holy Roman Emperor, had borrowed money from Soto, and paid him with the right of tax on the silks of Granada. But these adventurers can never bide easy with their wealth; they are forever looking for five feet on a cat. Though Soto had everything a man could desire, he was already preparing another expedition into the Indies. He had obtained, in the month of April, a grant from His Majesty to all the land known as Florida. . . .

It was one of those phrases that numb the mind, smothering all its happy life, drowning its accumulated imaginations, while the faithful body performs its disciplined tasks before the unsuspecting world. As his vessel beat up the swift current of the Tagus into Lisbon Pool, Cabeza de Vaca stared grimly at the trim white city, terraced on its splendid hills. All he could see against that screen was the fading vision of himself as governor of Florida, meting to its wild inhabitants such kindly and understanding justice as no Spanish officer had yet conceived.

In Lisbon he learned further particulars. Soto's warrant from the king appointed him governor of Cuba and all the land from Cape Fear (in North Carolina) to the Río de las Palmas, in northeastern Mexico, all the north shore of the Gulf, all the land north for twelve degrees from the Tropic of Cancer. It was an empire as large as half Europe, which the King signed away for his King's Fifth of precious metals and his half share of idols' finery.

No news, however bad, could utterly destroy the pleasure of Cabeza de Vaca's home-coming. Presumably he dropped down the coast to Cadiz, and rode the few miles to Jerez, under the unwinking eye of the August sun. He expected no change in his city and found none, for nothing changes or decays much in that hot dry country. No documents inform us of his meeting with his wife after ten years' absence, of the couple's transports or of the reservations in their bliss. Such matters would have seemed to him an amazing and improper subject for the concern of his neighbor, let alone the historian and future ages. He could not foresee the prurient curiosities of our Clio, an aging virgin in a tabloid era.

His sister María, married to Ruy Díaz de Guzmán, received him with hysterical joy and much blessing of the heavenly hierarchy. Long and closely he embraced his first cousin, Pedro Estopiñán Cabeza de Vaca, commonly known as Pero Vaca. Ruy Díaz de Guzmán presented his nephew, a fine strapping young fellow, Alonso Riquel de Guzmán, page and secretary of the Duke of Medina Sidonia, and Alonso Riquel's cousin, Pedro de Fuentes. The two avowed, at the admiring urgency of their families, that all their desire was to visit the Indies to seek adventure in the king's name.

But the cloud came back to Cabeza de Vaca's heart at the news that two of his kin, Baltasar de Gallegos and Cristóbal de Espindola, had signed an agreement to go out to Florida with Hernando de Soto.

The fact was a reminder, had he needed one, that he must hasten to court, to get the ear of the great ones and of the king himself. Perhaps it was not yet too late. Perhaps some provision might be added, some codicil, to the grant to Soto.

While he remained for a decent interval in his home, his wife gave an account of her stewardship. He possessed, in readily negotiable property, well over five thousand ducats (with a present purchasing value of about $75,000).

He was not happy amid the gossips of Jerez. The unappeasable curiosity of the citizens did not fail to weary him who had, in the wilderness, lost any tendency to garrulity. He found a formula of defense which had its basis of truth. "I have made a vow with my companion Dorantes," he would say. "I cannot tell what I have seen to any private person before I have told my king." And the interlocutor would nod his head in sage understanding, and would report to his friends that Don Alvar had so much as said outright that he bore news so marvelous that only the king's ear might hear it. The citizens of Jerez tormented their hearts with conjectures. Soon it was the creed of the city that Alvar Núñez had discovered at last the Seven Golden Cities, beside which Mexico and Peru were but dunghills.

When he had set some order in his affairs he mounted a horse proportionate to his rank, and turned his face northward toward the court. In his saddle-bags his provision of clean linen, chorrizo sausage, and wine rubbed against the quires of foolscap on which was neatly written his Report to the King. This document, when at length it came to His Majesty's hand, brought a faint prickly memory of travelers' rations, leather, and horses' sweat.

How gracefully said Cabeza de Vaca, in his dedication, that he hoped the king would be pleased to accept his little gift, for this was all that a naked man could bring him, out of the wilderness! [1]

---

[1] Proemio to 1542 edition. The only perfect copy known to exist is in the New York Public Library.

The rumor of wonders seen preceded him into Seville. Here he was met by his kinsmen, Baltasar de Gallegos and Cristóbal de Espindola. These led him promptly to the palace of Hernando de Soto, where a hearty reception awaited him. When the long courtesies of Spanish gentlemen were ended, Soto, much taken by the aspect of Cabeza de Vaca and warmed with the sympathy of the fellow-veteran, put to him an interesting proposal. Would he return to Florida as Soto's right-hand man? With only the hesitation of politeness Cabeza de Vaca refused, because, says the Gentleman of Elvas, chronicler of the Soto expedition, "he hoped to receive another government, being reluctant to march under the standard of another." [2]

Emerging from the interview with Soto, he was eagerly assailed by Gallegos and Espindola. He would not join their enterprise? Well then, what counsel would he give them? His answers were very disappointing; he talked of danger, poverty, and all the hazards of the wilderness. Wealth *might* lie beyond the mountains over which he had not passed; he did not know. He could give them no advice. Shrewdly they interpreted his answers; he was hiding his knowledge, not for the king, but for himself. He was hoping that Soto's expedition would fail, that then he might step in, and go directly to the cities where all the glory and all the gold lay waiting. Well, there were others who could play at that game. Baltasar de Gallegos sold houses, vineyards, a rent of wheat, and eighty acres of olive orchard in the Xarafe of Seville, and he and Espindola sailed with Soto the next spring. In the woods of Georgia and the swamps of Arkansas they cursed the name of Cabeza de Vaca, their cousin.[3]

We may suppose that Cabeza de Vaca's stay in Seville was as brief as possible. He rode on to court, and gained his precious interview

[2] Hodge, "Spanish Explorers," 137. The Gentleman of Elvas says further: "after they had come upon terms they disagreed, because the Adelantado would not give the money requisite to pay for a ship the other had bought." Both parts of this statement seem unlikely. If Cabeza de Vaca had already bought a ship, it must have been with the hope of better reward than that of being Soto's lieutenant. There is no other evidence that he bought a ship before receiving the king's grant. The Gentleman of Elvas had this news only by hearsay.

[3] Both are listed among the survivors of the great anabasis. Buckingham Smith, "Narratives of Hernando de Soto," 292

with His Majesty, probably in Monzón, midway between Saragossa and Barcelona.[4]

When, radiant and gay, Cabeza de Vaca emerged from the imperial presence, the watching courtiers drew from his demeanor conclusions which might be turned to their own fortune. He had been closeted with His Majesty an amazing time. Certain phrases His Majesty let fall, with royal condescension, confirmed the court's belief that Charles had heard stories of illimitable wealth at the back of Florida. The Marqués de Astorga, needing no better tip than this, sent an express to his brother and two cousins, who realized all their wealth and joined Soto.

And now for two years we lose track of Cabeza de Vaca. Did he, with the king's promise to comfort him, return to Jerez, there to await elevation to such a post as he had asked of His Majesty? Did he follow the court, pleading with the royal secretaries, confessors, judges of the Council of the Indies, all men of real or reputed influence? Did he, in the manner of suppliants, spend his days placing himself where he might strike the king's eye, as a mute reminder of fidelity? To such questions I have found no answer.

Perhaps he gave advice, out of his own experience, to Soto's men, before they set sail on April 6, 1538. Perhaps he saw Hernando Pizarro, brother of the great Francisco, who returned to Spain in 1538 and was promptly clapped in prison. He followed with faint interest the excitement attending the Cortes of 1538, which refused the taxation proposed by the king. He rejoiced with all Spain at the Peace of Villefranche in 1538, and grieved at the death of the empress in 1539. Yet in the midst of these concerns of his companions, only the surface of his spirit was touched. He had been too long away; he had missed too many chapters in the tangled story of Spain's distresses. He felt unreal in this reality, or real in this unreality. These endless squabbles over the heretics of Ghent and the imperial rights of Italy bored him. He had given too much of his life to the wilderness ever to be at ease in walled cities.

[4] King Charles was in Monzón, presiding over an important meeting of the Estates of Spain, and negotiating a truce with France, until the end of November. He returned then to his palace in Valladolid, and about the end of December departed for Barcelona and foreign parts. Baumgarten, "Geschichte Karls V," III, 232 n., 234.

He was uncomfortable in his court clothes; had he dared, he would have walked barefoot through the streets.

In his long idleness his great purpose had time to clarify and define itself. He was happy to learn that in 1537 Pope Paul III issued his brief declaring Indians human,[5] and forbidding their enslavement, under pain of excommunication. In 1539 Las Casas came to Spain, with news that must have fired the heart of Cabeza de Vaca, as it made glad that of his royal master.

Las Casas, in a monastery of Santo Domingo, had written his treatise, "De unico vocationis modo," asserting that to make war on heathen men because of their heathenism is a sin; they must be brought to Christ, not by force, but by reason and persuasion. To prove his thesis, against the mockery that echoed in the camps of the two Americas, he sought out the most evilly reputed region in the west to establish an experimental test. The province of Tuzulutlan, between Guatemala and Yucatan, a forbidding fastness of mountain and jungle, was known as "The Land of War," for its fierce man-eating denizens had three times routed the Spanish expeditions sent to conquer them. Las Casas asked permission of the governor of Guatemala to there make his test of the power of the Holy Ghost. The governor sardonically granted the plea, agreeing that in case of success, no lay Spaniard might enter the region, nor should any private person hold Indians in *encomienda*.

Las Casas and his Dominicans prepared their campaign. They wrote in the Quiché language a simple and dramatic story of the fall of man, the life and death of Christ, the resurrection of the dead, and the certainty of heaven and hell. The tale was told in spirited couplets, and set to Aztec melodies to be accompanied on the native flute and drum. Four Indian traders who had access to the Land of War were fortunately converted to Christianity; these were trained in the proper rendition of the versified gospels, and were despatched into the interior with a very lavish outfit of trade goods. Their performance had the most brilliant success, so rousing the curiosity of the cacique that he

---

[5] Though for a century afterward the clergy of Peru would not give the Holy Sacrament to natives. Azara, "Voyage dans l'Amérique méridionale," II, 186.

sent his younger brother back to Guatemala with the traders, with instructions to watch the black-and-white robed preachers closely and determine if the traders' tales were true. Soon the Dominicans were formally invited into the Land of War. And before two years were over the bloodthirsty idols of the Quichés lay shattered, and all the wild men had learned to say "Ave María" to the Queen of Heaven, when the hand of their beloved monk was uplifted.

So Las Casas came to Spain on behalf of his converts, and Charles V, who had always held the great-hearted monk in honor, confirmed by a solemn order Las Casas's agreement with the governor of Guatemala. The Indians should be saved from the greed of the king's subjects. And the name of the Land of War was changed to the Land of True Peace, and as Vera Paz a part of it is still known to-day.

All the probabilities of circumstance and character would indicate that Cabeza de Vaca met Las Casas, although there are no texts to prove it. If Cabeza de Vaca was then at court, he must have sought out the one man in Spain who could best understand his desire. And if they did meet, that spiritual power which poured forth in such abundance that it commanded Pope and king and a nation of cannibal warriors in the Guatemalan jungles must have flooded with new zeal the heart of Cabeza de Vaca.

The year 1539 wore on, taking with it some parcel of Cabeza de Vaca's hope. Still there was no fulfilment of the royal promise, no news of an empty quarter of the Indies where the slave of Indians might prove his theories of mastery. The early comers to the banquet had portioned a hemisphere among them. All he could do was to trust in the kind assurances of the Councillors of the Indies and wait for Fortune to remove some unlucky governor.

His long patience was at length rewarded. In September, 1539, a battered and hungry galleon, the Santa Catalina, was reported in harbor, back from the Río de la Plata. Its supercargoes, after a first gorge of fruits and green foods, hastened to court with a message of urgency. Things were going very ill in Buenos Aires and Asunción, the only Spanish footholds in eastern South America, below the Equator. The king was earnestly adjured to send a strong expedition of fighting men and supplies, or soon the faithful subjects, grimly clinging there, must yield to the fierce Indians whooping by night around the fort of Buenos Aires, Our Lady of Fair Winds.

As the king was absent, dealing with the mutinous Low Countries, the proper secretary interpreted his will. This was just such a commission as Cabeza de Vaca had asked, and such as His Majesty had, in principle, consented to. A meeting was arranged between Cabeza de Vaca and the envoys, and an express despatched to Charles for the royal opinion.

The spokesmen from the distant south were Antonio López, pilot; Gonzalo de Acosta, a Portuguese who had made two round trips to South America, and who spoke the native tongues; and the gentleman in authority, Felipe de Cáceres. Toward him Cabeza de Vaca felt an instant prickle of hostility. His was a type with which he was already familiar, a type common to all colonies of all nations. Loud, sanguine, strong of frame and delighting in his body, he had readily abandoned the satisfactions of civilization for the simpler joys of the bush. He loved to command, not for the pleasure of seeing his plans realized, but for the thrill of watching men scamper at his word. He was "timid and bold and cowardly and very haughty and vengeful and cowardly in his person," said one who knew him well.[6] In his happiness with Spanish wine, he would forget Cabeza de Vaca's lean grimness and treat him as a mate who could appreciate colonial humors; and he would plunge into roaring tales of the befooling of the natives, of jolly rapes on the pampas. By the light in his eyes it could be seen that he told his abject stories less for their intrinsic interest than for the memory of those squirming girls. For him, all Europe held nothing half so sweet.[7]

When Cabeza de Vaca arrived in Paraguay he learned what perhaps he now suspected, that Felipe de Cáceres had been chosen by the colony as its ambassador, not for his abilities, but because he was the member of whom it would most gladly be rid.

From this envoy, from certain disillusioned adventurers who had

[6] Gregorio de Acosta, in a *Relación* quoted by Serrano y Sanz: "Relación de Cabeza de Vaca," I, xxvii.

[7] For Cáceres's personal morality, see Gandía, "Historia de la Conquista del Río de la Plata," 146, n. 132.

CABEZA DE VACA
IN SOUTH AMERICA

——————— Route of Cabeza de Vaca
– – – – – Route of García (conjectural)
•••••••••• Route of Hernando de Ribera

L. A. Dickinson

been out to South America and back, and from the records of the
Council of the Indies, Cabeza de Vaca learned the history of the La
Plata settlements, which was, in sum, the history of all the Spanish
colonizing effort in South America east of the Andes and south of
Venezuela.

The great estuary of the River Plate was discovered in 1516 by Juan
Díaz de Solís, pilot-major of Spain, commanding an expedition sent
out to find a westward passage to the Spice Islands. For a few brief
days the fleet, tacking westward across the broad gulf, celebrated its
success; then the water lost its salt, the bay became a wide river, and
the expeditionaries turned back. Solís himself, incautiously landing on
the shore of present Uruguay, was killed by the dour natives of that
coast. One vessel was cast away near Santa Catalina Island, in what
is now southern Brazil; its crew there found the means of life and the
hope of rescue. The remainder of the expeditionaries, presuming their
companions to be dead, returned, disheartened, to Spain.

Magellan passed that way in 1520. Guided by a better instinct than
that of Solís, he paused only long enough to recognize the falsity of the
bay's promise, and pushed on to the south.

Six years later another vessel nosed inquiringly into the Plate. It
was commanded by Sebastiano Caboto, or Cabot, Venetian, son of
John Cabot who discovered the North American continent for a present of ten pounds sterling from Henry VII. Sebastian accompanied
his father on his second trip to North America, and later was employed
as pilot-major by Charles V of Spain. Having found no westward passage in the northern continent, he sought one half the world's length
away. Running down the eastern coast, he picked up the remnant of
Solís's party, on Santa Catalina Island. And as he had grievances against
three gentlemen on his own ship, he put them ashore, to occupy the
huts of the rescued sailors. Marooning, with its sporting chance of
salvation, appealed to these old captains, I suppose, because it supplied
the practical equivalent of a death sentence with a good ground for
self-justifying argument on Judgment Day.

The survivors of Solís's shipwrecked crew told absorbing tales of an
inland kingdom of gold and silver, reported by honest Indians. Cabot's
food ran short and the spirits of his men turned mutinous; he deter-

mined therefore to explore this pleasant region of the Plate and present it to his master, rather than to seek farther for a break in the continental barrier. He sailed a thousand miles up the Paraná and the Paraguay, a great feat of navigation, on treacherous rivers filled with shifting sand-bars, on which pilots even to-day perpetually run aground with resignation. He penetrated above the site of Asunción, the capital of present Paraguay; and here at last he found a reward for the pains of the long hunt, an earnest of riches for his sovereign and his companions. Friendly Indians welcomed him to their luxuriant country; each one wore, for his sole costume, a garland of feathers round his breech, and, hanging like an amulet, a plate of silver.

Whence came this silver? The amiable Indians grinned, and made clear that they had it from far away, from a country lying beyond deep jungles, to the west. They told a strange story, too strange for some historians to believe.[8] Pieced together from other testimonies, it makes a great tale of foolhardy enterprise, to put among the mighty deeds of obscure heroes unexploited by literature.

The score of shipwrecked sailors from Solís's expedition, living agreeably enough near Santa Catalina Island, were frequently entertained by the natives' wonder tales of a White King, living far to the northwest. His house and his person glittered with sparkling stones; those metals the white man loves were the dross of his streets, and could be had for the trouble of transport.

These stories, a much adorned version of the wealth and magnificence of the Great Inca of Peru, worked strongly on the mind of Alejo García, a Portuguese. Some time between 1521 and 1526 he and four other resolute spirits quitted their kindly haven on the coast, to hunt this White King through the jungles of South America, perhaps to depose him, to take his place—to conquer a continent!

[8] Azara ("Voyage dans l'Amérique méridionale") omits all mention of Alejo García, no doubt, says Funes ("Ensayo de la Historia civil," I, 11) because he regards the story as false. Luis L. Domínguez ("Conquest of the River Plate," 202 n.) refers to him merely as "the fabulous." Nevertheless, a careful reading of the "Commentaries of Cabeza de Vaca" should persuade one that the stories heard up and down Paraguay are beyond the reach of fabrication or coincidence. Gandía ("Historia crítica de los mitos de la conquista americana," 161 et sqq.) adds decisive supporting testimonies from manuscript sources and clarifies the story by exposing Ruy Díaz de Guzmán's confusion of two separate expeditions.

The stories of these indomitable explorers cannot be dismissed on the score of unlikelihood.

And one of the most heart-uplifting wonders of these tremendous times is the fact that the five Iberian sailors lacked only a little of crossing the continent twice, and of emerging with all the precious metal a thousand men could carry!

Enlisting the aid of certain warlike tribes, they made their way well over a thousand miles to the junction of the Cuyabá and the Paraguay, where Cabeza de Vaca found their spoor in 1543. They had traversed what is perhaps the most trackless region of the modern world, posted with every governmental warning to mad adventurers. (It was hereabouts that Commander Fawcett disappeared in 1925.) Their prestige was enforced, by what means we can only imagine, so far that they persuaded a great troop of natives to accompany them westward.[9] The company plunged five or six hundred miles through the Gran Chaco, that country of ill omen, and emerged on the slopes of the Andes, in the land of gold and silver. They are said to have reached the towns of Presto and Tarabuco, in Bolivia, about a hundred miles east of Potosí. Here the marauders fought a great battle, obtaining as the fruits of victory much silver and a little gold. Recruiting more allies to carry their treasure from the Andes to the Atlantic, the conquerors turned east again through the Chaco. When the army reached the Paraguay (farther south than on the westward journey) the five white leaders died, either in a battle with the riverain Indians who resented the intruders and coveted their baggage, or in an uprising of the metal-carriers, at length unable to understand why they were transporting on their backs these pretty, but heavy, burdens.

Thus García and his fellows died, their aim unaccomplished. No matter; with no other weapon than the human will they had performed one of the most wonderful journeys ever made, the memory of which, for want of a chronicler, has lain buried deep in the inactive files of history.[10]

The silver that Cabot found on the upper Paraguay had been trans-

[9] Ruy Díaz de Guzmán says 2,000. But the early chroniclers counted Indians as the Greeks counted Persians.

[10] Ruy Díaz de Guzmán tells of meeting, many years later, García's son, who, he says, was spared from the massacre on account of his youth, and who spent his life among his captors. But Ruy Díaz learned nothing of interest from him. The story is hardly possible; if the boy was a half-breed, born in Santa Catalina, he must have been too young to make the great raid; if he was a Spaniard, one of Solís's crew, he would not have been spared on account of his youth.

ported thither, according to the natives' own account, by the valiant Alejo García. Whatever its source, the sight of it gave rise to a sad misconception. Cabot, convinced that silver mines lay not far away, named his river the Río de la Plata (silver), the name which the estuary still bears. He soon obtained a good quantity of the metal, in exchange for his trade goods, little bells, looking glasses, bits of bright cloth, scissors. And he turned his prow down-stream, determined to bring the glad message to his sovereign with all speed.

When half-way to the river's mouth, he met, by the strangest of hazards, another Spanish explorer. After an amicable parley, the newcomer returned to Spain with the good news and an impressive baggage of silver, while Cabot sat down to wait in his fort of Santi Espíritu on the Paraná (midway between Rosario and Santa Fe). The mound that marks the site, still known as the Torre de Caboto, may yet be seen.[11]

After three years, Cabot, at an end of patience, sailed to Spain (in 1530) to press his claims. On his arrival, however, he found himself in ill odor, for the three gentlemen whom he had marooned on Santa Catalina Island had somehow escaped, returned to Spain, demanded and obtained official vengeance.

A few years later he succeeded in reëntering the service of England. He became governor of the Company of Merchant Adventurers, and organized Chancellor's great expedition to the White Sea. When the Searchthrift was despatched around the North Cape to Russia in 1556, he gave a banquet at the Sign of the Christopher; and the jolly old gentleman, then eighty years old, "for very joy that he had to see the towardness of our intended discovery, entered into the dance himself, among the rest of the young and lusty company."

For five years after Cabot's return to Spain, nothing was done to investigate the promise of riches on the River Plate. The Council of the Indies was hampered in its best purposes by the Emperor's worldwide wars, which drained the realm of money and men. As the Emperor himself, whether from poverty or calculation, consistently refused to advance a penny for any exploring party, it was necessary to wait for a moneyed volunteer with a speculative disposition.

[11] Graham, "Conquest of the River Plate," 35 n.

The volunteer at length presented himself: Don Pedro de Mendoza, Cupbearer to the King, a gentleman of fine lineage. He had enriched himself largely in the sack of Rome in 1527. The adventure tempted him; he assembled fourteen vessels and fifteen hundred Spanish expeditionaries,[12] many of them gentlemen of the best blood in Spain, some few of them accompanied by their wives and families. His inspector was Felipe de Cáceres, the messenger who brought back the news of the colony to Cabeza de Vaca in 1540. The quartermaster was García Venegas. Others of the distinguished party were Francisco de Mendoza, perhaps a relative of the governor; Gonzalo de Mendoza, a high official in disgrace, ex-major-domo of Maximilian, the Emperor's son-in-law; he was to become a skilled interpreter of native tongues; Captain Juan de Salazar de Espinosa; and an inconspicuous young gentleman, Domingo Martínez de Irala, of Vergara in the Basque country, destined to be the bitter enemy of Cabeza de Vaca in a great drama of the wilderness. The commoners of the expedition were drawn largely from the Basque provinces and from Cordova; the sense of loyalty to native cities accompanied them across the world, to divide them into hostile parties. A sprinkling of foreigners somehow joined the fleet: Frenchmen, Englishmen, and Italians.[13] And in the convoy voyaged a hundred and fifty Germans and Flemings, eighty of whom manned a vessel sent out for trade by the firm of Welzer and Neidhart of Nuremberg. The Welzers were associates of the Fuggers, those tremendous bankers who held a mortgage on the Holy Roman Empire. This German merchant ship carried out a cargo of trinkets, what are now called "notions," and was instructed to return with silver bars for ballast. In its crew was a simple, sour-humored, hard-fisted and hard-headed Bavarian, Ulrich Schmidel of Straubingen, who spent twenty years in the bush without learning more than approximately his commanders' names, and who has left us a precious first-hand account of the Mendoza expedition.[14]

[12] Some say twelve vessels; some say two thousand men.
[13] "Cartas de Indias," 763; Gandía, "Los Italianos en el Río de la Plata," 24.
[14] See the "Bibliography of Ulrich Schmidel," by E. Arana, in Boletín del Instituto de Investigaciones históricas, Jan.–June 1931. Schmidel is often mistakenly mentioned as Schmidt. I refer regularly to the English translation of the (very rare) early German edition, edited for the Hakluyt Society by Luis L. Domínguez ("The Conquest of the River Plate").

The proud armada set sail from San Lúcar de Barrameda on August 24, 1535.[15] During the long journey the confinement of ticklish-spirited men in tiny quarters bred its usual mischief. Mendoza conceived a great jealousy of his second in command, Don Juan Osorio, unduly popular with the fleet. He passed the word that this upstart must die. So four of the faithful finished him on the beach at Río de Janeiro, *"cosiéndole a puñaladas,"* sewing him with dagger-blows. Two of these assassins, Juan de Ayolas and Juan de Salazar de Espinosa, will reappear in our story.

The fleet reached the Plate in March, 1536, just before the season of the unrelenting cold south winds. On the south bank of the estuary they came to shore, and built a mud-walled fort which they christened Buenos Aires, for the Virgen del Buen Aire, the Debonnaire Virgin, or Our Lady of Fair Winds, protectress of sailors.[16] Here they thought to pass the winter while considering their next step toward the mines of silver. Soon, however, the dreams of wealth vanished under hunger's immediate urgency, for the natives, fierce Querandís, tired of feeding such a multitude. Don Pedro, lacking any veterans of the frontier to advise on methods of persuading Indians, applied the military maxims of the Italian wars. He issued a peremptory requisition for food, and sent a detachment of three hundred and thirty men to enforce his orders on the inhabitants.

That night eighty-five survivors returned to the fort.

A frightful winter ensued. Men greedily ate reptiles and any horrible things; the pet dogs and cats soon disappeared; two soldiers who committed "the sin against the Holy Ghost," [17] the killing of a horse for food, were promptly hung. By the following morning all the flesh was stripped from their dancing bones. A high-born lady sold her virtue for a fish's head. The women, testifies one of them who survived, were stronger than the men; they washed the clothes, tended the sick, prepared the little food there was, stood guard, patrolled the

---

[15] Many authorities say 1534. Gandía ("Historia de la Conquista," 13) settles the matter.

[16] The story that the city takes its name from the exclamation of Sancho del Campo: *"¡Que buenos aires son los de este suelo!* How good are the airs of this land!" is a creation of the etiological myth-makers.

[17] Graham, "Conquest of the River Plate," 62.

watch-fires, cranked crossbows, and commanded troops.[18] The spirit of the conquerors appeared in these gentle ladies, bred to a life of Oriental languor.

From time to time the Indians would descend on the feeble garrison, setting the thatched roofs afire with burning arrows, killing any foragers caught without the walls. Four of the ships were burned at anchor. When spring came, out of that whole army only five hundred and sixty were left alive.

The post was clearly untenable. Making a desperate cast at relief, Mendoza took four hundred men and attempted to ascend the Paraná. In two months he reached Santi Espíritu, the site of Cabot's settlement. Fifty men had died on the way. He appointed Juan de Ayolas governor pro tempore in his stead, and ordered him to continue on up stream to that better land of which Cabot had told. He himself, sick and shaking with fever and the pox, descended the river to Buenos Aires, where he found pestilence added to famine.

In this lamentable wreck of all his hopes and his great enterprise, Don Pedro could think of no recourse but to return to Spain, to beg succor from the king. A vessel was made ready and stocked with what supplies could be found. An old hunter, in a begging letter to the king, years later, tells how he shot a hundred and fifty quail and partridge for this voyage.[19]

So Don Pedro sailed for home (on April 22, 1537), and on the way he died, from chronic syphilis, say some,[20] from a phrenzy induced by eating a pregnant bitch, say others.[21] His body was consigned to the sea, off the Azores. God Almighty be merciful to him and to us. Amen. (So Ulrich Schmidel has frequent reason to exclaim in his chronicle.)

The Council of the Indies responded to the colonists' plea with unusual generosity and despatch. Three vessels, under the command of Alonso Cabrera, were sent out with provisions and orders. With the

[18] Isabel de Guevara, in "Cartas de Indias," 619.
[19] "Cartas de Indias," 602.
[20] Gandía, "Historia de la Conquista," 54; Graham, "Conquest of River Plate," 48.
[21] Ruy Díaz de Guzmán, in Angelis, "Colección de Obras," I, 39, followed by Charlevoix, "Histoire du Paraguay," I, 66 et al.

official documents was included a general pardon for those who had eaten human flesh in their extremity. The expedition arrived in Buenos Aires in November, 1538, to discover the colony in a parlous state. Its numbers had been increased by the crew of a shipwrecked Italian vessel, but privation, the attacks of Indians, and disease soon evened the account.

Cabrera found important news at hand of Ayolas and his exploring party, sent forth by Mendoza.

Ayolas had worked his craft, with sail, oar, and pole, against the swift current of the Paraná. He saw many marvelous beasts and fish, a sort of water-boar, half hog, half hare (the capibara), ostriches, tall sheep like deer (llamas), tremendous serpents, and rabbits like rats, but tailless. Reaching the division of the stream, he took the western branch, which the natives called the Paraguay. At length he reached the fruitful country of the Guaranís, well planted with maize, manioc, yams, papaws, and squash; the rivers abounded with fish and the woods with deer, wild boar, rabbits, hens, and geese; honey was plentiful, from which the natives made a good wine; there was cotton enough for any need. The Indians were a comely race; one might buy a woman for a shirt, a bread knife, or a hoe. They wore not even a bit of cloth to cover their privities.[22] They were cannibals, but rather through gourmandise than ferocity.

Ayolas, of the true breed of the conquerors, would not stay for any such lotus-land. He pushed on northward while the happy country turned to feverish tropics and the park-land to steaming marshes. "In our affliction of heat and hunger," says a companion of the voyage, "we could sometimes hear the demons talking in the air above us." [23] They passed among many tribes of natives. Some received the adventurers well, others in a hostile manner, but with little profit to themselves, for the Spaniards slew a goodly number of them with their guns, they having never in their lives before seen either a gun or a

---

[22] Roger Barlow, an English merchant of Seville, who accompanied Cabot, says quaintly of the Tupis, a related race: "In some placis before ther privitees thei wil hange a cloute of coton or a lefe for other clothe thei have none. And the yong women wil suffre nothing of that, but rather set it out with paynting colours." ("A Brief Summe of Geographie," 152.)

[23] Villalta, quoted by Gandía, "Historia de la Conquista," 56.

Christian.[24] Peace was commonly made by gifts of women. From one tribe Ayolas received six maidens, the oldest less than eighteen.

In the hot and marshy land came a message that seemed the reward of indomitable faith. The Indians brought a slave, who said that he had accompanied Alejo García, the Portuguese, to the western mountains, and had returned with a back-load of silver, as had his fellows. He had since been taken prisoner by the river Indians. Asked if he could serve as a guide to the silver land, he said he could. Therefore Ayolas moored his boats at this point, and established the settlement of Candelaria, for it was Candlemas Day, February 2, 1537. It stood about on the present site of Puerto Pacheco.[25]

Ayolas divided his men into two parties. He set Domingo Martínez de Irala in charge of the boats, with thirty-three men, strictly ordering him to wait there as long as he could cling, and to keep the boats ship-shape, for on the return trip they would be loaded to the gunwales with silver. Ayolas himself took a hundred and thirty Spaniards, with thirty Payaguá Indians as porters, and on the twelfth of February he disappeared westward into the bush.

Days and months went by, and no Spaniard returned, and no message and no sound came from the dark Chaco, ominous as the ocean's edge.

Irala lingered in the pestilential harbor of Candelaria. His boats were rotting; food began to fail, for the hospitality of the Payaguás was wearied by these exorbitant guests. There was another story: the chief of the Payaguás had sealed friendship with Ayolas by giving him his daughter, and Ayolas had left his spouse in the precarious guardianship of Irala. Tedium, that ancient bawd, soon made her match. Irala would spend the livelong day with the dark princess, locked in the lugger's cabin. This angered much her father and all the proud Payaguás.

On June 23, 1537, Captain Juan de Salazar de Espinosa arrived with two luggers, from the southern settlements. The two captains then ran down-stream to the fruitful country, to take on supplies and careen and repair their boats. On this journey Captain Salazar, reaching a pleasant

---

[24] This great phrase is lifted whole from the narrative of Ulrich Schmidel (Domínguez, 17).

[25] For the location of Candelaria see Gandía, "Conquista," 57, n. 7.

bight of the river, where the waters loitered behind a natural break-water, established a town on the day of the Assumption of Our Lady, August the fifteenth, and this he named Asunción, in honor of the Queen of Heaven.[26]

So ran the official report. But soldiers' gossip told that Irala had abandoned his post in Candelaria after only four months of fidelity, from no dire necessity, but because, tiring of his princess, he was pricked by the memory of a certain Cario girl in the port of Tapua, just above Asunción. For this reason Tapua was known along the Paraguay as *el puerto de la hodienda*.[27]

Thus, beguiling his wait with simple pleasures, Irala idled on the river until Ayolas should return. He made a second and a third trip to Candelaria, finding the Payaguás so hostile that he could not bide there long. When four of his men were killed in a skirmish, he returned to Asunción, where, by his natural gifts of command, he soon came to rule, uttering orders and signing decrees like a viceroy.

This, then, was the story that Cabrera heard in Buenos Aires. Ayolas and his men were still lost in the Chaco, but there was no reason yet to despair of their safety. The control of the upper river was in the strong hands of Irala, who had risen by the natural selection of the frontier to command the remnant of Mendoza's fighting men. Clearly, the first need of the colony was ample succor from Spain, and the second need the legal appointment of a chief to rule in the absence of Ayolas.

Cabera determined, therefore, to send immediate and urgent word of the colony's state to Spain, while he himself should carry to Asunción his precious cedula of the king. This document confirmed Ayolas in his provisional appointment by Mendoza as governor pro tempore of the colony, until a regular appointee should be sent out from Spain. Further, in case Ayolas should die without having named a successor, the Founders and Conquerors of Paraguay should meet and elect their captain by a plurality of votes.

As Cabrera's vessel turned up-stream toward Paraguay, the Santa

---

[26] The date, often given erroneously as 1536, is settled by Gandía, "Indios y Conquistadores," 1 *et sqq*.

[27] Serrano y Sanz, II, 321; Gandía, "Conquista," 60, n. 18. "Whore's Harbor" might render it for chaste ears.

Catalina, with the troublesome Felipe de Cáceres aboard, set sail for Spain. It arrived in Seville, as has been noted,[28] in September, 1539.

The Council of the Indies, hearing this story, with such additions and suppressions as Cáceres thought advisable, deliberated duly. Here was a task for a bold man who knew the Indies, one who had the wealth to equip an expedition. He would be rewarded with many honorable titles, and with the promise of great riches, to be assessed upon the golden kingdom lying beyond the jungle.

The Council of the Indies talked and pondered. A royal messenger summoned Alvar Núñez Cabeza de Vaca.

He stood before the Council and heard its terms. There was no doubt of his answer. This was the opportunity of which he had dreamed, so long. Here was a great kingdom offered, a quarter of a continent, the home of any wonder. Within its borders might lie the palaces of the White King, or the realm of El Dorado, the Gilded Man, who anointed his body daily with liquid gold, and who nightly washed himself clean of it. The vision of gold, wealth, power, and fame shimmered, alluring him, as it does all men. But in the dark of his mind there burned, like a sanctuary lamp, the unwavering thought of the land where, by God's grace, he might realize on earth the rule of justice, mercy, and peace.

The King's Patent, Agreement, and Capitulation is dated in Madrid, March 18, 1540.[29]

This precious document first defines the limits of the territory of La Plata, which extends from Peru to the Straits of Magellan. It then records the death of Don Pedro de Mendoza, and the fact that Ayolas, his heir, has disappeared, leaving his people in great need. Alvar Núñez Cabeza de Vaca, having offered to expend eight thousand ducats, plus the costs of transport, on a relief expedition, is appointed adelantado, governor, captain general and chief justice of the province, *provided only* that the death of Ayolas be attested. He will receive an annual salary of two thousand ducats (with a present significance of $30,000), to be drawn from the revenues of the province. He may build

---

[28] *Ante,* p. 173. Dates established by Gandía, "Conquista," 82, n. 70.
[29] Reproduced in "Colección de Documentos . . . de Indias," XXIII, 8. The King's Person was in fact in Ghent.

two forts, of which he will be commander, with an annual salary of a hundred thousand maravedís (meaning $4,000) for each. For twelve years, his colony will be remitted the payment of import and export duties. Provisionally, he will receive one twelfth of the revenue of provinces newly settled. He will have the right of distributing encomiendas of Indians. If he shall capture and hold to ransom a great cacique, one sixth of the ransom, gold, silver, pearls, and precious stones, must first be reserved for the king; the rest may be divided among the captors, the King's Fifth being deducted.

If Ayolas shall be found still alive, Cabeza de Vaca must submit to him, conceding him all the rights of Mendoza. Cabeza de Vaca will then receive appointment as chief lieutenant, with full rights to Santa Catalina Island for twelve years. And if Ayolas be still lost and missing, Cabeza de Vaca will be provisionally governor, taking precedence over any lieutenants found in command in the colony, until Ayolas shall return or assurance of his death shall be had.

He must set sail within six months of the date of this instrument.

And then a decree of 1526 regarding the treatment of natives is textually quoted at length. This relates the manifold abuses inflicted upon those unhappy subjects of the king, their labors in mines and pearl fisheries, the cruelty and mischief of their masters, the offenses against our Holy Faith. It is the same eloquent protest against the cruelties of the conquerors that had been incorporated in His Majesty's grant to Pánfilo de Narváez, fourteen years before.[30] After a recital of the natives' wrongs, it lays down stringent rules for the guarding of their welfare, under the loving protection of the clergy.

I make no doubt that these pages were inserted at the request of Cabeza de Vaca, who remembered well the words of Narváez's grant, and who planned to keep them quick in the minds of his subordinates by frequent public proclamation.

At about the time of the issuance of this Royal Appointment to the coveted post, Cabeza de Vaca found himself assailed by a rival claimant. A certain Orduña, representing the missing Ayolas, deposited several pleas, injunctions, writs and restraints with the Council of the Indies, to prevent the new governor's appointment. Unavailing though

[30] *Ante*, p. 24.

they were, they probably inspired Cabeza de Vaca to ask a supplementary kindness from the king. His Majesty was pleased to hear him, and on July 1, 1540, a Royal Provision was published that no lawyer or solicitor should be permitted to enter the colony for ten years from date.[31]

It was a happy spring and summer for Cabeza de Vaca, in possession of his heart's desire. With the thousand duties of preparation on his shoulders, he had no more time for dreaming. His days were filled, from dawn to midnight, with the obligations of a general who must choose his army, create his navy, and buy his supplies for a ten-thousand-mile journey to an almost unknown land.

First, the question of his personnel. To his headquarters in Seville there pressed a swarm of would-be adventurers, attracted by the fame of Cabeza de Vaca and by the whisper of a new Inca treasure-land behind the Andes. The new commander was obliged to enlist many gentlemen because of their powerful connections at court. Many he picked for their brisk and well-turned-out appearance. Many he refused, with the memory of some of Narváez's trouble-makers in his mind—fattish men, grumblers, the over-nice, the over-proud, the clerkly. He must have felt a chill of foreboding, wondering what the candidates would do after a week of starving, wondering what the bluff faces masked, what the high protestations hid. As it turned out, he made many serious mistakes, taking subordinates who mocked him covertly from the first. I think that, given as he was to a dream, he was too easily befooled by those who were coached to chime with his reported purposes.

It would have been to his advantage to view the world like that clear-eyed old cynic of Santo Domingo, Oviedo the historian, who thus addressed young volunteers: "Don't say that you come to the Indies to serve the king and to employ your person and your time like valorous gentlemen, since you know that the truth is just the contrary, that you come only with the desire to get more wealth than your father and your neighbors." [32]

---

[31] This wise provision had been inserted in the Royal Patent to Soto ("Narratives of De Soto," ed. Buckingham Smith, 270).
[32] "Historia general," II, 226.

Perhaps the first candidate chosen was Cabeza de Vaca's cousin, Pedro Estopiñán, or Pero Vaca, who had twice waved farewell to the adventurer, and who could not endure a third such leave-taking. With him enlisted the two eager young kinsmen from Jerez, Alonso Riquel de Guzmán and Pedro de Fuentes. A number of other Jerezanos were accepted, and various gentlemen of station.

As for the rank and file, the men-at-arms, crossbowmen, and artisans, one may be sure that Cabeza de Vaca tested their competence more carefully than had Narváez. He remembered only too well the clumsy, inapt efforts of the boat-builders by the Bay of Horses. He interviewed the likely volunteers who gathered on the steps of Seville Cathedral; for this was the employment exchange for the Indies. There the captains and merchants examined candidates, darting inside the church to seal bargains with God for witness. Of the cathedral steps Oviedo, the salty old historian, says:

When these conquerors and captains come there, they don't look for acquaintances nor men of good conscience, but they take the first comers who seem likely to aid them to rob and sack, profligates and brabblers whom they have never known nor seen; they take one because he says he was in the battle of Ravenna, and another at Pavia, or at the sack of Genoa or Rome, and one such shameless charlatan is enough to do great hurt to many. And the poor captain notices only that he wears a jaunty feather and carries a clean arquebus, and has his doublet and hose well pinked, with many taffeta puffs and silk-lined brocades, for which they pawn and pledge all they have, thinking that when they come to shore they will sate their greed with bars of gold.

But if I had to advise them and pick these men, I would do it quite otherwise. I would say: "Señor capitán, listen to me and mark me well. You should first consider a man's face, and by that effigy you will discern a little of his inward shame. And because the outward signs may deceive you, you must inquire secretly his habits, and how he lives, and what he knows how to do, and what his nation is; for in that sacred place some do not scruple to deny their country and even their own names. And let it not seem so good to you that he be tall and wear his beard well combed as that he be virtuous and well born and simple, not presumptuous. And if he tells you he was in the Ravenna business, heed him not; if he is Spanish, why did he survive? Why was he not taken prisoner? And the same for Pavia; and if he says he was in the sack of Genoa or of Rome, why did he not emerge a rich man? And if he was rich, and gamed away his money or lost it, trust him not. . . . Let the man you take not be questionable in religion above all, and let him not be less than twenty-five nor more than fifty, nor clutch-fisted nor a high talker." [33]

Remember also how Cervantes defined America,[34] as "the recourse of the ruined, the refuge and shelter of the desperate men of Spain, the sanctuary of the fraudulent bankrupts, the pardon of murderers, the haven of loose women, the last trick of gamblers, the common cheat of many and the remedy of few."

The roll of the expedition still exists, in the haunted gloom of the Archives of the Indies. In the list one notices a Flemish drummer, several slaves, four negroes, two Indians, one of them from Mexico.[35] A half-dozen brave women went as passengers; probably Juana Núñez, Cabeza de Vaca's negro servant, was among them.[36]

It was none too easy to recruit foremast hands for the perilous journey. A sailor complained, five years later, that he and a companion were shanghaied, with the connivance of the high commander.[37]

Transport was a matter of deep concern. Apparently there was difficulty in finding suitable vessels, for a royal cedula of July 1 orders the Casa de Contratación to coöperate with Cabeza de Vaca in finding bottoms, so that he may depart with all speed. With this aid, he bought two large ships, a new one of three hundred and fifty tons (the Santa Lucía), one of a hundred and fifty (the Trinidad), and a smaller caravel. He agreed with his pilot, Antonio López, to buy his vessel, which was lying in harbor in the Canaries. He stocked his fleet from the ship-chandlers' stores of Seville, buying a double set of arms for each man,[38] ammunition, iron, woolen and linen cloth, ship biscuit, flour, wine, oil, vinegar, medicines, and trade goods that the natives love: knives, fish-hooks, mirrors, scissors, red caps, shirts, and shawls.

And with great care he picked in the horse market thirty-six sturdy looking beasts, including stallions for breeding. He bought eight or

---

[33] "Historia general," II, 225.
[34] In "El Celoso extremeño," opening words.
[35] Arch. Ind., Justicia, 1130, 3A. It is not complete. (Gandía, "Conquista," 97, n. 9.)
[36] Arch. Ind., Justicia, 1130; Gandía "Indios y Conquistadores," 122–5. Perhaps she was an Indian girl, nicknamed "la Negra."
[37] Arch. Ind., Justicia, 1131.
[38] It was customary for the chief to supply all weapons but the sword and dagger. (Bayle, "El Dorado fantasma," 46.)

ten cows in Jerez. They did not survive the hardships of the voyage and the ogreish hungers of the passengers.[39]

He spent 14,000 gold ducats for his preparations, plus 9,000 for his shipping expenses (on a basis of purchasing values, about $350,000). Thus he more than doubled the expenditures to which he consented in his contract with the king. His patrimony soon disappeared; following the example of his grandfather, he was led by faith to contract a debt of 5,000 ducats (or $75,000).[40]

While these business matters were in hand, his troops, congregating in the Seville taverns, added to his difficulties. The idle hotspurs could not wait for the adventure to begin. It was necessary for the king to issue a cedula, dated July 25, 1540, enjoining the *asistente* of Seville from disarming the expeditionaries. His Majesty's secretary probably felt kindly disposed toward young fellows displaying to the townsfolk the character of heedless roaring blades, staking their lives against the roll of destiny's dice.

By October all was in readiness. The governor and his officers, in silks and armor, heard in the cathedral a last solemn mass, with the blessing of their banners. The three vessels cast off from the Seville wharfs, amid innumerable kisses and tears. From the mastheads flew the royal standard of crimson damask. Rowboats pulled the caravels to midstream, pointed the bows down-river, and dropped the hawsers. The sails ran up, heave after heave; the ships stirred with the wind and sluggish current. *¡Adiós! ¡Adiós!* It was farewell forever, as all felt in their hearts, for few indeed returned from the Indies. Men went out and gold came back, but the price of gold was high in Spanish blood.

---

[39] The first cattle in South America were seven cows and a bull, driven overland from Santa Catalina to Asunción by Ciprian de Goes in 1554–5, a most mighty feat. ("Cartas de Indias," 767.) Have the packers of South America erected a statue to Ciprian de Goes?

[40] Serrano y Sanz, II, 112, 247.

CHAPTER II

THE JOURNEY TO PARAGUAY

ALVAR NÚÑEZ CABEZA DE VACA, adelantado and governor of the Río de la Plata, stood on the quarter-deck and watched the brown, marshy banks of the Guadalquivir slip by. At San Lúcar de Barrameda, near the river's mouth, government inspectors boarded the ships, to determine that the King's Regulations were fulfilled as to equipment, lading, armament, and seaworthiness. Their certificates given, they dropped overside into their tenders. With all hands attentive on deck, the harbor pilot ordered the anchor aweigh. Then solemnly he intoned:

"Hoist the foresail in the name of the Holy Trinity, Father, Son, and Holy Ghost, three persons and one true God, that he may be with us and accompany and guard us and give us a good voyage to our safe harbor and bring us back to our homes." [1]

As the sail went up, all recited in unison an Ave María.

The canvas filled, the ships moved past the harbor bar, and out on the Atlantic.

Hardly had they debouched, however, when western gales struck them, and forced them to take shelter in Cadiz harbor. There they waited an intolerable month, all the men with nerves on edge. At last, on Dec. 2, 1540,[2] the winds relented, and the pilots headed south-southwest. Nine days later they made the island of Palma, in the Canaries, where they picked up the fourth ship of their convoy. Twenty-five days they halted here, awaiting a favorable wind.

Staring up at the high tower of Teneriffe, Cabeza de Vaca saw again his fierce old grandfather, the conqueror of the Grand Canary. He heard again that dead voice, in the patio of the palace in Jerez, telling

---

[1] Castro y Bravo, "Naos españoles," 132.
[2] Nov. 2, in the "Comentarios." This is disproved by various documents.

his stories of Spanish valor. Even his own memories of adventures on Bad Luck Island and the deserts of the west seemed dim beside his boyish imaginations of his grandfather, hunting the Guanches among these mountain crags. He remembered how he had clapped his hands at the thought of heaps of heathen dead, at the vision of heads rolling free at a single mighty Spanish moulinet. He remembered how, thirteen years before, he had passed this way, and how then he had been all iron of purpose, with his heart hardened and tempered for its task of conquest. What were these new feelings which sometimes dissolved him in weakness, and sometimes invaded him with a sense of more than earthly delight? He was a different man from his ghostly grandfather, and a different self from the Alvar Núñez Cabeza de Vaca who had paused here on the way to Florida. Well, his soul had passed through purgatory while his body was still alive; purged of much of its dross, it had struggled upward out of pride to humility.

Watching the sorrowful brown Guanches, doing the menial labors of the shore, he mentally asked their pardon for the cruelties of his grandfather and for all those of his fellows. He prayed for the soul of Pedro de Vera and for his own, and his secret resolves were strengthened.

During the delay among these islands an unfortunate incident occurred. A band of soldiers, on shore leave, gave chase, with their dogs, to a herd of cattle. They brought down three beasts and banqueted hugely. When the inevitable complaint was laid before the commander, he angrily confiscated the soldiers' cloaks, and repaid the injured cattleman with five or six doubloons from his own pocket. Several years later his enemies recalled the incident and charged that the depredations had been committed by his order.[3]

From Palma the course lay south-southwest to the Cape Verde Islands. On the way thither the flag-ship sprung a bad leak; five hundred quintals of biscuit were damaged, as well as other commodities. Pumping night and day, they reached Cape Verde in ten days (Jan. 15, 1541). The ship was unloaded, and the horses exercised; and the ship's captain, who was the best diver in all Spain, stopped the leak.

By a fortunate chance, two well-found ships lay in harbor. From one

[3] Arch. Ind., Justicia, 1131, various examinations; Gandía, "Conquista," 216, n. 89.

of them Cabeza de Vaca bought some wine, flour, and almonds; the captain of the other, with a true seaman's camaraderie, offered wine and oil, and asked no payment until the expedition should return rich from the Plate. These innocent transactions were later to be interpreted as acts of piracy.

On Feb. 9, 1541, the journey was resumed. The Line was crossed without incident. Daily at sunrise and sunset the four ships would come together, to salute the commander and receive orders. A number of the horses, packed side by side, head to tail, in the hold, died of kicks and colic. At least, a dead horse was meat, though not, as we remember, for Cabeza de Vaca.

One day the captain, taking stock of the water, discovered that out of a hundred barrels only three were left. He came in a panic to the governor, who ordered that the ships' heads be turned directly toward the Brazilian coast, that they might make the nearest land with all speed.

For three days they drove westward; "and the fourth day, one hour before dawn, a wonderful thing happened," says Pedro Hernández, Cabeza de Vaca's notary and adorer, who has left us the amplest consecutive account of the South American adventures.[4]

It happened that, as the vessels were going toward land, they were on the point of striking some very high rocks, and nobody would have seen or been aware of them had not a cricket begun to chirrup which one of the soldiers had put on board at Cadiz, being desirous of listening to the music of the cricket; during two months and a half, however, we had neither heard it nor known of its existence; and the soldier was grieved at its silence. That morning, however, the cricket felt the land and began to chirrup, and its music woke all the people on the vessel, who saw the rocks an arrow flight off, and shouted to let go the anchors, as we were drifting toward the rocks. And so they lowered the anchors, and this saved us, for had not the cricket chirruped our four hundred men and thirty horses would assurely have been drowned; and we all thought it a miracle of God for us. And while we navigated more than one hundred leagues along the coast, the cricket gave us his music every night.[5]

[4] Commonly known as the "Comentarios de Cabeza de Vaca," and often ascribed to his authorship, because they first appeared in conjunction with Cabeza de Vaca's acknowledged "Naufragios," concerning his North American odyssey. However, Cabeza de Vaca states that the "Comentarios" were written by Pedro Hernández at his direction. (Serrano y Sanz, I, 148.) I shall quote and refer to the admirable version of Luis L. Domínguez.

[5] Domínguez, 99. Domínguez, evidently troubled by this implausible story (for a

When the ships had passed beyond the limits of the Portuguese possessions (about in the region of the present Santos), they turned into the harbor of Cananea, in longitude forty-eight. This was the governor's first sight of his new realm. He disembarked, and formally took possession in the name of His Majesty.

Three years later his foes were to accuse him of having performed this act of possession in his own name, not in that of the king, and of having set up a stone engraved with his own device, a cow's head.[6]

Here the coast turns south. The fleet ran two hundred miles to the island of Santa Catalina, and there the governor landed on March 29, 1541, four months out from Cadiz.

Cabeza de Vaca found his island a fruitful and genial land. He was soon able to lure the timid Indians from the woods; and he must have been moved to find their simplicity responsive to his old air of kindly command. From them he learned that near by, on the mainland, lived two Franciscan monks. He sent to fetch them, and they came with great willingness, for two Christians living in that land had just been slain by the natives.

These friars were Bernardo de Armenta of Cordova and Alonso Lebrón of the Canary Islands. They had come out with Cabrera, and had since been laboring, in their own way, along the Atlantic coast. Cabeza de Vaca discovered them before long to be the foes of his purpose. Sanctimoniousness, not true godly zeal, shone in their words; shifty, fleshly men, they carried on the old tradition of the jolly friar, so hateful to the austere governor, so amusing in modern retrospect. To the self-indulgence of the venal cleric, out of sight of his superiors, they joined the scorn of frontiersmen for the native.[7]

The great task loomed ever more formidable to Cabeza de Vaca. To his program of justice he must first convert the consecrated servants

lookout and helmsman who could sleep through the sound of surf would not wake for any mere cricket), translates *grillo* as *cock,* a bold emendation. However, Hernández was repeating this story at second hand, in spite of his first person plural. He went out with Mendoza (Serrano y Sanz, II, 245).

[6] Arch. Ind., Justicia, 1131, reported in Gandía, "Conquista," 98, n. 11. Cananea was the scene of an unsuccessful British attempt at colonization in the nineteenth century. "Its name has been heard in England on account of the singular folly or knavery of attempting to stock the land with British peasants, the meanest of races." (Note by Richard F. Burton to "The Captivity of Hans Stade," 40 n.)

[7] But see the pious protestations in Armenta's letter of 1538, lauding his own triumphs in converting natives. (Mendieta, "Historia eclesiástica indiana," 553.)

of justice. He enjoined upon them straitly that they preach the Word, and that they labor to pacify the natives and win their friendship.

In the month of May (1541), in a lull in the great south wind, he sent Felipe de Cáceres with two vessels to carry relief to Buenos Aires. But when they had hardly left the island the gale caught them and ran them ashore, destroying the ships; and they were glad to escape to Santa Catalina with their lives.

While the governor sat there puzzling as to what next he should do, nine naked Spaniards arrived in a small boat, fugitives from Buenos Aires. They had stolen their craft and fled because they could not endure the ill treatment of their captain. In many long interrogatories, Cabeza de Vaca learned from them the present state of the colony.

So the fort of Buenos Aires still held out?

Ay, that it did indeed, but barely, for rations were very short, and unless help came soon it must be abandoned.

(Then the question that had lain on Cabeza de Vaca's mind through all the outward journey.) Had Juan de Ayolas returned?

No, he had not returned. (Then Cabeza de Vaca should rule in fact, if not with full title!)

Had news been received of his death?

Yes. (Then Cabeza de Vaca was governor of La Plata!)

Questioned more closely, they told the story of Irala's fourth trip to Candelaria, as it had been reported down-river.

Irala had arrived in Candelaria in January, 1540. Then for the first time he learned from the Indians that Ayolas was near by, with handsome loot in gold and silver. Though it was flood season, Irala attempted to make a contact with his master. For eighteen days the party struggled through waist-deep water, with no place to sleep or build a fire. Finally they returned exhausted to the harbor, their mission unaccomplished. When they were about to fall back discouraged to Asunción, they heard a voice calling from the shore. It was an Indian boy, begging to be rescued by the Spaniards. He said he was of the Chané tribe, and his home was on the slopes of the Andes. There Ayolas had come with his men, and all had lived together in great peace and amity. Ayolas, taking a fancy to the boy, had taken him for a personal servant, and christened him Gonzalo. Then Ayolas and his men had returned from the Andes, their porters carrying a considerable weight of precious metal. Arriving at Candelaria, they had seemed much dejected to find no waiting fleet, and to discover the Payaguá Indians in a hostile mood. Afterwards, these fierce people, apparently revenging themselves for the affronts of Irala, had massacred Ayolas and all his men. Only the teller of the tale was spared, as a harmless boy. Irala, on hearing this news, burned alive those Payaguá Indians on whom he could lay his hands. Then he returned to Asunción, and sent word of his doings, with two boat-loads of food, to Buenos Aires.

How long had Ayolas been obliged to dwell among the Indians, awaiting the rescue that did not come?

No one seemed to know exactly.

Did any blame attach to Irala for not keeping his vigil for the return of his master?

The refugees from Buenos Aires looked at each other and grinned. And, with encouragement from Cabeza de Vaca, they told of Irala's sins of the flesh and how he had been led by lust away from his duty. Some would even blame the death of Ayolas on Irala's derelictions, because he had abandoned his post, and because he had ruffled the honor of the Payaguás, turning them from friends to foes.

Cabeza de Vaca began to feel the premonition of a great conflict to be waged in the Paraguayan wild. The adversary was taking the shape and feature of Domingo Martínez de Irala.

He rewarded the refugees with clothing, and enlisted them in his army, for they were useful men and good sailors, and one was a pilot who knew the navigation of the great river.

And now, having formed a project in his mind, he called a meeting of his chiefs. To them he set forth that the winter winds would hold them in port for some months to come; that the garrison of Buenos Aires was small, and that the great body of expeditionaries was assembled in Asunción, surrounded by tribes, many of which were turning hostile; that to reach Asunción by sea and river would be the business of a year; and that therefore he proposed to reconnoiter a route across country to the west.

A storm of protest greeted his words. All agreed that the trackless interior was inhabited by savage races, cannibals, foes of the white man. The country was one of tremendous mountains, broad, impassable rivers, and dense jungles, the home of tigers, poisonous vipers, and colossal bone-breaking snakes.

Cabeza de Vaca replied that he had once accomplished a much more difficult journey, that he had a way of mollifying savage natives, and that he was captain and would be obeyed.

His cold air of command could not fail to inflame the tender susceptibilities of his subordinates. The whisper ran around the camp: "The governor still thinks himself half a god, issuing divine decrees to a horde of ape-like Indians! He will find that he must pitch another tone to Spanish gentlemen!"

He chose a hundred men for a scouting party. In command he placed his quartermaster, Pedro Dorantes of Béjar, probably a relative of Andrés Dorantes. (Stout Andrés! Would that he were present! No dangers could affright his heart!) And Pedro cheerily ferried to the mainland; his expedition, having been blessed by the priests, followed the Indian guides up the mountain side. Cabeza de Vaca sat down on the island to wait, stoically bearing the hinted reproaches of his lieutenants.

Three months later Pedro Dorantes returned, with good news. Crossing the barren mountains, he had reached an inhabited country, and had departed again without hindrance from the natives.

The governor immediately published marching orders. He put a hundred and forty men, including the weak and sickly and the women, under the command of his cousin Pero Vaca, who was directed to collect all the food available, and carry his cargo to Buenos Aires as soon as the winds should permit. The light artillery, the iron and heavier trade goods were also to be transported in the flag-ship's hold.[8]

"Before I left," writes the governor, "I gave the island Indians many shirts and caps and other things to leave them happy, and of their own will a certain number offered to come in my company, as well to show me the road as to carry the loads of food." [9]

[8] Ruy Díaz de Guzmán tells of the transport of a forge across country, on which chisels, hatchets, fish-hooks and needles were created to the admiration of the natives. Obviously a legend.

[9] Serrano y Sanz, II, 9.

Among those who sneered at this ridiculous coddling of the natives were the monks Armenta and Lebrón. Cabeza de Vaca, who would gladly have been rid of them, bade them remain on Santa Catalina, to instruct the natives in Christian doctrine, directing and confirming those already baptized. But they begged to join the overland party, and he assented. This was a great misfortune.

On October 18, 1541, the flag-ship freighted the expedition to the mouth of the Itapucu, fifty miles north of Santa Catalina. The governor held a review; his forces consisted of two hundred and fifty men, crossbowmen and arquebusiers, twenty-six of them mounted; also the Indian carriers and the two Franciscan friars. On November 2 he gave the command— "Forward!"—and led the way up into the mountains, along the Itapucu River.

Oh what a happy moment was this, when Cabeza de Vaca again fronted the unknown wilderness, heading westward toward a salvation mined round about with every danger! At a sudden impulse he stopped, removed his shoes. He walked the thousand miles of the journey, over mountain passes, through the deep jungle, barefoot, "to inspirit my men," he says.[10] And did he so inspirit them? One can hear the outraged, contemptuous mockery in the ranks!

But no doubt the Indian bearers rejoiced to march with a white captain who could outfoot them under an equal burden, who knew their pains and guarded them from any presumption of the heavy-handed soldiery.

After nineteen difficult days the mountain-range was passed, and the expedition descended among Indian villages, where the men were well received and fed. The governor entertained the chieftains affably, and scrupulously paid for the food with trade goods.

These Indians were Guaranís, of that great race which overspread South America from Venezuela to La Plata. "They are cultivators," says Pedro Hernández, "sowing maize twice in the year, and also cassava. They rear fowls as in our Spain, and geese; keep many parrots in their houses, and occupy much land, and the whole are of one language. They eat human flesh, as well that of their Indian enemies as of Christians; they also eat one another. This people is very fond

[10] Serrano y Sanz, II, 15.

of war, and they seek it; they are very vindictive." [11] But of them more later; Cabeza de Vaca was to know them better during his days in Paraguay.

The governor took formal possession of this country in the name of his king, and named it the Province of Vera. But his purpose that this quarter of the world should perpetuate forever the name of his father and grandfather has been frustrated by time.

After a few days he reached a large river, flowing west; it was known, then as to-day, as the Iguazú.[12]

On the march, a few days later, the governor was astounded to be greeted by a Spanish-speaking native. The newcomer explained that he was making his way from Asunción to the coast. After giving a full account of conditions in Paraguay, he volunteered to guide the expedition thither. This happy chance seemed to Cabeza de Vaca of good augury.

The inhabitants, readily conquered by the good reputation of the advancing host, brought them more food than they could eat. "And besides paying for it I gave them readily many things for the pacification of the land." But though the natives made no trouble, the soldiers gave their commander a deal indeed. Where were the bruited pleasures of the conqueror, if not to be exercised in the Indian camps?

The men caused me great labors, which I felt more than the labors of travel and the clearing of paths and the building of bridges, so that I forbade them to enter the houses and camps of the Indians, and to make any trades with them, and I appointed four men who knew and understood the language and native trade, and I ordered them to be very scrupulous in talking with the Indians and in buying supplies for all our people. And this they did always; and all the supplies were bought at a very low price and amicably, and they were given out and distributed without any interest. And wherever there were Indians I ordered our camp pitched far from the Indian villages, so that no injury or provocation should be given, wherefor they might revolt and be affronted, because this is the way to bring most pacification and peace to the land.[13]

[11] Domínguez, 107.
[12] An anonymous contemporary gives this list of rivers crossed: Las Lajas; Domingo; Corimbata; Uba; Iguatú; Piquerí; Paraná; Monday. (Buckingham Smith mss., in N. Y. Historical Society.)
[13] Serrano y Sanz, II, 12.

Pedro Hernández adds other particulars:

It was curious to see how feared were the horses by the Indians of that land and province, that for the terror they had of them they dropped on the road, and set food for them, such as fowls and honey, saying that, provided they would not be angry, they would give them plenty to eat; and to tranquilize them they said that they would not abandon their settlements.[14] Owing to the good order that was kept, and seeing that the governor punished every one who offended them, all the Indians, with their wives and children, had such confidence that it was a sight to see. And from very distant parts they came, laden with provisions, only to see the Christians and their horses.[15]

Such is the version of the commander and his partizans. When, a few years later, the soldiers had the chance to vent their spleen, they reported long-cherished grievances. The governor would always pitch camp far from a native village, only in order to keep the monopoly of foodstuffs. These the servants and hirelings of the governor would sell to the Christians at exorbitant rates. Luis Osorio testified that he paid three German rings for three chickens, and others traded linen shirts for food.[16]

In rebuttal, one may admit that the governor's servants may have been guilty of such peculations. Cabeza de Vaca, often a poor judge of character, was not seldom ill served by his subordinates. However, the depositions in question were obtained in highly suspicious circumstances.

The happy progress continued through the Province of Vera, the tribesmen bringing honey, geese, fowls, flour, and maize. "And the governor spoke to them affably, and ordered that they should be paid for what they brought, which gave them great satisfaction. . . . We left the Indians of this tribe so merry and pleased that they danced and sang for joy through the settlement."

For some reason, the travelers forsook the direct course down the Iguazú, and went northwestward to the Taquarí, a tributary of the

---

[14] On Cortés's expedition to Honduras, his great black charger fell ill, and was entrusted to the natives. Although maidens garlanded with flowers plied him with roast chicken and the finest fruits, he died. (Graham, "The Horses of the Conquest," 39.)

[15] Domínguez, 110.

[16] Arch. Ind., Justicia, 1131, examinations of witnesses.

Paraná-panema. Everywhere the news of their bounty preceded them, and everywhere ample supplies were made ready. In mid-December, however, they reached a difficult and uninhabited land, wherein steep mountains alternated with marshy jungle. Twenty men went in advance, cutting and clearing a road; they had to make as many as eighteen bridges in one day. They saw the monkeys dropping nuts [17] from the trees, and the wild boar waiting below to profit by them, "the monkeys all the while uttering cries from the branches of the trees."

They found a village at last where they were joyfully received. Pausing here to rest, the men feasted; but, "taking no exercise and eating plentifully, they could not digest what they ate, and they immediately caught fevers, which did not happen while they were marching." The governor, relentless, gave the order to break camp and move on. There was much grumbling, the soldiers vowing that he would not delay "because he wished to give them more trouble." On the march their sickness disappeared, "till at length they were fain to acknowledge that he had so acted for their own good, since by eating much they had suffered; and of this the governor had great experience."

But (if I remember soldiers) there were others who would never so acknowledge their error. Rather would they hold their master a tyrannical prig; and they would dream of an opportunity to make clear to him their opinion.

Early in January, 1542, they reached another inhospitable mountainous region, clothed in bamboo forests. Here their chief food was the weevil of the bamboo, which they ate fried. All ate of them, and thought them excellent food. Crossing several rivers flowing north, they came to a country abounding in wild boar and deer.

Somewhere hereabouts the trouble-making Franciscans, Armenta and Lebrón, rebelled against the irksome discipline. They went on in advance of the army, and with certain malcontents [18] and a rabble of about a hundred Indians, they pillaged the stores gathered for sale to the expedition. The governor sending these schismatics peremptory

[17] According to a testimony of 1581, a nut like a chestnut, but growing in clusters. Gandía, "Conquista," 104, n. 31.

[18] Thus Luis Osorio deposed that, being sick, he wanted to ride a horse, and Cabeza de Vaca told him that horses were not brought for that purpose. Deponent saved himself by following Armenta. He condemns himself by asserting that, though too weak to travel, he outstripped the army. (Arch. Ind., Justicia, 1131, examination of witnesses.)

orders to return, they vanished into the woods. Thereupon the governor drew up an indictment of them before his notary, charging them with various disorders, and especially with taking possession of too many women.

Working south again, they arrived on the banks of a river as wide as the Guadalquivir. Here the governor wrote a letter to the officials of Asunción, which he somehow understood to lie not far away. He ordered them to send two luggers, to pass his men and horses across the river Paraná, by the banks of which dwelt Indians reputed hostile. He could not know that the journey by water from Asunción to the appointed spot was a matter of some six hundred miles, mostly up-stream. Two Indians volunteered to deliver the letter.

In this country he felt so secure that he left behind fourteen sick, with orders to follow by easy stages.

Still he journeyed south among the welcoming Guaranís. "For some distance before the villages were reached they cleared and swept the roads, dancing and making great merriment on seeing the Spaniards. What increases their pleasure and contentment is to see their old women merry." On the last day of January they reached again the great river Iguazú, which, as a stripling, they had crossed two months before. Their friends warned them that on the Paraná, near by, dwelt the fierce Indians who had massacred a band of Portuguese sent exploring, a few years back, by the governor of Brazil. Half had been killed in ambush on the Paraná; the others took refuge in canoes kindly offered by the natives. But in midstream the Indian crew pulled out the calks and jumped overboard, and the men-at-arms, cased in honorable armor, sank instantly to the river bottom.[19]

Undaunted by this story, the governor and eighty men descended the Iguazú in canoes, while the remainder of the men and horses proceeded by land.

First, probably, of any white men, the expeditionaries saw the Great Falls of the Iguazú, one of the great cataracts of the world. The chronicle wastes no words on beauty, telling only of the long and difficult portage. Below the falls the two parties reunited.

At the confluence of the Iguazú and the Paraná they found an army

[19] Gandía, "Hist. Crit. de los mitos," 163, n. 34, settles the historicity of this expedition.

of Indians, painted and feathered for war, and holding their bows ready. But the sight of the horses gave them pause; and Cabeza de Vaca, advancing with his old assurance, and with his arms full of fascinating objects, roused more uneasy curiosity than defiance. His interpreters spoke politic words, and, smiling, he distributed his presents to the nonplussed chiefs. "As they were covetous people, delighting in novelties, they began to be appeased and to approach us." And these warriors, who had come to slay and eat the invaders, ended by aiding them to lash their canoes together and transport men and horses over the wide and dangerous river. It was a brilliant vindication of the governor's Indian policy.

Cabeza de Vaca was downcast to find neither boats nor messengers awaiting him from Asunción. The sick were in no state to attempt the journey overland. Therefore, at the suggestion of a kindly chief, he determined to ship them down the river in rafts and canoes, in the hope that soon they would meet the rescuing luggers. The party consisted of thirty sick and fifty hale, with Nuflo de Chaves in charge.

Now the main party headed directly west, over the *campos quebrantados,* the rolling plains of Paraguay, well grassed, and covered with stunted yatai palms.

Thick clumps of hardwood trees break up the prairie here and there into peninsulas and islands, and in the hollows and rocky valleys bushy palmetto rises above a horse's knees. In general the soil is of a rich bright red, which, gleaming through the trees, gives a peculiarly warm color to the land. . . . If the shrubs are myriad, the flowers are past the power of man to count. Lianas, with their yellow and red and purple clusters of blossoms, like enormous bunches of grapes, hang from the forest trees.[20]

Still the Indians showed their good will, bringing food, clearing and sweeping the road before the oncomers.

In token of peace they raised their hands, and, in their own language, some, too, in ours, welcomed the governor and his people. Along the route they entered into conversation with us, and were as cordial and familiar as though they were our own countrymen, born and bred in Spain.

[20] Graham, "A Vanished Arcadia," 171.

On the way a Spaniard, emissary from Asunción, met the advancing party. His news was chiefly of hardship and tribulation, and of the great eagerness of the colonists to see their new master, "for they had given up all hope of deliverance." Also he told of the universal wonder in the city that Cabeza de Vaca could have accomplished his journey along the road held hitherto to be that of certain doom.

Finally "it pleased God that on the eleventh of March, being a Saturday, at nine o'clock in the morning, in the year of grace 1542, we arrived at the city of Asunción." The overland journey had lasted four months and nine days.

Thirty days later the detachment sent down the Paraná appeared. The men reported a most troublesome journey. The riverside Indians had repeatedly attacked them in canoes; at one time two hundred craft had surrounded them. For fourteen days and nights they had not ceased fighting. The natives tried to drag the rafts ashore with long hooks, "while the incessant shouting and cries of these men made so much din that one would have said the powers of light and darkness were at war with one another." Twenty Spaniards were wounded, but none seriously, and all the time the swift current was bearing them nearer to safety. At last they reached the village of a former servant of Gonzalo de Acosta, and he fed them and protected them while they recovered from their wounds and fevers. Then they met the two luggers sent out by Irala from Asunción, and so came safely to port.

Cabeza de Vaca was very happy. By daring his cross-country journey, he had defied all the prudent experience of his countrymen. He had staked the lives of two hundred and fifty Spaniards on his faith that he could soften the hard hearts of the wild, and by the simple rules of honor and courtesy find a safe path through a land of death. He had lost two men: one drowned in the passage of the Paraná, and one killed by a tiger. And he had gained an increase of faith—faith in the power that inhabited him, in the reality of his mission, and in the favor vouchsafed to his purpose by God.

CHAPTER III

PARAGUAY

Aꜱᴜɴᴄɪóɴ, the capital of Cabeza de Vaca's empire, might have seemed to his exultant eye the egg of a great city. Three hundred and fifty Spaniards and a host of native servants were, at his arrival, contained within its stout palisade. Straw-thatched wooden cabins stood as the residences of the pale-faced gentry; the natives dwelt in dependencies of adobe. A considerable commerce throve on the sarsaparilla-colored waters of the Paraguay.

The founders and conquerors of Paraguay, who thronged forth to meet the newcomers with loud *¡oles!* of joy, were a savage and uncouth band. Uniformly bearded, for lack of razors, they were clad in roughly tanned deerskins and trousers of native cotton, tricked out with scraps of velvet and brocade, the spoil of an Italian trader wrecked on the Plate.[1] Cords of woven grasses held their garments together. The marks of untended disease were on many faces. Their smiles displayed the stumps of rotted teeth.

The streets swarmed with wheat-faced subject Guaranís. As the objects of Cabeza de Vaca's concern, it will be well to describe them:

The figure is somewhat short and stout, but well put together, with neat, shapely, and remarkably small extremities. The brachycephalic head is covered with a long straight curtain of blue-black hair, coarse as a horse's mane, looking as if, once wet, it would never dry. The face is full, flat, and circular; the cheek-bones are high, and remarkably salient; the forehead is low, remarkably contrasting with the broad, long, heavy, and highly-developed chin; and the eyes are often oblique, being raised at the exterior canthi, with light or dark-brown pupils, well marked eyebrows, and long, full, and curling lashes. The look is rather intelligent than otherwise, combined with an expression of reserve; it is soft in the women, but in both sexes it readily becomes that of the savage. The nose is neither heavy nor prominent, and

---

[1] Gandía, "Indios y Conquistadores," 65.

205

in many cases besides being short and thin it is upturned. The masticatory apparatus is formidable, the mouth is large and wide, the jaws are strong, and the teeth are regular, white, and made for hard work. The coloration is a warm yellow lit up with red; the lips are also rosy. The only popular deformity is the goiter, of which at Asunción there is one in almost every family.[2]

The voice is very low; they do not cry loud, even under torture. In the back country they painted the body, to represent, for instance, the jaguar. In our own day they paint coat, vest, and trousers on their bodies for their formal trips to town. The women's faces and breasts were lavishly tattooed. Most of the tribes perforated the lower lip, enlarging the hole until it would accommodate a stone or wood disk an inch and a half in diameter. Understanding missionaries, in more recent times, have taught them to tattoo crosses on their noses.

Though competent in many of the crafts, such as weaving and pottery, they had not progressed far on the road of intellectual development. The woodland tribes could not count beyond four. They held many curious beliefs, as that the spots on the moon are a man's intestines, which celestial dogs draw forth, thus causing an eclipse. They had no gods.

Among them there was no sense of sexual exclusiveness. Chastity was unknown; they had "neither bashfulness, nor modesty, nor reserve."[3] They gave their daughters readily to the Spaniards, and the Spaniards as readily accepted them.

Cabeza de Vaca found among these people many a reminder of manners he had known long before. Thus the ceremony of meeting and greeting began with a period of mutual tears. Thus the medicine-men cured ills by incantations, and by sucking the wound and producing from the mouth a pebble asserted to have been the poisoning agent.[4] The savage mind, in whatever country, reaches like conclusions by savage logic.

The Guaranís were brave, and dextrous hunters, especially with the long bow, six feet long and sharp ended to serve as a spear against the jaguar. To shoot arrows, they planted one end of the bow in the

[2] Burton, "Battlefields of Paraguay," 11, 275.
[3] Featherman, "Chiapo- and Guarano-Maranonians," 435.
[4] Featherman, 434, 444; Azara, II, 25.

ground. If they captured a tapir, they boldly grappled with the beast, throwing him down and knocking out his brains with a club.

The food of their country was varied and plentiful. Manioc or cassava root made an excellent bread. Corn, beans, pumpkins, yams, and peanuts were cultivated; honey could be had at no expense of effort. The rivers were filled with fish and the woods with game, especially wild hens and turkeys. Their drink was *yerba maté*, Paraguayan tea, a tannin-rich decoction of the *ilex Paraguayensis*, which stimulates a man for a day's activity and leaves no reaction of lassitude. For festivities they had *chicha*, usually brewed of manioc. The young women chewed the soft boiled roots thoroughly, and spat the product in warm water to ferment. It is said to have a very pleasant refreshing taste resembling milk.[5]

But the best of their meat was human flesh.

Pedro Hernández gives an exact account of the ritual of their feasts.

They eat the flesh of their enemies whom they take captive in war, bringing them to their settlements and making great merriment and rejoicing over them, dancing and singing till the captive grows fat. They give him their wives and daughters, in order that he may have every pleasure. It is these wives who take the trouble to fatten him. Those held in the greatest honor among them admit him to their couches, adorn him in various ways according to their custom, and bedeck him with feathers and necklaces of white beads and stones, which are much prized among them.[6]

Roger Barlow, an Englishman who penetrated to this region with Sebastian Cabot in 1527, adds that the proud paramour paints and dresses her temporary bedfellow as though he were her own husband, and leads him with a cotton cord around his neck, dancing and singing together.[7]

Hernández proceeds:

When he begins to grow fat they redouble their efforts; dancing, singing, and pleasures of all kinds increase. Then the men come; they adorn and

[5] Mulhall, "From Europe to Paraguay," 66. A North American dentist recently invented a machine, consisting of hand-operated artificial jaws, to chew the roots on a large scale. It would not work, for lack of artificial saliva. "Captivity of Hans Stade," 135 n.

[6] Domínguez, 129.

[7] "A Brief Summe of Geographie," 157.

make ready three boys of the age of six or seven, placing a little hatchet in their hands. The Indian considered the bravest among them now takes a wooden sword in his hand, called in their language macana, and leads the captive to a place where he is made to dance for one hour; the Indian then advances, and with both hands deals him a blow in the loins, and another on the spine to knock him down. It happens sometimes that after striking him six blows on the head they cannot kill him, so hard are their heads, though this two-handed sword is made of very tough, heavy, black wood, and the executioner is strong enough to kill an ox with a single blow. When they have knocked him down the three boys come with their hatchets, and the eldest of them, usually the son of the chief, begins striking blows on his head, the others do the same till the blood flows; the Indians meanwhile exhorting them to be brave and learn to kill their enemies and make war upon them, and to remember that this victim has killed many of their own people, and that they should revenge themselves upon him. As soon as he is dead the one that gave him the first blow takes the name of the dead man and keeps it henceforth in token of his bravery. Then the old women cut the body in pieces and cook it in their earthenware pots, distributing the flesh among themselves. They eat it and consider it excellent food. Afterwards they resume their dancing and pleasures, which last several days, saying that now the enemy who had slain their relatives is dead, they will take their rest and make merry.

Ulrich Schmidel adds the detail that when they eat a young and good-looking woman, they marry her in the same festival, serving her as the chief dish at her own wedding breakfast.[8]

Such were the Guaranís as Cabeza de Vaca came to know them.

[8] Domínguez, 20. The graphic Roger Barlow completes the picture. The celebrants are all drunk as apes; about the victim's neck "he shal have a coler made of cotton and to that coler shal be tied v or vj cordes and round about the place shalbe set erthen pottes paynted and full of water and then the aunciest of the kynred shal take every one of them a corde that is so tyed about his necke and so lede him into the myddis of the place and stonde rounde about him w^t ther cordes in ther handes, and then ther cometh in the owners sone or a ladde of his kynne, paynted and dressed all in fethres, and bringeth in his hand a sworde of hard tymbre like unto brasyl which is proportioned like a palmar or custos thet thei use in gramat-scoles, which likwise is painted and dressed w^t fethers. And when the prisoner seeth him there, and all the pottes prepared for him, then he begynneth to rave and runneth about, and if he can come by ony of the pottes he overthroweth them with his feete. And those that hold the cordes, when he wil ronne one waie pluckes him another waie, til that he be so weried that he falleth downe, then the ladd w^t his sworde of tree manglyth him in the hede til the brayne falleth out, and when he is dead thei cut and tere him in pieces and put him in the pottes to seethe, and then thei singe and daunce a fresshe and go not therens till thei have eten him up everie morcelle, and well be thei that maie get a pece of him or drynke of the brothe." ("A Briefe Summe of Geographie," 158.) The ceremony described is almost identical with that witnessed by Hans Staden among the Tupis of the Brazilian coast. See also Montaigne's chapter on the Cannibals, Book I, chapter 30.

For the moment, however, his business was with the Spaniards, men of his race and kind, who could be, if things so fell out, more deadly foes.

The assembly that greeted him, on that March morning, made him formal welcome. Irala knelt, received the King's Ordinance, regarded the seal, the "Yo el Rey," and the signature. He kissed the paper, laid it on his head, and swore to obey it. Rising, he handed it to the notary, who read aloud the commission of Cabeza de Vaca as adelantado and governor of the Río de la Plata. Then to the new governor were formally delivered the Rods of Justice, ash wands as tall as a man, symbol of authority. Escorted to his residence, he called a meeting of the captains, and informed himself of the news of the colony.

First, what of the fort of Buenos Aires?

Domingo de Irala answered. "In response to urgent requisitions for relief, I descended the river early in last year, fifteen forty-one. I found the colony full of disorder and sickness, with the prospect of a needy winter before it. Beginning to despair of aid from Spain, I took counsel with the chief men and elders, and determined to abandon Buenos Aires and assemble all our expeditionaries here in Asunción. I put a placard on a ship's mast amid the ruins of the fort, telling Spaniards where to find a letter. In that letter I gave all the news of us, with instructions for ascending the river, and I told our reasons for abandoning the fort, and had the whole attested by a notary. And I informed any comers that in the Islands of San Gabriel they would find a wooden house full of corn and beans for their use, and a pair of swine, which must not be killed.[9] Then at the end of May, I quitted that shore, and arrived here on the second of September." [10]

And what of the present state of the Spanish in Asunción?

[9] This letter, unearthed from its hiding place on that desolate shore, is reproduced in Serrano y Sanz, II, 361.

[10] Gandía asserts, without convincing proofs, that Irala lingered about Buenos Aires until the end of June ("Conquista," 91, n. 104). In that case Irala must have made a record trip up the river. But it was a hard trip, according to the indomitable Isabel de Guevara (Cartas de Indias, 619). The women of the party fetched wood, cooked, handled helm and sails, took the oars from collapsing soldiers, and heartened the men with virile words. To be sure, Gandía alleges she went to Paraguay with Ayolas in 1536, which seems altogether unlikely and for which I find no authority ("Indios y Conquistadores," 120).

Why, there was food enough, but a great scarcity of clothing, ammunition, metal for repairing crossbows, and so forth. By the operation of some mysterious economics, a few of the Christians had come to possess all the property and rights, while the majority were sunk so deep in debt that it seemed they would never get out. Some men made a living by their ingenuity. Clever Domingo Martínez had invented a machine for stamping out fish-hooks, a silversmith's bellows, a screw-press for crushing sugar-cane, and other wonderful devices.[11]

Had any gold or silver been found?

None except a bead of 8-carat gold, some silver beads and plates, and a small silver ax-head. These had been obtained from the Indians who had killed Ayolas.[12]

How then was wealth reckoned in the province?

Mostly by means of personal notes and I O U's, which would all come due when gold should be found. Besides, there was a complicated currency system, of which the eight-ounce iron wedge was the unit. One gold doubloon equaled twenty pounds of iron. Twenty-five wedges equaled one small slave girl.[13]

How, then, were the taxes of His Majesty gathered?

The answer to this question was evasive. But from many malcontents Cabeza de Vaca soon learned that the collectors, especially Cabrera, the supervisor, and Venegas, the quartermaster, took their tribute in kind, every fifth fish from the river, every fifth deer hide and pound of fat. And sometimes they would levy twice on their enemies.

And what happened to these collections?

The tax-gatherers kept them, or gave them to their servants, or sold them. They offered as an excuse, that this was permitted in Santo Domingo and the West Indies. And as there was no bishop, no power existed to excommunicate them.[14]

And what of the treatment of the Indians?

[11] "Cartas de Indias," 623.
[12] Serrano y Sanz, II, 259.
[13] Gandía, "Indios y Conquistadores," 70; Serrano y Sanz, II, 299. Pedro de Fuentes, writing home, asks for five quintals of iron, a cape, and five pounds of glass beads. Iron was so precious in the Indies! Hernando Pizarro, on a Peruvian expedition, shod his horses with silver.
[14] "Cartas de Indias," 582; Serrano y Sanz, II, 28, 322.

CANNIBAL RITES

Those of the Tupis of Brazil, nearly related to the Guaranís. The sacrificial club was called Iwera Pemme and was covered with designs painted with birds' eggs. Notice the men's lip-stones and the hammock of cotton yarn, an American invention. The bearded man is Hans Staden, who escaped sacrifice by luck and shrewdness.

The answer came in many private conversations with those who thought themselves injured.

The native population included legal slaves (captives from hostile tribes), and the Guaranís, nominally allies, great numbers of whom were kept in servitude amounting to slavery. They were obliged to work without pay, and were whipped if they slacked. The labors of the women were not finished with the curfew. Some of the captains had fifty concubines, being worse than Mohammedans. Disregarding God's ruling that, by the mystical relation of espousal, connection with the kin of one's mate is incest, they would fall foul of a mother and her daughter, or of three sisters at a time.[15]

And had not Acting Governor Irala brought order in this matter? Ha! Irala was the worst offender of the lot! He kept a throng of girls secluded in a harem, and would beat any man who approached. And he would sell these supposedly free girls, drawing up deeds of sale before a notary. And his bad example encouraged one and all who might otherwise be inspired in better courses. Thus Pedro Díaz del Valle, the alcalde or judge, because he desired an Indian girl of Gonzalo Rodríguez, went to Rodríguez's house and found him lying there naked; calling him *bellaco* and traitor, he took him by the beard and pulled him off to jail and threw him in the public stocks. And a comrade who brought Rodríguez his clothes was clapped in the stocks beside him.

Again, while Irala was absent in Buenos Aires, García Venegas, his appointee as substitute, carried things with a high hand. He took the wife of Lorenzo, an Indian chief and his own father-in-law, to give to a friend. The weeping Lorenzo offered his twelve-year-old daughter in exchange for his wife, but Venegas, indignant, had his father-in-law beaten to death. And Irala, returning, showed no displeasure. There were many other misdeeds, murders, rapes, and dreadful things, which Irala condoned or directly approved.[16]

It was clear that the Spaniards were not beloved by their subjects, and the fault was the Spaniards' own. *"Para ser una nación*

---

[15] Serrano y Sanz, II, 28–9, 298.

[16] Serrano y Sanz, II, 29, 316–20. *"Yrala por celos que tuvo de Diego Portugues lo colgó de su natura, de lo qual quedó muy malo e lastimado."* Some of the horrid accusations may be discounted as appearing in a partizan document.

aborrecida, basta por lo común ser conquistadora," says the wise historian, Dean Funes.[17] "To be abhorred, a nation need only conquer."

Here was the most difficult of the problems confronting the new governor. Could he enforce a general house-cleaning? Could he make the soldiers surrender their brown darlings without jeopardizing all his authority? Did he dare to set against himself Irala and his partizans? For at Irala's back were all his favorites, all the profiteers in office, all his fellow-Basques, famous for their wrong-headedness,[18] and probably the majority of the common soldiers, who admired his strength and prowess in every sort of engagement, and who enjoyed to the full the military relaxations he permitted. To Ulrich Schmidel, the private who wrote a narrative of this campaign, Irala was an admirable hero and Cabeza de Vaca an interfering busybody.

Cabeza de Vaca concluded upon a compromise with his impulse. He summoned a meeting of the monks and clergy, and in the presence of all the people, "he entreated them, in kind but earnest words, to bestow special attention to the teaching of Christian doctrines to the natives, subject to the king, and he caused certain passages of the Royal Patent to be read aloud, in which special mention was made of the treatment of the Indians. He further enjoined the monks, clergy, and other ecclesiastics, to take the Indians under their particular care, and to protect them from ill treatment, and to inform him of anything done contrary to these orders."

He did not attempt to free immediately all the natives from servitude; he decreed only that Indians who were ill treated should be taken from their masters and put in worthier hands. This announcement was followed by a decided improvement in the domestic conduct of the conquerors. He began a vigorous campaign against incestuous concubinage. He appointed a priest and an interpreter to inquire into such cases, ordering them to permit only one of a family in each troop of maidservants.[19] And great was the anger and resentment in the colony.

[17] "Historia del Paraguay," I, 92.
[18] "I had rather be a lion keeper than undertake to govern the Basques," said Gonsalvo de Cordova, the Great Captain. (Prescott, "Ferdinand and Isabella," III, 28.)
[19] Serrano y Sanz, II, 29, 68.

He forbade his subjects to leave the city without permission, or to be abroad after dark. He authorized the natives to visit their relatives outside the walls. He declared it unlawful for the Spaniards to buy slaves taken in tribal warfare by the Guaranís. A disappointing effect of this ordinance was that the Guaranís, finding no market for their slaves, ate them.

Now he could turn his mind to the other urgent problems awaiting solution. First, the relief of the colonists. He distributed from his private stores clothing and arms, gratis, to the destitute. For fear of creating civil discord, he made no effort to punish offenses committed before his arrival. Instead, he prorogued all debts to the king until gold and silver should be found, and offered to make good the sum due out of his own pay, if the Council of the Indies should refuse to indorse his action. By this proclamation he made several powerful enemies, among the weighty persons of the banker type.

Now he was forced to choose an attitude and a course of action toward Irala.

No doubt his impulse was to degrade Irala from his functions, on many and serious counts. And yet to do so would be to invite a civil war. Would he emerge victor in such a trial of strength? It was very doubtful. Besides, Irala was a brilliant leader of backwoods warfare; he would undertake, fearless, the wildest journey, followed unhesitatingly by his loyal band. Such power was precious in this great solitude. All things considered, it would be wisest to make no exception to the policy of a general amnesty—oblivion for all misdeeds now past. It would be wisest to recognize the competence of Irala, to reward his defense and preservation of the colony, and to enlist his influential friendship.

The governor appointed Domingo de Irala his first lieutenant and adjutant. Perhaps he would have done better to have risked the civil war.

In the matter of the new governor versus the old tax-collectors, pride was soon ruffled and honor vexed. A scrutiny of the accounts of Alonso Cabrera, supervisor, provoked mutual ire and bad blood. Cabeza de Vaca talked loosely of beheading Cabrera, called him greedy swine and Jew, said that he would cut off all the white tails and brown (for Cabrera was nicknamed the white-tailed fox).[20] They were foolish words, never forgotten, never forgiven.

An inventory was made of the possessions of Don Pedro de Mendoza and others deceased in La Plata. Much of this property was unaccountably found in strange hands. Justice was served at the cost of many friendships. Cabeza de Vaca would not learn to keep his eyes determinedly shut.

Most of the officials, whatever their misdoings, were left in office. But the governor found the notary, with whom he must be closely associated, unendurable. This was Martín de Orue, Basque, a member of the ruling clique, a conniver and profiter in the tax-gatherers' high commissions. Cabeza de Vaca replaced him in office by Pedro Hernández, one of Pedro de Mendoza's expedition. Hernández was to be the most loyal of the governor's friends, while Martín de Orue's implacable hostility was to pursue him back to Spain and into the pages of history.

Perhaps it was due to Pedro Hernández's inexperience that an unfortunate mistake was made. The orders and instructions to the colonists were published without the heading *"los señores oficiales,"* thus grieving the umbrageous honor of the proud Founders and Conquerors of Paraguay.

Cabeza de Vaca, as chief justice, settled civil and criminal cases; the resentment of litigants against him in his person as judge affected him in his person as leader. A native girl, Juliana, had poisoned her Christian spouse and escaped to her people boasting among them of the deed. Cabeza de Vaca had her seized, tried, and condemned. At that Domingo de Irala asked her release, on the sole ground that a friend of his wanted her. "I censured and reprimanded him," says the governor. One needs no record of the reception of this virtuous rigor.

He forbade any one to buy wildcats or parrots without his consent. Religion, as one may suppose, received his fervent care. For many months he never missed mass a single day.[21] He supplied vestments,

---

[20] Gandía, "Conquista," 129, n. 90.
[21] Arch. Ind., Justicia, 1131, 8A, testimony of Fray Luis Herrezuela.

flour, and a barrel of wine for the celebration of the holy mysteries he loved. He encouraged the formation of a Brotherhood to aid the church. This "cofradía de San Sebastian" pledged thirty pesos of gold—payable when gold should be found—and bought a precious piece of purple velvet for a chasuble.[22]

During these days the governor lived austerely, possessing himself of no complaisant maids-of-all-work. His solitary life was determined not, as he puts it, by moral considerations, but by policy, to fulfil the king's commands and to avoid giving his subjects a bad example.[23] Howbeit, "he never defiled himself by touching any Indian woman," says a clerical witness.[24]

Clearly the old humility of the slave of Texas savages was being overlaid with an applauding self-righteousness. The alleged malefactions for which he was later brought to trial date mostly from this period. They are the deeds of pride. He was accused of removing His Majesty's flag from a lugger and substituting his own; of carving his arms on a stone with those of His Majesty;[25] of calling himself king, and saying, "I am prince and master of this country"; of saying, "as weapons and powder lose their force when they cross the Equator, it is easy for the instructions and provisions of the king to lose theirs"; of saying, "Hernando Cortés was a fool not to have raised himself high in his new land." One may well suppose these words to have been put into his mouth by his enemies, for many witnesses give each other the direct lie. Nevertheless, false though the specific charges may be, the type of accusation betrays the common esteem of the governor in his province: a haughty man, conscious of birth and place, full of strange ambitions.[26]

As the governor labored at his tasks of organization, the number of his subjects was swelled by the arrival of various scattered groups. One day a party of Indians brought in the detachment of Spaniards

[22] Domínguez, 128; Gandía, "Indios y Conquistadores," 46.

[23] Serrano y Sanz, II, 55. It is true that, at the time of his imprisonment, he complains that the conspirators robbed him of the women servants voluntarily given him by the Indians. (Serrano y Sanz, II, 67.)

[24] Fray Luis Herrezuela, in Arch. Ind., Justicia, 1131, 8A.

[25] To this he answered, on the witness stand, that the carved stone was merely a token of authority for collectors of requisitions. Arch. Ind., Justicia, 1131; reply to accusations.

[26] "Indictment of Cabeza de Vaca," reproduced in Bol. Est. Hist. And., I, 28; Gandía, "Conquista," 130, 190, n. 18.

whom he had left behind, sick in the jungle, on the way to Asunción. Only one of the fourteen was missing; he had died of a dog-bite.

News came that the two jolly friars, Armenta and Lebrón, had reached the Paraguay, and were settled thirty leagues up stream with their sympathetic companions. Cabeza de Vaca, wiping out old scores, sent them word that they should build a church and indoctrinate the natives, as his other clerics were doing in zeal and piety.

To aid the party sent from Santa Catalina to Buenos Aires under Pero Vaca, and to guide them up the river to Asunción, he commanded the building of two new luggers, himself accompanying the woodcutters to the forests. In July, 1542, he despatched these downstream, loaded with victuals. The two parties made a junction, and returned in December, with a tale of many troubles. When Pero Vaca's ship had left Santa Catalina, the pilot died.[27] The vessel went blindly down the coast, under the guidance of a boatswain who could take the latitude. They came near returning baffled to Santa Catalina, when the sailors vowed they had already passed the mouth of the Plate. However, after forty days' navigation, they discovered the abandoned fort of Buenos Aires, and Irala's message, and they supported life on Irala's cache of maize. Mounting the River Paraná, they were happily relieved by Cabeza de Vaca's two luggers. On the way Felipe de Cáceres, royal inspector, gambled away the king's artillery at cards and dice.

At this news Cabeza de Vaca ordered the artillery restored, without compensation to the winning gamblers. Thereupon Felipe de Cáceres staked it again on cards and dice, and again lost.

Some order having been brought to the internal economy of his province, the governor was enabled to turn to pressing problems of relations with Indians of the Chaco.

This great region, extending from the right bank of the Paraguay to the foot-hills of the Andes, remains one of the jungles of the modern world. Opposite the thriving city of Asunción, behind a screen of tall trees, lies the mysterious void. Bloody wars between Paraguay and Bolivia have not yet determined where, in that dark wilderness,

---

[27] Not Antonio López, who lived to return to Spain.

their boundary is to be drawn; nor is there peace between the historians of either country, flourishing deeds and grants of Cabeza de Vaca and his contemporaries.

Passengers on the river steamers to-day look with a sense of dread into the west, over the unending swamps, now covered with rank pampas grass, now wooded with tangled brakes of thorny trees, on islands of sure ground. The boughs are twined about with flowering vines and orchids. "The climate is heavy and humid, the air dank with vinchucas [28] and mosquitoes and the little black infernal midget called the jején; no roads, no paths, no landmarks, but here and there at intervals of many leagues a clearing in the forest where some straggling settlement exists, more rarely still the walls of a deserted Jesuit mission-house or church. Ostriches and deer, tigers [jaguars], capibaras and tapirs, are seen." [29] Add to these alligators, monkeys, armadillos, peccaries, ant-eaters, parrakeets, pigeons, and snakes of manifold species. Many of the streams teem with the *palometa* (known on the Orinoco as the *piranha*), the small but ferocious fish which eats men. They will not disturb swimmers with a whole skin; but if a creature with an open wound enter the water, the palometas taste him from afar; "unless the luckless victim succeeds in reaching the shore immediately nothing but the skeleton will remain within a very short time." [30]

This region was and is inhabited by innumerable shifting tribes of Indians, who have in common only a treacherous hatred of white interlopers. And no invader has proved their master, save only the indomitable Jesuits of the seventeenth and eighteenth centuries, who established missions among them and subdued them by wisdom and love, and—to take the word of the Jesuits, who after all have the best means of knowledge—the grace of God.

When Cabeza de Vaca arrived in Asunción, the fierce and bloody

[28] A kind of flying bedbug, swelling from the size of a thumbnail to that of a gooseberry. Its syringing is painless; the victim becomes conscious of intolerable itching when the vinchuca has departed.

[29] Graham, "A Vanished Arcadia," 39.

[30] Leo E. Miller, "In the Wilds of South America," 205. Barco Centenera, who wrote a (most unauthoritative) history of Argentina in rime, tells in numbers how a woman, cooking a palometa, floured, was surprised by the fish's jumping from the frying pan and biting off her finger. He recounts a more horrible incident of a swimmer who was given cause for a lifetime of lamentation. (Angelis, "Colección," II, 193.)

Guaicurús were molesting the Guaranís, vassals of His Majesty and providers of food for the Spanish conquerors. The governor called an assembly of the clergy, to indicate the divine will in the matter. The clergy rendered a signed report that war was justifiable and proper. However, before proceeding to stern measures Cabeza de Vaca sent a deputation of fifty-three Spaniards to give the Guaicurús the choice of war or submission. The deputation returned, having read the ultimatum three times loudly and deliberately, and having received in response only a flight of arrows.

The governor therefore made ready a punitive expedition, of two hundred infantry, twelve cavalry, and a host of Guaraní auxiliaries. They crossed the river above Asunción, and pursued the foe as stealthily as such an army can. One evening a great uproar arose, which Cabeza de Vaca blames on the malice of enemies within the camp, and Pedro Hernández on a tiger.[31] The Spaniards, suspecting a revolt of their allies, fired upon their dark companions, who straightway fled. Strangely indeed, two bullets grazed the face of Cabeza de Vaca. "And since the officers and Domingo de Irala took me prisoner they have said and published that they shot at me with arquebuses that night."

The governor leaped from his horse and followed the Indians, shouting encouraging words. His familiar voice stayed their flight; they halted, and suffered themselves to be persuaded. The expedition was resumed, the Spaniards now marching in the van, to bear the brunt of the attack, and to allay the suspicions of the auxiliaries. When the enemy were reported, the army crept upon them, the horses having their bits stuffed with grass to prevent their neighing. White crosses were painted on the friendly Indians' breasts and backs, a precaution which availed little in the hand-to-hand combat.

The armored beasts and the cries of "Santiago!" cast a panic among the enemy, who fled, firing their straw houses on the way. Concealed by this smoke screen, they killed two Christians, and decapitated twelve Guaranís. "This operation is performed by the aid of two or three teeth of a fish called *palometa,* which bites fish hooks in two. These teeth are attached to a small stick. The Guaicurús, holding their prisoners by the hair of the head, pass this instrument round their neck, and

[31] Serrano y Sanz, I, 215; II, 25.

with a twist or two of the head, completely sever it from the body, and carry it off by the hair. They will perform this operation while they are running, as if it were the easiest thing possible." [32]

As Cabeza de Vaca led the pursuit of the fugitives, a Guaicurú sprang from the bush with three arrows in his hand. Seizing the governor's mare by the mane, he plunged his weapons repeatedly in the animal's breast, nor could they loosen his hold until he was dead.

Four hundred prisoners were taken, and the enemy was sufficiently impressed with the power of the Spaniards and the significance of their friendship. The governor therefore returned to Asunción. He held a muster of the captives, and to the amazement of Spaniard, Guaraní and Guaicurú, proclaimed that none of these prisoners should be enslaved, "because all had not been done that ought to have been done to ascertain their condition, and His Majesty would be rather pleased if these prisoners were given their liberty."

Before releasing these valuable hostages, however, he sent their leader with a message of amity to their cacique, or chief. Four days later the messenger returned, bringing all his tribe, even those who were badly wounded. Twenty spokesmen were admitted to the presence of the governor. Squatting with one foot doubled under, in token of respect, they offered their submission to the valor and mansuetude of the governor, and to the glory of the king of Spain. The governor kindly declared to them that he had come by order of His Majesty to bring all people to the knowledge of Our Lord, and to be Christians and vassals of His Majesty. If they would cease from war, he would protect and favor them, and restore their kinsmen without ransom. And this was done, with a profuse exchange of promises. "Cabeza de Vaca was much pleased with their promises, and he distributed gifts and jewels among the chiefs, and peace was cemented. Since then they have always kept the peace, and whenever the governor sent for them, hastened to obey his commands."

Thus the governor's Indian policy scored a signal triumph. The Guaicurús became the chief provisioners of the city; Cabeza de Vaca

---

[32] Domínguez, 147. The Paraguayans even of recent years have been fond of such trophies. Richard F. Burton (who knew the South American bush as he did the Orient) tells how the soldiers in the war of 1866–70 would hang strings of enemy ears to the shrouds of their river-craft. ("Battlefields of Paraguay," 15.)

delighted to watch their weekly market, and especially the fine show of their two hundred canoes crossing the river, loaded with supplies. "The celerity of their movements is such that they sometimes collide with one another, and all the merchandise falls into the water. Then the Indians to whom this happens, and those awaiting them on the bank, burst into fits of laughter, and the jokes and merriment continue all the time the market is being held. In their marketing they talk so loud and so much, that they cannot hear one another for the noise, and all are very gay and jolly."

Other Indian affairs required the governor's attention in Asunción. The troublesome Agaces Indians, who had twice rebelled against the Spaniards, took advantage of the absence of the punitive expedition against the Guaicurús to lay waste by night the Spaniards' farms and carry off their Guaraní women. The governor called a meeting of clergy and officers, and asked their opinion in writing. The vote was cast unanimously for war and condign punishment. Cabeza de Vaca, still reluctant, ordered a judicial inquiry into the offenses of the tribe. As this inquiry confirmed their guilt, the governor declared war, and sentenced a dozen Agaces prisoners to death. The Agaces tribesmen were soon chased from the neighborhood of Asunción, and though they were not subdued for years they ceased to be a reason for concern.

Now that the natives were put in order, Cabeza de Vaca could proceed with the business that lay closest to the hearts of his superiors in Spain. He could bring to reality the dream of Cabot, and Pedro de Mendoza, and Juan de Ayolas, and open a way from the Paraguay River to the Golden Kingdom. Confirming the reports of such a wonderland, brought to Spain by the earlier explorers, the natives told circumstantial tales of emperors in jeweled palaces, of golden temples islanded on sacred lakes. To-day the stories are recognized as faraway pictures of the glories of Cuzco and the shrines of Lake Titicaca.[33] The Spaniards of Paraguay, however, did not conceive of such an identification, and regarded the Golden Kingdom as a fief of their empire.

Some, surely, reflected that if they should miss the obscure road

[33] This thesis was propounded by Manuel Domínguez, "El Alma de la raza" (Asunción), and developed by Gandía, "Historia crítica de los mitos."

to El Dorado, they might still find their way to Peru; and an easy route for the transport of metals from Cuzco to Spain would be much appreciated by the authorities.[34] How far Cabeza de Vaca held such an idea is conjectural. Nowhere, I think, does he mention Peru; he proposes only "the discovery and conquest of the land."

Following out his purpose, Cabeza de Vaca called a meeting of the Indian chiefs, and to them kindly explained his intention and asked their aid. The caciques as courteously promised the good-will and assistance of their people. Loudest in protestation of friendship was Aracaré, a chief of the upper river.

On Oct. 20, 1542, Captain Domingo de Irala was sent out to reconnoiter the way. It was his fifth journey up the Paraguay. He commanded three luggers and ninety Christians, together with certain Indian chiefs. Seventy leagues up-stream, according to his orders, he set ashore three Spaniards, good woodsmen and linguists, and with them Chief Aracaré. Their instructions were to find out, if possible, a land trail to the west. But Aracaré, a traitor, incited his Indians to rebel, and set fire to the fields as a signal of war. The Spaniards, by happy chance, escaped alive to Asunción.

Meanwhile Irala with the main body made good headway north into the interior.

When the governor heard from the three refugees the story of their check, he sent a second expedition, in force, into Aracaré's country. This too turned back baffled, after much harassment by the Indians. The governor then drew up a legal indictment of Aracaré, and had it served upon him personally, "a somewhat dangerous commission, because Aracaré came with arms in his hands, followed by a number of friends and relations, with the intent to kill the Spaniards sent to him. The process, however, was duly served according to law, and Aracaré was sentenced to death, the natives being made to understand the just cause for which this had been done." [35] The order for his execution was then sent up-river to Irala.

---

[34] Ruy Díaz de Guzmán, followed by Padre del Techo, says that Cabeza de Vaca had agreed in Spain with Vaca de Castro, governor of Peru, to open communication and render mutual aid. (Churchill's "Collection of Voyages," VI, 13.) Ruy Díaz reported only family legends, of more value as corroborations than as assertions.

[35] Domínguez, 164.

Here was the first eminent case of the failure of Cabeza de Vaca's pacificatory policy. He showed the Spaniards at last that he could be stern. Ironically enough, this conclusion to his long forbearance was later made an accusation against him of outrageous and bloodthirsty cruelty.

In Asunción the summer passed quietly, being marked chiefly by growing ill will and exasperation between the governor and his subjects, chafing under unwonted restraint. "He did not do much, because he was not the right sort of man," says Ulrich Schmidel, member of the extreme anti-gubernatorial faction. "Besides, all the officers and soldiers hated him for his perverse and rigorous carriage towards the men." [36]

On December 20, Pero Vaca and his party arrived from Buenos Aires, as has already been stated.[37] Enemies, such as Felipe de Cáceres, as well as friends were added to the uneasy colony.

On Feb. 4, 1543, the city was burned in a disastrous fire, which consumed seven thousand bushels of Indian corn. The governor promptly replaced the thatch dwellings by substantial houses of clay. He surrounded his city with stout wooden walls of tree trunks, driven six feet into earth, and built a fort in the central plaza.

An enduring result of the fire was the new church, Our Lady of September, the object of Cabeza de Vaca's tenderest care. Following the medieval tradition, he aided in the building of it with his own hands, to give the others an example, *"para que los otros tomasen exemplo,"* he says. Fray Alonso de Medina watched him pounding with a rammer the earthen floor. Yet was not this an example calculated to rouse unrighteous mockery, and not shame, in his lordly followers? [38]

Then on February 11 Domingo de Irala returned.[39] He brought cheering word. He had pushed two hundred and fifty leagues upstream, far beyond Candelaria, and had reached an agreeable region of lakes and hills. He had found a good harbor on the day of Epiphany, and had named it Puerto de los Reyes, the Harbor of the Kings, in honor of the festival. Many Indians there had been the slaves of Alejo

---

[36] Domínguez, 41.

[37] *Ante*, p. 216.

[38] Serrano y Sanz, II, 116, 181, 226. Also testimony of Alonso Bautista, Arch. Ind., Justicia, 1131, 8A.

[39] Gandía, "Conquista," 127, n. 88, and Cabeza de Vaca's report, in spite of Hernández, who says Feb. 15. Serrano y Sanz, I, 248; II, 33.

García, and told of his marauding expedition to the edge of the great mountains. Irala had gone inland three days' journey, and had found a tribe of Guaranís who told him there was a well-populated region two weeks' travel to the west. With this information he had returned, as ordered. On the way he had received Cabeza de Vaca's message ordering him to seize and execute Aracaré; and Captain Vergara had competently fulfilled this detail. But the upriver tribes were seething with anger at the deed; and Atabaré, brother of the deceased cacique, was uniting them against the Spaniards.

Cabeza de Vaca called a meeting of monks and clergy, officers, and captains, and to them read Irala's report. It was their opinion, well considered, and subscribed by the notary, that an entry should be made in force from Los Reyes, to explore the country and take possession of its riches.

The governor, pleased at this independent expression of concord with his own desire, ordered the ten luggers equipped and stocked. But before venturing so far from his base, he desired to soothe the rebellious tribes commanded by Atabaré. He therefore sent out Gonzalo de Mendoza with orders to use every effort toward conciliation. Only when Mendoza found the natives stiff-necked against the kindliest of exhortations was a punitive war determined. The heavy-handed Domingo de Irala, with a hundred and fifty men, worsted the Indians in a fierce battle. The chiefs, Atabaré and another, came to the governor's presence to sue for peace. The governor followed stern admonitions with kindly words, forgiving them for their past disobedience, and warning them only that a second uprising would provoke the harshest of vengeance. "After this he gave them presents, and dismissed them very happy and contented."

In these pacifications and punishments the winter months of 1543 passed by. Many another incident vexed the governor during his preparation of the great expedition. A soldier who had violated an Indian woman in her husband's presence was punished with a hundred lashes, merely on the indignant native's complaint. And the jolly friars, Armenta and Lebrón, again fell within the purview of justice.

For lack of a bishop or other ecclesiastical superior, the clerics were free to interpret as they would their mission to the Indians. The jolly friars chose to establish a nunnery, for girls between the ages of twelve and twenty, whom they kept "locked up as if they were their wives." So jealous were they of the Faith, that they would rush out with pikes upon any loiterer and give him a sound drubbing. And there was one Indian chief, fain to usurp their rights of instruction, whom they attempted to make a eunuch for the kingdom of heaven's sake.[40]

Now these lusty fellows, being reproved and dispossessed of their nunnery by the governor, joined the growing party of the malcontents. It was decided, in secret confabulations, that the friars should make their way overland to the coast of Brazil and thence to Spain, and that they should lay before His Majesty the sad state of the colony under their intolerable governor, and render to him the plea of the founders and conquerors of Paraguay that Domingo de Irala, the strong and just, be appointed governor in the stead of Cabeza de Vaca. To this petition, it was said, Irala had given his consent.[41]

The plot might have succeeded had not the monks insisted on taking thirty-five girls, the daughters of chiefs, to carry their baggage and beguile their journey. To prevent insubordination, they manacled the girls and whipped them well. So when the expedition was hardly two leagues from the city, the weeping fathers came to the governor to beg the return of their daughters. They found, as they had expected, ready aid from their friend in office. He had the monks and their feminine scouts apprehended, instituted criminal charges against the clerics, and, pending the issue, took them with him on his northern expedition.

Finally there came a lull in the governor's distresses. His ships were ready; relative quiet was reported from the Indian tribes to the north; his city seemed outwardly at ease. He appointed Juan de Salazar de Espinosa and his surest friends to garrison the capital, while the troublemakers should accompany him in the strike through the Chaco. Perhaps their taste for trouble would be sated in the tropical jungles that lay before them.

[40] Serrano y Sanz, II, 39, 148.
[41] Serrano y Sanz, II, 243, 327.

CHAPTER IV

THE CHACO

O N the day of the Nativity of the Virgin Mary, the 8th of September, 1543, Cabeza de Vaca gave the word for his little fleet to cast off and ascend the stream coursing from the warm heart of the continent. He commanded ten luggers, four hundred Spaniards, ten horses, and twelve hundred Guaraní auxiliaries in a hundred and twenty canoes. The horsemen proceeded alongshore as long as they could find footing.

It was a serene journey through a park-like country, where tall palm-trees shaded clean grassy lawns. With oar and sail, the boats made good speed against the current of two miles per hour. As the expedition worked up-river, the heat day by day grew heavier and the aspect of the land more tropical. Food of all sorts abounded, especially the gamy water-hog, the capincho. The health of men and horses was excellent; "our people were so strong and lusty on this voyage that they looked as though they had just arrived from Spain."

The governor seized every chance to halt by the shore, to summon the natives, and speak to them lovingly, and distribute presents. In the country of Atabaré he completely won that vengeful chief, who volunteered to accompany the expedition with thirty relatives and dependents. By night the army would camp on shore, the canoes of the Indians being first securely attached to the well guarded luggers. "The numerous camp-fires presented a very pretty sight."

After a month of such travel, Cabeza de Vaca arrived, on October 12, at the spot christened Candelaria, whence Juan de Ayolas set off into the west, and whither he returned to find Irala vanished, and to die.

Here the governor landed, and opened communication with the Payaguá Indians, assassins of Ayolas, long reputed the fiercest and strongest of the inland tribes, and now nearly, if not quite, extinct.[1]

---

[1] In the nineteenth century the Payaguás had been moved down-stream to the neigh-

The Payaguá spokesmen asked if these Spanish were the same white men who had before passed that way. The interpreter assured the Indians that these were different men, newly arrived from far away. The news seemed to give the natives pleasure. They admitted that Ayolas and his men had died through some misunderstanding, and said that all his treasure was kept in one place, and that they would render it up in return for a guarantee of peace from the Christians. And how considerable was this treasure? It consisted of loads for sixty-six men, and was all in plates, bracelets, crowns, and axes, with some small vases of gold and silver. At this word, the governor summoned the chief of the Payaguás to a parley, and the envoys promised to bring him. The chief, he learned, "is a very grave man, feared and respected by his people, and if any one offend him and make him angry, he takes a bow and shoots two or three arrows into him. If the man be killed, he sends for the wife (if there be one), and gives her a bead to appease her wrath at the murder of her husband. If he have no bead to give her, then a couple of feathers. When this chief wishes to spit, one that is nearest to him joins his hands together so that he should spit into them. These, and such like extravagances, are practised by this chief." [2]

The extravagant chief did not come to the parley. Instead, he assembled his people and disappeared into the green darkness of the Chaco. And the treasure of Ayolas has never been seen, and no one has ever learned whether the envoys lied, or the interpreter, or whether (as his enemies alleged) Cabeza de Vaca invented the tale to justify himself and cast opprobrium on Domingo de Irala, who deserted his post of duty.

After five days of waiting the governor ordered the anchors aweigh and a continuance of the river journey. The park-like country ceased, and the great central lake and marsh region began. Henceforward the way lay among indeterminate rivers, dividing and rejoining, widen-

borhood of Asunción. Travelers described with special gusto their festivals, marked by great sham battles between the girls and men. Universal drunkenness would close the day. In June was held a great feast of courage; the men would meet to attack each other with splinters and fish-bones. This ceremony was an important event in the humdrum life of Asunción; the townswomen would scream with fascinated horror at the sight of the young men, proudly displaying their pierced tendernesses. (Featherman, "Maranonians," 434; Robertson, "Letters on Paraguay," III, 182.)

[2] Domínguez, 187.

THE AMAZONS.

"They do accompany with Men but once in a Year," says Sir Walter Raleigh, whose adventures the drawing illustrates. "After the Queens have chosen, the rest cast Lots for their Valentines. . . . If in the Wars they took any Prisoners, they used to accompany with those also at what Time soever, but in the End for certain they put them to Death: For they are said to be very cruel and blood-thirsty, especially to such as offer to invade their Territories."

ing into broad lakes and lagoons, thinning to capricious channels. As the soil is underlaid by a hard impenetrable clay bed, the waters spread far and wide in the rainy reason to make shoreless seas, which disappear in time of drought, giving place to foul marshes, wherein trapped fishes die. Travelers tell sad tales of days and weeks spent sleepless in such *esteros,* floundering through league-long mud, under the escort of clouds of insects. The country teems with tropical life, bats, monkeys, marmosets, opossums, deer of many sorts, tapirs, and white-lipped peccaries. This is the home of beasts, the ant-bear and armadillo, which, with the sloth and the hoazin, have survived from a previous age of the world. The trees are full of macaws and gray-throated green parrakeets, building nests six feet across, which weigh hundreds of pounds. The unwary wanderer stumbles on rattlesnakes and lizards, crocodiles (more properly caymans),[3] tarantulas like diabolical dinner plates, ant-hills taller than a man on horseback, nests of maribundi wasps that paralyze a man and leave him to die.

The expedition's chronicler tells strange stories of the vampire bats, which eat the combs of cocks, and bite horses' ears, but a man only on the toes and nose-tip. These bats served the Christians a very bad trick; they ate the teats of six pregnant sows, which were to people the tropics with Spanish bacon. "When the little pigs were born, and tried to suck their mothers, they could not find the teats, because these had been bitten off by the bats; so the young pigs died, and we had to eat the sows." The governor himself learned his lesson. Having fallen asleep with one foot uncovered, he awoke "from feeling his leg cold, and finding the bed soaked with blood, thought somebody had wounded him; but those on board searched for the place where he was wounded, and when they found what they knew, by experience, to be the bite of a bat, they laughed. The governor found that a slice of his toe had been bitten off."[4]

A few days of navigation brought the expedition to the mouth of the Cuyabá, a considerable river flowing from the northeast. Down

[3] Ulrich Schmidel says that if a crocodile "is found in a well, there is no other means to kill·it than to show it a mirror, in order that it may look at itself therein; it must then die from the sight of its own atrocious face." (Domínguez, 43.)

[4] Domínguez, 199. For the savagery of these bats, which caused some casualties among the conquerors, see Bayle, "El Dorado fantasma," 68, n. 2.

this stream, said the Indians, Alejo García the Portuguese had come, years before. With his troop of Guaraní fighting men, he had passed through and plunged into the difficult country to the west. He had not returned this way. But some of his Guaraní followers were said to be living still in the west country.

On the 8th of November the governor, with the first division of his men, arrived at the Port of Los Reyes, which would seem to have been on the shores of Lake Gaiba.[5] Landing, Cabeza de Vaca addressed the assembled Indians, conjuring them to receive the Christian doctrine and the suzerainty of Emperor Charles V, warning them of his harshness if they should prove refractory, and promising kindness if they should cherish virtue in their hearts and show it forth in their lives. In such a case he would give them many presents, "as he always did to those who were good." He ordered the clergy to see immediately to the building of a church where mass could be said. He set up a great cross by the water's edge. He took formal possession of the country in the name of the king, and registered the fact with his notary. And he settled the Spaniards and the Guaraní allies along the shore, "cautioning them to do the natives no injury or violence, because they were friendly, and vassals of the king. Moreover, he gave them strict orders not to enter the native settlements and houses, because what the Indians fear and hate most, and what irritates them more than anything, is to see the Christians, accompanied by Indians, entering their houses, disturbing their things, and taking away the few possessions they have. If they trafficked with them, they were to pay for what they bought, or they would be punished." [6]

Eight hundred lodges made up this Indian village. The Spaniards called the natives Orejones, Great-Ears, because their ears, enlarged with gourds or disks of wood, hung to their shoulders. When they fought, they removed the gourds or disks and rolled up their ears, or tied them behind their heads.[7] These people worshiped wooden images.

[5] The reckoning of time and various circumstances of the journey lead to this conclusion. See Gandía, "Historia del Gran Chaco," 103, n. 5; Charlevoix, "Histoire du Paraguay," I, 135.

[6] Domínguez, 198.

[7] The Payaguás preserved this custom into the nineteenth century. W. P. Robertson ("Letters from Paraguay," III, 179) describes the lobes of their ears, narrow rims of

The governor tried, with kind words, to turn them from their idolatry, persuading them to burn their idols, and believe only in God, who created heaven and earth, man, the sea, fish, and every living creature, and that he whom they worshiped was the devil, who deceived them. They burned some of their idols, but their chiefs were frightened, saying the devil would kill them, and that he would be angry with them. As soon as the church was built, and mass had been said, the devil fled from that country and left the Indians in peace and tranquillity.

Only a dozen miles away dwelt a tribe of Chané Indians, whose proper home lay to the west, at the foot of the Andes. A deputation came to pay their courtesies to the Governor. Under interrogation, they told things that stirred the hearts of the conquerors.

How had they been cast up here beside the great river, so far from their mountains?

Why, years ago, Alejo García had come to their mountain home, and had enlisted them to march eastward in his train. So they had done, striking the Paraguay well to the south of Los Reyes. And there the indigenous Indians had set upon them, slaying García, and they had fled north along the river to their present station, where they had been well received, and where they had settled down and married into the local tribes. In proof they displayed some glass beads of European make, given them by García's own hand.

Could they guide the Spaniards to their former homes in the west?

Ah no; they did not know the direct road across country, and they feared to return down-stream among the hostile tribes, murderers of García and their own companions.

What was the country that lay to the west?

Many bogs lay near by, but strips of high ground led to a dry, heavily tangled forest region. Some Guaranís dwelt there, foes of all the riverain Indians. They would have, themselves, no dealings with these Guaranís; but among the Xarayes, a few days' journey distant, was a Guaraní from the interior who had married into the Xarayes tribe. Perhaps communication could be opened by his aid.

After a vain attempt to make contact with the Guaranís, the gover-

flesh around wooden disks two inches in diameter. "I endeavoured, on three or four occasions, when I heard of the death of a Payaguá, to purchase his ears, through the medium of friends; but they would never consent to have them cut off from their deceased relative—they would lend no *ear* to my proposal."

nor sent an embassy to the Xarayes. The envoys, floundering through scalding mud, in which sometimes they would sink to the middle, reached their destination and were most ceremoniously received. The chief offered each a girl to sleep with; they declined on the score of fatigue. Marvelously well pleased with the red cap sent him by the governor, he readily rendered up his Guaraní subject.

This waif of fortune reported that in his boyhood his tribe had left the shores of the Paraguay, with many others, to make a great marauding expedition against the rich mountaineers of the Andean foot-hills. Eventually they had found their retreat cut off; numbers of them remained in the Chaco, and it was said that Guaraní hamlets still persisted there, islanded among hostile races. Some few elected to steal back to their homes by the great river. But they were surprised by their enemies, and he alone found safety in flight. And now he was adopted into the tribe of the Xarayes.

Did he know the road taken by his countrymen into the interior?

Ah, there was no road; they had cut their way through the jungle, and any scars of their passage would long since have been healed by the luxuriant life of the bush.

But were there no landmarks, no general directions for a determined man to follow?

Yes, there was a kind of way, beginning at a high round mountain visible to the west. And, if his memory served him right, in five days' journey one would arrive at a settlement, where provisions were plentiful. Beyond the marshes lay a tolerable country, rich in game, well watered, with plenty of honey and fruit. "To the question, if at the time when his people made their expedition into the country he saw much silver and gold among the natives, he answered that from those tribes they had plundered much gold and silver plate, lip-ornaments, ear-rings, bracelets, crowns, hatchets and small vessels, but that these things had been retaken when they were defeated."

This word was sufficient encouragement for one accustomed to doing without. The governor determined upon an immediate advance into the interior, while his men were fresh and their purpose high. True, he left his base with some misgivings, for the second section of his fleet, while working up-stream, had lost five men in an attack by

Guajarapos Indians, provoked by Christian presumption; the victorious savages were spreading the portentous news that the Spaniards were not valiant, and that their heads were soft. "From that time the natives began to cherish evil designs against us." However, Cabeza de Vaca could not abandon all his enterprise out of mere caution.

He left one hundred Christians and two hundred Guaranís under Captain Juan Romero to guard the boats; with the remaining three hundred Spanish soldiers and the Indian auxiliaries he plunged into the jungle, on Nov. 26, 1543.[8]

It was with a lightening of the heart that he began his third great westward march. Every danger lay before him, but they were dangers that he knew: the perils of the wilderness, hunger, thirst, fever, the heat of tropic midsummer, and arrows dropping from unseen and silent bows. These could be met by courage, dogged endurance, and the kindly diplomacy that had opened paths across two continents. How almost gladly could he front these foes, rather than the sly devils in the spirits of his countrymen!

The way lay first through cool and shady forests; but on the second day the jungle closed in, barring all passage with rank undergrowth and serpentine creepers and lickerish flowers that caught and clung to the pilgrims like hungry harlots. There were harmless fruits in abundance for their food, although the noise of their progress frightened the game.

After five days of such going, the guide confessed that he was much non-plussed, as he had failed to find the old landmarks he had hoped for. But by good fortune, or Providence's doing, on that day two Guaranís appeared from the forest glades. They told the governor that they were remnants of that old unsuccessful Guaraní expedition of conquest into the west. Only fourteen of them remained; all had been children

[8] Cabeza de Vaca was accused by the plaintiffs in his trial of crippling this expedition by the amount of his personal baggage. He was accused of taking a camp bed, bedclothes, chairs, table service and washbowl, and also the wife and daughter of Hernando de Ribera, slung in hammocks, and according to camp gossip the señora was his concubine. Although four witnesses make such an attestation, I find it impossible to believe. No fault could be more foreign to the character of this dry ascetic. One of the witnesses was openly known to be a member of a plot to assassinate Cabeza de Vaca. Hernando de Ribera was present on this northern journey; had he nothing to say to his wife and daughter? (Complaisance was not in the character of these conquerors.) The manner in which these accusations were drawn up will later be related. (Gandía, "Historia de la Conquista," 145, n. 131; Bol. Est. Hist. And., I, 20.)

at the time of the great massacre. Now they dwelt in the most inaccessible part of the jungle, in constant fear of their savage neighbors. Two days' journey distant was another group, of only ten Guaranís.

Did they know the way to the inhabited country to the west?

Alas no, they had been but children when they had gone thither with their warrior fathers, and they had never returned that way since, and they could not tell the road. But their cousin in the western settlement knew the way and would surely serve as guide.

As no more could be got from this pitiful pair, the governor dismissed them with presents, and they returned to their homes well satisfied. He then sent an interpreter with escort to the farther settlement and himself followed with the slow-moving main body, delayed by the horses and by the weight of muskets, ammunition, and supplies.

After three days of slow progress an Indian messenger appeared with a letter from the interpreter. That competent officer had reached his destination, and had found the Guaraní who knew the way into the interior. This native reported that the first inhabited place was a rocky hill, sixteen days' journey to the west, and the road was very difficult. The interpreter noted that he had been obliged to crawl part of the way on his hands and knees, and that the Indian asserted the track to be much worse farther on.

Having read this letter, the governor followed the path by which the messenger had come, but found it so thickly wooded and beset with difficulties that it took a whole day to clear a passage the length of a slinger's shot. Heavy rains having now set in, the governor ordered his people to retire to the shelter huts they had left in the morning, for fear of their suffering from wet and damping their ammunition.

On the following day the interpreter joined the little army, bringing with him the Indian pathfinder. Under questioning, the native sustained his reported story. He would willingly serve as guide, though he greatly feared the natives of the western country.

Now, according to the democratic rules of the conquerors, it was necessary to call an assembly of clergy, officers, and captains, to hear opinions and to take a vote on the propriety of a further advance.

How would stout Cortés have dealt with this problem? He would already have so indoctrinated his men with his own purpose that, in the meeting, he would have seemed a deferential chairman, the agent of his peers. Before the vote, a wave of emotion would have swept the gathering, mingling adventurous foolhardiness, greed, esteem of folly, and hearty good-fellowship. And after the vote, the entire party would have turned gaily to the unknown, daring every hardship for the promise of gold, glory, and orgies fit for kings.

But Cabeza de Vaca had lost the way of such miracles. The speakers rose, and, with a malign pleasure at the distress of the commander, pointed out that food for only six days remained, for the troops, in expectation of plenty, had wantonly consumed nearly all their supplies. Who could put faith in an Indian's reckoning of sixteen days to the next habitation? The time might well drag out to a month or more. It must, therefore, be concluded that life and safety depended upon an immediate return to the boats at Los Reyes. And if necessary, they would exercise their right, and require the governor to conform to their will, in the name of His Majesty.[9]

Cabeza de Vaca indicated the dangers of such a course. "He said that it would be impossible to find sufficient provisions at Los Reyes for so many people; that the maize was not yet ripe for harvest, and that none could be obtained from the natives. He reminded them that the natives had told them that the floods would soon begin, and these would add seriously to their embarrassments." He tried to whip up their spirits with reference to the gold of Ayolas and García, with the thought of luxurious ease after a bare two weeks of hardship. Did they shrink at the thought of a little hunger? Ah, roots and bark and forest herbs were enough for a resolute man. Had he not, in the northern continent, kept life in his body with loathly insects and cactus leaves and green tunas mashed with earth? Shame on such Spaniards, who could turn back with food in their hands, not out of direst necessity, but merely out of apprehension!

Perhaps his exhortation would have kindled the laggard spirits to flame if he had been able to first warm them to sympathetic heat. But the fire in his own breast was secret and incommunicable. He could

---

[9] And yet, four years later, Martín de Orue, Cabeza de Vaca's implacable enemy, told Oviedo the historian that the governor had turned back in opposition to every one's opinion. ("Historia general," II, 207.)

not open the mysterious ways that carry emotion from soul to soul. The sullen faces did not lighten; he knew that he had been defeated by his companions. Some, no doubt, were honestly afraid of the spectral gloom of the Chaco, while others were determined only that Cabeza de Vaca should not get the profit and glory of discoveries they coveted for their own cabal.

This was the turning point of his life. The impetus of his purpose had carried him from the Court of Spain across the oceans and into the fastnesses of the trackless wild. Here his power was spent, and in this parley he met his first defeat, in set conflict. Had he compelled the forward journey, he would have emerged triumphant in Peru, the first man to cross the southern continent from Atlantic to Pacific,[10] as he had been the first to cross North America. Or he would have left his bones in the Chaco to rot honorably, with the bones of García and Ayolas. Instead, he surrendered to the will of his men. Never again was he to know the feeling of victory.

Before giving the order for retreat, he called for volunteers to travel light through the forest and spy out the way to Tapuaguazú, the rocky hill to the west. From the willing fellows, men of his own stamp, who stepped readily forward, he chose Captain Francisco de Ribera and six men. These, with eleven native chiefs, he commanded to follow the Guaraní guide, to make their way to Tapuaguazú, and to report back to him on the practicability of the road. When they had disappeared into the green tangle, Cabeza de Vaca faced about to the return journey. He was defeated. He was turning his back on the west, on his duty and all his desire. In eight days the expedition was back in Los Reyes.

Bad news awaited him here. The indigenous Indians, puffed up with presumption, threatened an attack on the garrison and on the fleet. They had ceased to bring supplies. A reckoning of the food on hand showed rations for only ten or twelve days for the Spaniards and their auxiliaries, numbering about three thousand in all.

While the Spaniards sneered, Cabeza de Vaca resorted to his methods of diplomacy. He summoned the native chiefs, and to them made

---

[10] Orellana crossed from Peru to the mouth of the Amazon, arriving in 1543. Cabeza de Vaca was following approximately the route, now a highway, described in Duguid's "Green Hell."

such a discourse as should warm amity and other kindly emotions. He concluded with threats of provisional harsh measures and a distribution of colored caps. And yet, when his interpreters were despatched, they could find no food in any of the near-by villages.

It was as if the native chiefs had subtly comprehended the failure of the white governor in the wilderness. Should a forest king obey a foreign cacique who could not command his own soldiers? When a great man falls in the way of failure, the meanest are abetted by fortune in their petty triumphs.

It was necessary to send out a provisioning party to bring food to Los Reyes. For this mission Cabeza de Vaca chose Gonzalo de Mendoza, a good linguist and a man who could get his ends from the Indians by friendly means. His orders were to summon the chiefs of the near-by Arianicocíes, with kind but peremptory words, to acknowledge the authority of the king of Spain, and to furnish manioc, corn, and meat. All food must be paid for, to the natives' satisfaction, and no violence should be permitted.

When you arrive at the villages you shall ask for the commodities you require for the sustenance of your men, offering payment, and entreating the Indians with kind words. Should they decline to provide you with what you want, you shall repeat your request twice, thrice, or as often as you think right, offering payment beforehand. Should they refuse to give it, you shall take it by force, and, if resistance be offered, you shall make war upon them, for the hunger we suffer from justifies us in resorting to these extreme measures. In all that may happen afterwards you shall use such moderation as becomes the service of God and His Majesty.

Here is an abdication from the extreme humanitarian theory Cabeza de Vaca had brought to South America. If the natives do not respond to kindness, then use force; not because force is just and right, but because of our great hunger. Such a doctrine is an abandonment of principle out of need; the need, I think, was in Cabeza de Vaca's spirit more than in his belly.

After a few days a messenger arrived with word from Mendoza. He said that on arriving at a village of the Arianicocíes he had asked for provisions, displaying, for payment, beads, knives, wedges, and fish-hooks. But the Indians came forth, feathered and painted, carrying lighted fuses in their mouths, and they answered Mendoza with a flight of arrows. And they shouted that they would allow no Christians in their land, nor would they give them anything, but would kill them all. And they said that their friends, the unconquerable Guajarapos, had joined them, and they had killed Christians, and were saying that the Christians' heads were soft, and that they were not a strong people.

Mendoza, after a second summons, was obliged in his own defense to let loose a volley of musketry. Two Indians fell dead, and the others ran off in frantic fear. Their houses were found well stocked with food. Mendoza was sending other intermediaries to make overtures of peace, but all so far had availed nothing. "The governor sent orders to the captain to do everything in his power to induce the Indians to return; he enjoined him not to let any of his men do the least harm to the natives, to pay for all the provisions he had taken, to pacify them, and to go elsewhere in search of provisions." [11] But peace was never made, and Mendoza was at length obliged to return to Los Reyes, on account of the illness of his men.

A second provisioning party was despatched from Los Reyes a few days after that of Gonzalo de Mendoza. Hernando de Ribera (not to be confounded with Francisco de Ribera, still hunting the overland way toward Peru) was set in charge. He was ordered to push up-stream, if conditions should permit, to obtain food, and to placate the natives. He should not venture away from his ship, and he should return promptly.

Of this expedition we have explicit, though surprising, records. Captain Hernando de Ribera himself, on returning to Asunción, attested his story before four witnesses and a notary, and laid his hand on a missal opened to the sacred gospel, and made the sign of the cross before the reverend Father Paniagua. Even at that some historians will not believe him, nor will they credit the recollections of the unimaginative private soldier, Ulrich Schmidel.

Ribera set sail on December 20, 1543, in the lugger Golondrino (*The Swallow*) with fifty-two men. They worked up the Paraguay for twenty-three days, pausing to pay diplomatic visits on the riverain in-

[11] Domínguez, 226; Serrano y Sanz, II, 183.

habitants. The women made a deep impression on Private Schmidel. They were painted blue from breast to belly, "and so artistically," he says, "that one could not find a painter to do it so well. They are absolutely naked, and are beautiful after their manner, and also commit transgressions in the dark." [12] Ribera came at length to a very large settlement of Xarayes Indians, consisting of about a thousand houses. The king descended to the river shore to greet his visitors, and led them up a flower-strewn path to his residence.

The king also held a court in his own way, like the greatest lord in the country. At dinner the musicians must play whenever it is his pleasure. Then the men and the most beautiful women must dance before him, and such a dance is to us Christians quite wonderful, so much so that looking upon them one could think of nothing else. . . . The women are very fair and venerous, very amiable, and very hot too, as it seemed to me.[13]

Wealth as well as feminine warmth rendered this country enviable. The king, says Schmidel, gave to Hernando de Ribera a silver crown, weighing twelve ounces, and a bar of gold a span and a half in length and half a span broad, and a bracelet and other things of silver. Ribera himself mentions only feathers like those of Peru, and metal plates in the rough. These treasures, said the Indians, were obtained in warfare with the Amazons.

The Amazons?

The hosts told a most wonderful tale.

Ten days' march to the westward lived a tribe of fierce women, who made all their domestic utensils from white and yellow metal. Before reaching those warlike women one had to pass a tribe of very small Indians, who made war upon them, except at certain seasons, when the two tribes united in carnal communication. The girls born of these unions were kept by their mothers, while the boys were delivered to their fathers. So says Ribera; [14] and Ulrich Schmidel adds that the women seared the right breast, the better to handle their bows. Pedro de Fuentes corroborates this statement.[15]

---

[12] Domínguez, 43.

[13] Gandía gives Schmidel the lie direct, alleging that Schmidel tells as eye-witness a story that he later had at second hand concerning the mysterious Candire. ("Conquista," 156, n. 151.) I do not see why. Schmidel is always very sober and matter-of-fact.

[14] Domínguez, 264.

[15] Domínguez, 45; Serrano y Sanz, II, 297.

The story must, I fear, be dismissed. The natives were seeking to tell, in struggling phrases, the inland rumors of the Virgins of the Sun and the Houses of Chosen Women, actually existing in far Peru. The interpreters, interpreting unduly, adorned the barbarians' simple words. The Spaniards recalled entire the story, current through the Indies, of the Amazons, and to the accepted canon the mysterious phrases of the natives were adapted. Christopher Columbus, that unscrupulous saint, began the business, roundly alleging to Queen Isabella that the Thracian Amazons were dwelling on the West Indian island of Martinique.[16] The report spread fast and far; it was common in Mexico, and the Amazons were hunted up and down the Gulf of California.[17] Orellana saw women aiding their men against him, on the banks of his great river; making a logical identification and deduction, he named the enormous stream "River of the Amazons." And in the Paraguayan jungle the adventurers, ignorant of the psychology of myth-making, innocently put into the gabble of the savages their own memories, even the childish wonder of the ἀ-μαζόνες, breastless ones, and soberly died to prove their dear story true.

Beyond the Amazons, said the natives, relishing their impressive story-telling success, were further marvels: large nations of black people with beards—like the Moors, thought the credulous Spaniards. They had houses of stone and clay, and used the white and yellow metals for their domestic utensils. And fifteen days to the west was a large lake, so wide one could not see from shore to shore. Here dwelt a numerous people, wearing clothes, in which were worked brilliant stones, which they found by the lakeside. And more to the southwest were large towns of clay houses, inhabited by a rich people, who raised great sheep for transport.

Among those people they said there were other Christians, and great waterless deserts of sand. We asked them how they knew there were Christians on that side, and they answered, that in times gone by the Indians living in that neighborhood had been heard to say that as they were passing

---

[16] Bayle, "El Dorado fantasma," 222; Las Casas, "Hist. de las Indias," Lib. I, cap. 67; Peter Martyr, Dec. I, cap. 2. Perhaps the marvels which Columbus, in his journal, vowed he saw, cyclops, sirens, magnificent cities, are to be blamed upon Las Casas, transcriber and reporter of the journal. See references in Bayle, 223, n. 1.

[17] See *ante*, p. 155; Gandía, "Mitos," 74 n.; Bandelier, "The Gilded Man," 114 *et sqq.*

the desert they met many white people, clothed, with beards, and they had certain animals with them (evidently, according to their showing, horses), and riders on their backs, and that owing to the want of water they had returned, and many had died on the way. . . . They showed us also, by signs, that in the direction west, one quarter south, there were high mountains, and an uninhabited country. . . . They said, too, that on the southwest skirt of those mountains there were many large settlements, and people rich in metal; and beyond these again lay the salt water and the great ships.[18]

Even though Hernando de Ribera was interpreting the equivocal gestures of the Indians with meanings drawn from his antecedent knowledge, he does not obscure the fact that the Indians told honest tales which had made their way through leagues of jungle.[19] One recognizes the Inca kingdom, the sacred lake of Titicaca, all that marvel which amazes us no less than it did the woodland Indians. Unfortunately, the Spaniards on the Paraguay chose to believe that the stories dealt with lands as yet undiscovered by their fellows. Thus, in after times, many a bold explorer was led on a heartsick chase through this dismal land. The tale developed into the legend of the Paitití, or el Gran Mojo, who lived in his kingdom of El Dorado, at the source of the river Paraguay. The buildings of this city were all of white stone; the doors of the emperor's palace were guarded by lions with golden chains; a great image of the moon on a tall silver column reflected the sun's rays across the lake.[20] This was the story that lured Sir Walter Raleigh far from England, the story that Voltaire tells in a sober passage of "Candide." And only some half dozen years ago, Commander Fawcett disappeared into the bush, in search of just such a wonderland.

At any rate, Ribera and his men were happy for a time in this rich region, among the affable natives. Afterwards memory magnified that

---

[18] Domínguez, 268.

[19] Confident misinterpretations of Indian speech led the explorers far astray. Pero Ordaz, hunting El Dorado up the Orinoco in 1531, was encouraged by his guide, who repeated forever, "Bumbum! Bumbum!" This he took to refer to gold-beaters, pounding gold on anvils. Later he was forced to conclude that it was merely an imitation of a water-fall. (Bayle, "El Dorado fantasma," 160.)

[20] Guevara, "Conquista del Paraguay," 190. Indeed, this is a not greatly exaggerated description of the wonders of the Inca's court. (Gandía, "Mitos," 151 et sqq.; also Bayle, "El Dorado fantasma," 354.)

happiness; the chroniclers of the next generation named it Paradise Island.[21] In fact the explorers soon pushed on, impatient to find the nation of rich women, neither maids nor wives. Leaving the faithful *Swallow* under guard by the shore, they turned westward, thus disregarding their governor's orders, which not only forbade them explicitly to quit their vessel but required them to make prompt return.

The tropical rains were falling, and the rivers rising and broadening to lakes, as if all the elements were surrendering to Water. For fifteen days and nights Ribera's men advanced through scalding, stagnant water to the knee, and sometimes to the waist. To make a fire, it was necessary first to build an island. "And it happened several times that as we were about to cook our meat, both the pot in which we had our food and the fire fell into the water, and then we had to remain without eating. We also could not find any rest either by day or night, because of the small flies [mosquitoes], against which we could do nothing."

When they emerged on sure ground, they encountered an innumerable throng of Indians, who were starving, for twice the grasshoppers had destroyed their crops and the fruits of the trees. These Indians were too listless to be hostile. The chief gave Ribera four golden medals, to be worn on the forehead, and four silver bracelets, and Ribera presented the chief with a hatchet, knives, paternoster beads, and other Nuremberg goods.

And what of the Amazons?

Why, they were still a month's journey distant, over flooded country.

No, said Ribera and his men, this was impossible. Food was out; the men were sickening from hardship and the foul water. Supposing they should win through to Amazonia; those stalwart women would make short work of a band of feverish ghosts, too weak for love or war.

---

21 Ruy Díaz de Guzmán, and Barco de la Centenera, in Angelis, Colección, I, 55; II, 207. Padre del Techo beautifully imagines the speech of these lotus eaters, reluctant from further toils: "What is it we seek amidst so many dangers, and in these barbarous countries; we have now been toss'd about these ten years, without seeing anything but deep morasses, uncouth mountains, fierce nations, new diseases, and the death of our companions; let us at last grow wise upon our own and other men's experience, and ceasing to seek after uncertainties, make use of what we have; let the young seek after gold, let us rest our ancient bodies in this place, where there's plenty of servants and provisions." ("History of Paraguay," in Churchill, Collection, VI, 13.)

So the party turned, to flounder back through the lagoons. They fed on certain fruits of palms, and thistles, and underground roots. At last, quaking with ague, they emerged among their friends beside the Paraguay, and after four days of rest reëmbarked in the *Swallow* for Los Reyes. Even the fever had not robbed them of all their wits. "On this journey," says Ulrich Schmidel, "each of us plundered nearly two hundred ducats' worth of Indian cotton mantles and silver, having secretly bartered these for knives, paternoster beads, scissors, and looking glasses."

They found the settlement at Los Reyes in unhappy state.[22] The governor and nearly all the garrison were sick with fever and shivering fits, food was very scarce, and the Indians had risen in general hostility.

The governor's relief at seeing Ribera was expressed by a burst of rage, the fury of a man burned dry with fever, who has been watching all the purposes of his life come tumbling down. He flailed Ribera with hard words, for daring to desert his ship, imperiling his necessitous companions in Los Reyes, and disobeying orders to follow a crazy chimera. (It is possible, but not, I think, probable, that the governor's anger was due to jealousy that another should approach so near the Eldorado he had marked as his own.) [23]

Ulrich Schmidel says that Cabeza de Vaca came on board the lugger and ordered the imprisonment of Ribera, "and took from us soldiers all that we had brought with us from the country; and finally, he would have hanged our commander on a tree. But when we heard of this, we being still on the lugger, raised a great tumult along with other good friends who were on shore, against our chief commander, Albernunzo Cabessa de Bacha, demanding that he should set our commander, Ernando Rieffere,[24] free, and restore to us all of that which he had taken away, otherwise we should take measures accordingly. Seeing such an uproar and our wrathful indignation, he

---

[22] Cabeza de Vaca's "Relación" and Hernández's "Comentarios" give Jan. 30 as the date of the return (Serrano y Sanz, I, 335; II, 51). This is too early, as it does not allow enough time for the exploration. Since Ribera did not have a chance to deliver his report, the journey down-stream to Asunción (March 24, 1544) must have begun shortly after his arrival in Los Reyes.

[23] Gandía, "Conquista," 159.

[24] The orthography is that of Ulrich Schmidel. (Domínguez, 49.)

was very glad indeed to let our commander go free, and to restore to us all he had taken away, giving us fair words that we might be pacified."

Ulrich Schmidel's words must be assayed with the knowledge that he was a mean-spirited creature, whose thoughts ran mostly on loot and women. The fact that Cabeza de Vaca tried to wrest away the soldiers' plunder would be reason enough for his malevolence toward the governor. Further, Schmidel, one of Irala's bravos, found it to his interest to allege tyrannical deeds, to justify his own part in the imminent mutiny.

Ulrich Schmidel could not recognize that Cabeza de Vaca's outburst proceeded mostly from relief at the lifting of an anxious burden. With such fury fathers receive returning prodigals.

The other Ribera, Francisco, had already arrived in Los Reyes from his westward reconnoissance.

He reported that he and his companions, six Spanish and eleven native, had gone directly west from the point where the main expedition turned back. They hacked their way through the jungle for twenty-one days, sometimes advancing only a league in a day, sometimes half a league in two days. They found plenty of game, very easily to be had, and also honey and fruit. Eventually they reached a river flowing west. (They had crossed the watershed, and found one of the streams that drain northward into the Madeira and thence into the Amazon.) Here they found footprints; following them, they came to a cornfield with the harvested ears gathered in piles. An Indian greeted them in a strange tongue; he wore a large silver disk in his lower lip, and gold earrings. He took Francisco de Ribera by the arm, and led him to a large house made of straw and wood.

On approaching it, they saw women and other Indians carrying out of the house cotton stuffs and other articles, which they placed in front of the stacks. The Indian made them enter the house, where men and women were carrying out all it contained. In order to avoid passing the Christians, they made an opening in the straw, and passed the things out that way. Our people saw them taking, from some large vessels full of maize, plates, hatchets, and bracelets of silver which they carried outside the straw walls. This Indian appeared to be the head of the family, from the respect shown him. He took them inside, and signed to them to be seated, and ordered two *Orejones* (Great-Ears) whom they supposed to be his slaves, to give them maize wine to drink out of some jars, which stood in the house buried up to their necks in the earth. They poured the wine into large gourds, and handed these to the Spaniards. The two Orejones said that at three days' journey from that place there were Christians living with a tribe called Payzunos; they then told the way to Tapuaguazú, which is a high mountain. Soon many natives arrived in their war-paint and feathers, with bows and arrows. The Indian spoke very volubly to them, and he also took a bow and arrow; he sent men, who came and went, with messages, by which the Spaniards knew that he was summoning the population from the neighboring villages, and intended killing them. The captain told the Christians who were with him to come out of the house altogether, and return by the way they came, before more Indians had assembled; by this time there were over three hundred. Ribera gave the Indians to understand that he would go and fetch many other Christians who were close at hand, and, as they were expecting more to arrive, they had only to wait till he came back. By this ruse our people escaped, but, at a stone's throw from the house, the Indians, who saw they were escaping, pursued them with cries, and shot many arrows at them. They followed them into the forest, where the Christians defended themselves, and the Indians, thinking there were a larger number of them there, durst not pursue further, but let them go; all the Spaniards, however, were wounded.

So they hurried back toward Los Reyes, at double the speed of the outward journey. On the way they were abandoned by eight of their eleven native comrades.

Twenty leagues to the west of Los Reyes, the homing Spaniards found a great lagoon, two pike-lengths deep, where on their outward course, they had waded in water to the knee. They were forced to make clumsy rafts and paddle their way with great danger and difficulty.

This report filled the governor with pleasure. Evidently communication with a land of gold and silver, where dwelt other Christians, was almost opened. Resolute men, who could live off the country, could establish a road, placating the natives and rendering them allies. His next thrust should find its way to success. He must, however, wait for the great floods to subside.

Every four days he sent a messenger to observe the great lagoon which had nearly barred Francisco de Ribera's return. Each time the messenger reported that the water was rising, not falling.

The governor's impatience increased with the discovery, near Los Reyes, of a group of Tarapecosí Indians, hailing from the very village where Francisco de Ribera had been so ill received. They immediately recognized the arrows of their tribe, which Ribera had preserved in souvenir of his narrow squeak. Why had their kin turned hostile? The Tarapecosís protested that their fellow tribesmen were animated only by friendship toward the Christians, but that the presence of the Guaraní companions was in itself a declaration of war. Had the Christians taken a Tarapecosí interpreter, all would have gone well, for their race made no war on those who did them no injury. Asked about the gold and silver, they replied that it was no rarity; they obtained it from the Payzunos, three days to the west of their country, who in turn had it from more western tribes.

They were shown a brass candlestick very bright and shiny, to see if the gold they had in their land was like that. They said that the metal of the candlestick was hard and base, but their metal was soft and without smell, and more yellow. Then they were shown a gold ring, and asked if it were the metal of their country, and they said it was. They were also shown a tin plate, very bright and shiny, and asked if the silver in their country was of that kind. They answered that this metal stank, and was base and soft; theirs was whiter, harder, and had no bad smell. A silver cup was then put in their hands, and they were greatly pleased with it, and said that of that metal they had quantities in their land in the form of small vases and other things in use among the Indians, such as plates, bracelets, crowns, small hatchets, and other objects.[25]

Then, reflected Cabeza de Vaca, the needful thing was to cling determinedly to Los Reyes until the waters should subside. Steadfastness should be the watchword. Steadfast men could outlast all the assaults of hunger, sickness, unsleeping insects, and emboldened savages. Let his men only endure for three months or four, and with one fierce thrust into the jungle all would come together to the Land of Gold.

Cabeza de Vaca reckoned without one enemy, the deadliest of all: the sullen and jealous spirits among his men.

In the flood season many of the friendly Indians had disappeared, loading their families and goods in large pirogues with clay hearths amidships, and sailing away to other shores. Food was scarce, and the Indians would not go hungry to feed their throng of visitors. In March or April the waters of this country fall, leaving the whole region a steaming land of mud, stinking intolerably, with dead fish rotting in every cup of the marsh. The poisoned water filled the men with bowel disease, and left them feverish and mad. The Indians shared the common malady; in July, it was said, the natives died in great numbers. "I never in my life experienced a more unhealthy country," says Ulrich Schmidel, adding that he saw no native over forty or fifty years of age.[26]

Only the mosquitoes throve. "Besides the illness by which we were attacked, there were so many mosquitoes of various kinds that we could neither sleep nor rest day and night; the sufferings we endured from this plague were even worse than fever." [27]

The governor succored his men as best he could. He assembled all the food obtainable about Los Reyes, punctually paying the Indians in such goods as they adored. To the objections of his lieutenants he responded by charging all these outlays to his personal account, thus contracting a great debt to plague him in his later days. On the same financial basis he bought for two hundred and fifty poor naked men, "pobres desnudos," shirts and trousers woven from thread of the pounded teazel or nettle, hardly an improvement, one would say, on the mosquitoes. And even in the face of this charity the royal tax-collectors insisted on making their deduction of the king's share, which promptly became their own.

The governor's bounty could not still the malevolence fed by hardship, fever, and idleness. In the long stillness, under the thatched huts, the soldiers examined the future and planned how it might be directed to their advantage. They had small taste for repeating the effort to find the Golden Land under Cabeza de Vaca's leadership. With justice in command there would be little loot for honest soldiers and no

[26] Domínguez, 50. Alonso Riquel de Guzmán corroborates this. (Serrano y Sanz, II, 291, 393.) But later travelers (especially Thomas J. Page, "La Plata") remark on the extraordinary longevity of the tribes living farther south on the Paraguay.

[27] Domínguez, 237. Pizarro's men would bury themselves under the tropic sands to escape the furious mosquitoes. When one of Orellana's men would eat an ear of corn, two companions were necessary to drive off these insects. And so forth. (Bayle, "El Dorado fantasma," 70.)

orgies with bevies of brown girls. The success of such an enterprise would mean the enhancement of Cabeza de Vaca's reputation and an increase in his already intolerable authority. Therefore it would be best to hang back, to bring his plans to failure, to destroy the governor's prestige. Perhaps it would be best simply to destroy the governor.

The leaders of the opposition, led by Irala and Cáceres, implanted in the idle minds words that bred like poison germs. Cabeza de Vaca learned that the plotters would take the soldiers aside one by one, and say: "The governor has said that he plans to hang you because you are a damnable traitor; I was present and told him you were a good fellow, but still he looks askance at you. So beware of him, for he has some grudge against you."

And the stern governor himself served the growing mutiny. He called a meeting of the Indian chiefs and asked them if they had any complaints to make of Christians' entering their houses and maltreating them; and certain accusations being made, he promised to punish the guilty ones.[28] An indignant whisper ran round the camp: "He takes the Indians' word against the word of a Spaniard and Christian!"

Irala, Cáceres, and others laid a plot against their superior's life. An alarm was to be given in the camp, and in the hurly-burly the governor should die of a bullet whose intention could not be proved. The machinations came to the subject's knowledge, and though the tropic fever dulled his purposes and rendered even death unimportant, he took immediate action. He issued a general order forbidding any man to obstruct and cry down the expedition to the interior, and he brought a formal indictment against Irala as instigator of the mutiny. In support of this indictment he ordered his notary, Pedro Hernández, to take evidence.

At the hearing of the first witness the notary shook so with fever that he could not hold a pen, nor distinguish truth from hallucination. As the governor's illness also increased, the hearings were suspended, with the presumption that they would be resumed when accusers and accused should find sufficient health.[29]

[28] Serrano y Sanz, II, 56, 239.
[29] Serrano y Sanz, II, 55–57, 335.

Meanwhile the hostile Indians of the neighborhood grew in audacity. They attacked the faithful Guaranís, who were fishing for the supply of the camp. The governor no longer had patience for the slow preliminaries to a declaration of war. Fever and despair worked together in his mind, to distill a raging bitterness. Was treachery, then, the result of all his kindness and forbearance toward the Indians? He turned on the ingrates with the fury of a man who sees his bounty mocked, who learns that love and mercy have made him a public dupe. He would chastise these faithless barbarians, and mostly he would chastise himself, punish the fool for his folly. His brain was dry with fever, and he tore mercy from his breast.

With the approbation of the clergy, Cabeza de Vaca declared the Socorino Indians outlaws who had forfeited the rights of freemen. He sent out a punitive expedition with orders to kill and imprison the rebels.

"God knows we did them wrong," says Ulrich Schmidel, ever sanctimonious in evil. Taking them unawares, the Christians killed many and took more than two thousand prisoners. "We afterwards burnt down their town, and took all they possessed that could be carried away, as in such violent assaults is usual; then we turned back again to our commander, Albernunzo Cabessa de Bacha, who was very well pleased with our deeds."

But the commander's pleasure was that of a man racked with ague, who could no longer well distinguish between fact and dream, between living men and phantoms from the past. His companions, Christian and pagan, were in no better case. He owed his life, it seems, to the listless, fever-smitten spirits of his enemies.

This could not go on. The cry of the soldiers to return to the happy country of Asunción could no longer be stilled. Therefore, in a lucid moment between fever and chill, the governor took the counsel of officers and clergy, and, on their demand, gave the order to break camp and fall back down the river.

Before the retreat, he had one command to give. All his men must return their Indian girls to their fathers.

The motive was to avoid the offence against God done in this way. He ordered, at the moment of departure, the fathers of these girls to receive them back into their houses until our return, being unwilling that their parents should be dissatisfied and the country scandalized because of this. To give more importance to this action of his, he published a rescript of His Majesty, forbidding, under the severest penalty, anybody from removing natives from their homes. [He was quoting the words of his own Appointment.[30]] The natives were well satisfied with this measure, but the Spaniards were greatly discontented, some of them felt ill disposed toward him, and from that time he was detested by the majority. This was the motive or pretext for their subsequent conduct.[31]

Indeed the ill will of many of his swashbucklers had swelled to hatred. "It would have been no great loss had he died at this time," says Ulrich Schmidel, "for he really commanded no great respect among us."

It was March 24, 1544, when the governor said farewell to his Indian friends, promising to return soon. He gave the order to take to the luggers and the escorting canoes. It was the last command his subjects ever obeyed.

Sick in body, with despair in his heart, he made the journey down a river of delirium. "Though sick to death, the people derived strength from their desire to return home. The perils and difficulties of this voyage were certainly not light, for the men were not strong enough to handle their arms to resist the enemy, or make use of an oar to help steer the vessels; and had it not been for the culverins we carried, our trouble would have been greater." But keeping good order, with the Indians' canoes protected and surrounded by the luggers, the fleet sped down-stream on the rapid current. One Christian was killed and a number of Indians wounded in attacks from the shore.

After fifteen days of travel, the convoy landed at Asunción. It was April 8, 1544, Wednesday of Holy Week, two hours before dawn. "I arrived very weak and sick, on the point of death, and even so arrived all the men." Though they returned from no success, all kissed the ground of Asunción and gave devoutest thanks to God.

[30] *Ante,* pp. 24, 186.
[31] Domínguez, 237. Juan de Salazar says the natives urged Cabeza de Vaca to return, saying they would guide him to the land of gold and silver (Serrano y Sanz, II, 238).

248

CHAPTER V

THE CAPTIVITY IN ASUNCIÓN

WHEN Cabeza de Vaca arrived in Asunción from the hostile north, he was too weak to assume vigorous control of his government. He retired to the luxury of his pallet bed, and lay there shivering and sweating. Ulrich Schmidel ascribes, to be sure, his retirement rather to offended pride than actual sickness. But the cross-grained Bavarian's malevolence cannot prevail against the otherwise universal testimony.

The governor was well enough to receive the report of Captain Juan de Salazar, his deputy left in charge of the Asunción garrison. The caravel building to carry the news of the colony to Spain was nearly finished. The Agaces Indians were in rebellion for the fourth time, burning, plundering, and enslaving the friendly tribes. The governor promised to undertake a punitive expedition when he should feel better; he relapsed with a sigh into his fever.

The pure airs of Asunción brought a more rapid recovery to Domingo de Irala and his fellow malcontents.[1] This arch conspirator called his cabal together and thus addressed them: "The Governor has said to me that he plans to hang you, because you are damnable thieves; but I told him he was ill informed and that you are men of honor. And he said he is going to take from you your houses and goods and Indian girls and give them to his milksop friends who parade their piety and virtue and say 'yes, yes!' to his every folly."

No more was needed to explode the gases of discontent. The plot took shape; the rôles were assigned, the hour set.

The leaders were those who, with Irala, were under indictment for obstructing the campaign on the upper river. With success, they

[1] Serrano y Sanz, II, 336; Gandía, "Conquista," 169, n. 175. Ruy Díaz de Guzmán absolves Irala from all share in the plot, asserting that he was absent from the city (Angelis, I, 57). But Ruy Díaz was Irala's grandson.

could at a stroke be transformed from felons to liberators, valiant tyrannicides. Among the chief plotters were the royal officers, Felipe de Cáceres, Alonso Cabrera (who had captained the relief expedition to Mendoza in 1538),[2] García Venegas, quartermaster, Francisco de Mendoza, presumably Don Pedro's relative, Pedro Dorantes, who had served Cabeza de Vaca well on the journey from Santa Catalina to Asunción, and others of less note. In a general way, the veterans who had come out with Mendoza were aligned against the new arrivals with Cabeza de Vaca. The rank and file of the conspiracy was composed largely of artisans, common soldiers like Ulrich Schmidel, weavers, sword cutlers, shoemakers, woolcombers—and of course the obstreperous Franciscan friars. As always, revolution attracted the foreigners, French, German, Venetian, Genoese.[3] These outlanders, forbidden by Spanish law to own land, could hope for no fat encomiendas under the rigorous rule of Cabeza de Vaca, hidalgo of Spain. The craftsmen and private soldiers, checked in their simple satisfactions, were ripe for rebellion. The gentility referred to the insurgents as *comuneros,* communists, in memory of the uprising in the Spanish communes against Charles V, in 1520. The class line was clearly drawn in this revolution.

Solidarity of origin also played its part in the choosing of sides. The Basques and the Cordovans clove to the rebels; the men of Jerez remained loyal to their townsman.

Only a fortnight after the return to Asunción the conspiracy was ripe. On the evening of St. Mark's Day, April 25, 1544, Cabeza de Vaca, sick in his inner room, was roused by the sound of tumult without and by repeated cries of *"¡Libertad! ¡libertad!"* Liberty! He knew well the meaning of that cry.[4] He knew that his time was come, and that the debility of fever must yield to valor.

Shouting to his servant to bar the door, he tried to struggle to his feet. The servant, a Basque and a rebel, flung it wide. In rushed a dozen of the ringleaders, all the little room would hold. They carried drawn swords, or crossbows flexed, or arquebuses with fuses lit and

---

[2] *Ante,* p. 181.
[3] "Cartas de Indias," 598; Serrano y Sanz, II, 293.
[4] "All the complaints were in the name of liberty, as generally is the case when tyranny or villainy of any sort is to be done." Graham, "A Vanished Arcadia," 41.

smoldering. "Liberty!" they cried, "¡*libertad!* ¡*libertad!*" They thrust
their governor back on his bed and held him there and filled the room
with their triumphant shout. Swords and daggers were put to his
breast, and drawn crossbows, with bolts ready slotted, looked at him
wherever his eyes would turn. But none seemed ready to thrust home
the dagger or loose the quarrel from the bow. (Irala, with future
reports in mind, was prudently absent.) So they pulled him to his
feet and hustled him down the street toward the house of García
Venegas, all the while shouting "¡*Libertad!* ¡*libertad!*"

Even in the midst of revolution counter-revolution began. Some of
the partizans of Cabeza de Vaca came hurrying to the clamor, although the leaders were confined to their houses by specially detailed
bands of insurgents. The lukewarm hesitated, and even some of the
enrolled conspirators turned against their fellows, realizing the possible results of their incrimination. "Do you want to make us traitors
against the king?" they cried against their leaders. There was a great
hurly-burly, and some blood spilled, but through it all the governor
was sped to his prison. Once he was safe inside, the orators addressed
the mob, saying: "You are betraying us; don't say that you did not
know what was going to be done; help us to keep him in prison.
If you attempt to deliver him we will cut you to pieces and chop off
your heads. It is a matter of life and death to you; aid us, therefore,
to complete what we have begun, and we will all share the goods, the
Indian girls, and furniture of the governor."

Cabeza de Vaca was thrown into a small dark room, a sort of
pantry, in the house of Venegas. Irons were loaded on his fleshless
legs, and a sufficient guard set over him. "And now, Alvar Núñez,"
said the ringleaders, "you will know how to treat gentlemen like us!" [5]
With this farewell, they left him to his fever, in order to complete the
work of that fateful St. Mark's Day.

García Venegas and Martín de Orue seemed now, by their loud
activity, to be the commanders. With the drummer before and the
faithful behind, they patrolled the streets, commanding all but their
friends to keep within doors. At intervals Bartolomé González, clerk,
would cry: "Now, gentlemen, shout all together: '¡*Libertad!* ¡*li-*

[5] Serrano y Sanz, II, 61.

bertad!'" And again the prisoner and the gaping natives heard the ill-boding cry of Liberty rising amid the palms of Paraguay.

First the mob sought out the house of the judge, alcalde mayor, who might mistake the super-legal for the mere illegal. They took from him the rod of justice, his symbol of office, beat him with sticks, pulled his beard, and haled him off down the street to the house of Alonso Cabrera. There the alcalde protested that he was too sick to bear confinement. "Go on, boys," answered Cabrera; "to jail with him, and put his head in pillory to cool!" This they did gaily, with loud cries of "*¡Libertad!*" [6] The better to fulfil their motto, they liberated a murderer and what other malefactors they found imprisoned.

Next they hunted down the constables, stripped them of their rods of office and cast them in prison with their master. Then they visited Pedro Hernández, the notary. Crying "*¡Libertad! ¡libertad! ¡viva el rey!*" they pushed him into his bed with sword-pricks. "When the shouting was over," says the notary in his report, "they told me that Domingo de Irala was sending for the writings and testimonies that the governor had made against him, and that I should tell the officials where they were and give them up. I told him that they were not in my power, that they were in a safe in the governor's house. At that moment the drummer passed, making a proclamation, and with him Martín de Orue telling him what to announce: 'The gentlemen officers of His Majesty order that no person venture to leave his house until morning, on pain of being treated as a traitor.' At the end of the announcement the communists gave a shout, crying: '¡Libertad! ¡libertad!'"

The faithful Pedro Hernández joined his loyal friends in jail, and the revolutionists hastened to the governor's house. There they broke open the safe, destroyed the incriminating documents, including accusations against Pedro Dorantes and Martín de Orue for attempted mutiny. They examined the governor's private papers, destroying many and saving what might serve their purposes. All his possessions, cloth, wine and oil, iron and steel, fell into their greedy hands. It is a pathetic inventory of his wealth that one may still read in the Archives of the Indies: a half-burned candle of white wax, a small broken sail-

---

[6] Serrano y Sanz, II, 338; "Cartas de Indias," 593.

makers' needle, a metal syringe, treasures of the deep wilderness. Also finery wherewith to impress the king of El Dorado, a state costume of black velvet with trimmings of the same, a pair of white gloves, fourteen new handkerchiefs trimmed with white thread. And his library: a notebook of the genealogy of the family of Vera, and a "Relation of Florida," books suggesting pride, one the pride of birth, one that of authorship.[7]

These goods, together with his valuable property in land and ships, were consigned to his enemies, under the fiction of a deposit in security.

The well-planned measures of the insurgents checked any organized opposition. Alonso Riquel de Guzmán, the governor's kinsman, says that at the noise of tumult he rose from a sick-bed and issued forth with a friend, crossbows in hand; they found at the end of their street ten armed men with a constable. At sight of the impossible odds the two retired, thinking it wisest to avoid capture. Another more impetuous partizan attempted to give battle, only to be thrown in prison.[8]

So the revolution ended. Morning found the little city in the hands of the insurgents. New masters were now to guide the state, while the old masters retired to *otium sine dignitate* in jail.

When Revolution, that upstart, wins success, it weds Virtue in the palace, with pimping Law to bless the match. In the morning a great assembly of the group that called themselves the founders and conquerors of Paraguay was summoned, with drum and trumpet. All the partizans being gathered under arms, the public crier read a proclamation in a loud voice. This stated that the governor had secretly ordered that his people be deprived of their possessions and be treated as slaves; "and that they, in the general interests of liberty, had laid hands on his person. When this libel had been read they called out: 'Gentlemen, cry: "Liberty, liberty, long live the King!"' And this was accordingly done by their friends. After these proceedings they inveighed against the governor, and many said: 'Hell's fury! Let us kill this tyrant who wished to ruin and destroy us!'"

In this mood the gentlemen proceeded to an election. Whom should

[7] Arch. Ind., Justicia, 1131, 5; Gandía, "Conquista," 218, n. 92.
[8] Serrano y Sanz, II, 292; "Cartas de Indias," 629.

they choose as deputy governor and captain general but Domingo Martínez de Irala, the valiant, the unmatchable in feats of love and war, that model of a good fellow in office? To second him, a complement of officers, judicial and executive, was chosen from the revolutionaries who had deserved most from their actions of the great night. Domingo de Irala, in his inaugural address, thanked his well-wishing electors, promised a new rule of tolerant and understanding justice, and publicly revealed a project already known to many.

He proposed a new entry into the jungle, a new hunt for the land of gold, which, under his leadership, should be successful. He was no puling milk-and-water sniveler, as they well knew; he did not prize one scurvy naked savage above a dozen Spanish gentlemen. He knew how to treat Indians—this for the men and that for the women! He would guarantee to the honorable caballeros, his friends, that he would bring them to the land of gold and bring them out!

The auditors laughed and cheered.

And let no one fear the anger of the distant king as to the night's doings. Let them send to His Majesty a fine present of gold and reassuring word of the happy colony, and he would shut his ears to whatever malicious stories their foes might circulate. Let all, then, live in happy brotherhood under the light of the new day, and let all shout together: "Liberty! Liberty! Long live the king!"

As it turned out, the predictions of Irala proved true in almost every particular.

The assembly having dissolved, the junta of conspirators considered their exalted prisoner. They feared to murder him in cold blood. No one liked to take the responsibility, nor did it seem well to alienate wavering spirits in the community. It was important to the future that everything should have an air of legality. It was then decided to hold Cabeza de Vaca close prisoner. He was sick and fevered; very likely he would die.

The little dark room in the house of García Venegas was chosen for his jail. Four padlocks were put on the door; the fifty men most compromised in the uprising were quartered round about. Within the house, around his bed, a palisade was driven which extended six feet underground, to check even mines and tunnels. The houses near by were daily searched for evidence of furtive digging.

While these events were happening the governor was very ill in bed, and for the sake of his health chains were fastened round his feet; by his pillow a candle burned, for the prison was dark, no light being admitted, and so damp that the grass grew under his bed; he had the candle because he might want it at any moment [for his last rites]. To crown his miseries, they had searched among the whole population for the man most evilly disposed toward him, and they found one named Hernando de Sosa, whom the governor had punished for striking an Indian chief. This man was placed on guard in the same room with him. [In the ante-room to his jail lay a supplementary guard.] They appointed four men, whom they considered the bravest of their band, to stand ready armed with poniards, and made them swear that on the first attempt to rescue him they would immediately enter and behead him. These men were posted so near the governor that he could hear them talking and sharpening their daggers.[9]

To enforce outward security the new government forbade any assembly of the governor's partizans. They put two sentry boxes on the roof of his jail, to command the town and country, and they commissioned spies to seek out all sedition. "When the officers saw two or three men of the governor's party talking together, they would immediately raise the alarm, enter the place in which the governor was confined, lay their hands on their daggers, and say: 'Now God be witness that if the people try to take you from our power, we are going to stab you and cut off your head and throw it to your rescuers, to satisfy them!' "

Though the precautions of the warders effectually guarded the body of their prisoner, not all their cunning could prevent him from communicating regularly with his friends without.

Notwithstanding this strict watch kept upon him, every night, or every third night, an Indian woman who brought him his supper conveyed him a letter written by one of his friends, informing him of all that happened outside his prison. They begged him to say what he wished them to do, three fourths of the people being determined to die with the Indians in order to deliver him. [Pedro Hernández, deported to Spain with Cabeza de Vaca,

[9] Domínguez, 245, 247.

and his defender before the world, is speaking.] . . . The Indian woman passed through the midst of the guards, who stripped her naked, examined her mouth and ears, and cut off her hair, for fear of her concealing anything. They even searched her in parts which modesty compels me not to mention. This woman, as I have stated, passed the guards quite naked, and having come to where the governor was, handed the gaoler what she brought, and then sat down on his bed, for the room was small. She then began to scratch her foot, and while engaged in this way, drew forth a letter which she handed to the governor behind the back of the gaoler. This letter, written on very thin paper, was deftly rolled up and covered with black wax; this was concealed under the lesser toes, and attached to these by two black threads.[10] In this way she brought the letters and the necessary paper for him to write his answer, and a little powder made of a certain black stone of the country, which, moistened with a little saliva or water, made ink. The officers and their friends suspected her, for they had learned that the governor knew what was passing outside the prison, and what they were doing. In order to be sure of this, they chose four of the more youthful of their party to seduce the Indian woman—not a difficult task, for these women are not sparing of their charms, and consider it an affront to deny their favors to any one; they say, moreover, that they have received them for that purpose. These four youths accordingly intrigued with her and gave her many presents; but they could never make her divulge her secret during the whole of their intercourse, which lasted twelve months.[11]

The word that came to him was mostly of the mistreatment of his loyal friends. Bands of insurrectionists patrolled the city, arresting pairs seen in conversation, bludgeoning without a by-your-leave any group of three or four. At night, thirty armed men walked the streets, clapping into prison whomsoever they found abroad. Treating them worse than dogs. Some were jailed and their property divided among the right-thinkers; some were banned and all men were forbidden to give them food. No justice could be had from the new officials, who judged by the simple maxim that every communist was right and every loyalist guilty. Thus they made converts among the time-servers, the abject to expediency, the poor in fortitude. There were some scandalous cases; Francisco de Sepúlveda killed his own daughter and was indicted for the crime, but when he promised adherence to the insurgents he was let go free.[12]

[10] Houdini is said to have used a similar method to carry pick-locks into confinement.
[11] Domínguez, 247.
[12] Domínguez, 246, 250; Serrano y Sanz, II, 67, 356.

Among the faithful and the high-hearted the opposition nevertheless took shape. A boy named Bravo, eighteen years of age, was overheard to say that he would form a scheme to release the governor. He was seized, tortured and treated to a hundred lashes. Certain ones whom he incriminated under torture, the persuasive *question,* were similarly punished. A wholesale cleansing of the city was undertaken, and many a man lost the use of his limbs on the leg-twisting machine that freshened witnesses' memories. In spite of all, mysterious messages appeared on the walls: "By thy own law and by thy own king thou shalt die!" Irala, accepting the prophecy for himself, had it scratched out with nails. Then the doggerel was found inscribed: *"Quien a su rey no fuere leal, ny le valdria Castilla ny Portugal."* Or: "For him who toward his king shall fail, Castile and Portugal shall not avail." [13]

A brave man, of that heroic stuff that Spain breeds among her burning hills, made a valiant protest. Pedro de Molina, a former judge from Guadix, was revolted by the lawless state of the colony. One day he calmly entered the stockaded inclosure where dwelt Irala and his officers. He handed to Martín de Orue, the new notary, a requisition or injunction, requiring that the murders, evils, and injustices occasioned by the arrest of Cabeza de Vaca should cease. Further he demanded that the governor be set free, and that a suitable person be invested with authority by the governor to rule the colony with peace and justice. The notary glanced at the document, sneered, and refused to read it. But Molina knew the law, and knew the reverence of law-breakers for formality.

"You, as notary, are obliged to read aloud documents formally laid before you."

"Not without pay. First give me my fee."

Pedro de Molina unbuckled his sword and laid it on the notary's table.

"It is illegal to part with arms," said the notary. "You should know that. I cannot accept this as payment."

Pedro de Molina took off his woolen cap, which every one knew to be worth far more than the fixed price for notarial service. Martín de Orue, in a fury, flung the cap on the ground. And yet—so strong is

[13] Domínguez, 252; Serrano y Sanz, II, 69, 348–50, 353.

the sense of Spanish law in the Paraguayan woods—he dared not utterly flout his duty. He began muttering the words of the injunction between his teeth. "Louder!" cried Pedro de Molina. "Louder so that my Lords may hear!" This was more than my Lords could brook. "Seize him!" cried some, and "Hang him!" shouted others. And as he had serenely supposed, he was taken, thrown in prison, and there forced to bear all the cruelties and indignities his captors could devise.[14]

The persistence and strength of the opposition troubled the cabal. Daily, says Cabeza de Vaca, his captors would threaten him with bared daggers, promising his death if any attempt at rescue should be made. Not the threats, but his desire for the welfare of the province moved him to discourage the plotters in his behalf. "I sent to them to say that they should not strive to set me free, because I wished to come as a captive before His Majesty, and I would not have a single drop of blood shed on my account, so they should be calm and quiet, for I was more afflicted by the scandals and disorders than by my cruel imprisonment." [15]

To confer legality upon their deeds, the conspirators conceived a most presumptuous idea. García Venegas and Alonso Cabrera entered the governor's cell and demanded that he formally appoint Domingo de Irala his lieutenant, with full power over the colony. "I told them that I would give no such power to any communist, but if they wished the land to be well governed, I would appoint Captain Juan de Salazar as proxy of His Majesty, with full power." This proposal was naturally received with scorn. The envoys replied that Irala already had power enough for his purpose, and that the king's mandates no longer had any force in them.

Yet they belied their own words by returning with Irala and the clerk, Bartolomé González, and repeating their demand. Cabeza de

[14] Cabeza de Vaca and Pedro Hernández say that Molina's boldness so took aback the junta that he left the stockade unscathed. (Serrano y Sanz, I, 357; II, 74.) But Hernández, in his contemporary attestation, deposed in Asunción on Jan. 28, 1545, says that Molina was immediately seized and was still imprisoned. (Serrano y Sanz, II, 351.) This seems more probable. Molina was later reconciled with Irala, and served as his ambassador to Spain in 1555.

[15] Serrano y Sanz, II, 66.

Vaca roused to command the clerk to write: "I give my proxy as lieutenant and governor and captain general to Captain Juan de Salazar, to govern until His Majesty shall send a contrary order!"

"I have no paper!" said González sullenly.

"And I," records Cabeza de Vaca, "ordered and required him once and twice and thrice, and he refused to do it; and I said to the witnesses there present that they were witnesses of this."

Though the new masters now considered the incident closed, Cabeza de Vaca saw therein a means toward an honorable resolution of Paraguayan troubles. By his secret channel of communication he sent a message to his faithful notary, Pedro Hernández, who had now been set at liberty. Hernández returned to him a legal form of appointment of Captain Salazar, tightly rolled, to fit in the crook of the maidservant's toe. This the governor signed, while his guards were sleeping, and returned by the same prehensile post.[16]

Nothing came of this counterplot. Salazar himself says that he protested to Irala and others against their high-handedness: "I said that Arabs wouldn't do what was done in this town and country, and that since they had committed one misdeed, that was no reason they should do so many." [17] Alonso Riquel, the governor's kinsman, openly called Salazar a traitor. Another witness states, with an air of likelihood, that after Salazar's life had been saved by Francisco de Mendoza, a leader of the cabal, he was reluctant to use his appointment to foment another revolution.

Salazar seems, in fact, to have led a middle party fairly effective in restraining the extremists in power. When a rumor went the rounds that the governor had been killed in his prison, the conspirators, to combat rising public indignation, admitted a committee, which attested that the governor was still alive. And Irala came in person, promising to set him free, "and he wept, excusing himself and telling his sorrow, charging the blame for my imprisonment on the officials, and at the same time he promised Captain Juan de Salazar de

[16] Salazar's appointment is still to be seen in the Archives of the Indies (Justicia 1131, 5, cxlvii). I regret to report that it seems unduly bulky for sub-digital transmission, and bears no sign, at this long interval, of tight rolling.

[17] Serrano y Sanz, II, 243; also 71, 76, 78, 293, 349; and Buckingham Smith mss.

Espinosa to release me and all the servants of His Majesty, which was false and sly, so that they should be quiet and not try to free me, and thus he kept them befooled for many days." [18]

During this time Cabeza de Vaca's mind was haunted by the fear that assails all illustrious prisoners. His friends sent him word that Irala was attempting to persuade his cook and others to poison his food. "So for many days I did not dare to eat the meat and fish they gave me, but only the bread and some fruits in which they could not put poison."

Strange fires broke out in and around his prison. The junta blamed the fires on partizans of the captive, preparing a jail delivery, "but it is certain that Domingo de Irala ordered them set so that I should be burned in my prison, and when there was a fire the officials and their creatures would carry out all their property and leave me inside with my shackles, locked in with four padlocks, so that I should be burned therein." [19]

Why did they not take the straight course, murder him and be done with it? Each conspirator knew his companions well enough to withhold his dagger, for fear of becoming the scapegoat, if an official residencia should arrive from Spain to review the colony's affairs. They had hoped that Cabeza de Vaca would settle matters by dying of disease or confinement. But that tough body and that unyielding soul had been tempered in greater distresses than any these men could devise. With poison they could make a show of natural death, but no sophistry could explain the wounds of swords or crossbow quarrels. And meanwhile the cynical injustice of the new rulers was making more enemies day by day. "Because of the great disturbances and scandals and clamors of the people they did not dare to kill me, because knowing that I was alive the people hoped that they would free me and get me out of their power, and the officials knew well that if they killed me in prison, they themselves would be killed."

The officials concluded, then, that they would bring tranquillity to their people by promising to send Cabeza de Vaca to Spain, there to

[18] Serrano y Sanz, II, 76–8.
[19] For documents in support, see Gandía, "Conquista," 186.

submit to the judgment of his king. In evidence of good faith, they set about preparing one of the luggers for the journey, for Cabeza de Vaca's caravel had been dismantled for the sake of its iron, and its woodwork had gone to make doors and windows for the friends of Irala.

The state of the city was indeed such as to appal all honest men. There was hardly a pretense of justice or of police, except for political purposes. Every private vengeance had its opportunity. One Juan Gallego was beaten and drowned by five Basques; an English calker, Nicholas Simon, had his hand cut off; many others were killed or maimed while the judges shut their eyes. Domingo de Irala set the example of violence, nay of blasphemy. He pursued an enemy even into the church, and when two priests resisted this violation of sanctuary he pulled them by the beards and said: "I deny the milk I sucked if you do not pay me for this!" And again, while mass was in progress on a high feast-day, in the very church, in sight of Irala and all the people, "a servant of his named Juan Vizcaíno began to put his hands between the breasts of the Indian girls, and one Baltasar de Sevilla reprehended him for it, whereat he said bad words to him, and the said Baltasar de Sevilla gave him a buffet before the said Domingo de Irala; for this [Irala] did not proceed with justice, but threatened him, swearing to God that he would have to pay for it because he had affronted him, and a week later he came to mass with a large train, and emerging after mass, the said Juan Vizcaíno beat with a cudgel the said Baltasar de Sevilla, before the door of the church and in the presence of his master, and knocked him down on the ground with his head laid open, for which no punishment was assessed, but Irala kept the said Juan Vizcaíno in his house as before." [20]

Yet this same Domingo de Irala, writing to the king for supplies and relief in 1545, sanctimoniously requested a pastor for his church; "and let him be such that we may all be in fear and shame of his life, admonitions, and example." [21]

Certain examples set by his own clergy must have inspired any-

[20] Serrano y Sanz, II, 72, 147, 348, 352; Buckingham Smith mss.
[21] Serrano y Sanz, II, 394.

thing but fear and shame. A priest wrote a satirical-pastoral farce and himself acted a part in it, before the Holy Sacrament on the altar, on Corpus Christi. The governor was represented as a wolf, the author as the good shepherd.[22]

If the condition of the non-conforming Spaniards was irksome, that of the unhappy natives soon became intolerable. The officials permitted their friends and partizans to go into the native villages and take what women, chickens, ducks, cotton, and hammocks might please their fancy.[23] Similarly they would carry off likely young men as servants to work their plantations. Indian girls again became common coin, and were bartered for mares, clothes, and arms. There was advertised for sale "a slave girl eleven or twelve years old and a side of bacon." [24] "When the Indians came and complained to Domingo de Irala and the officers, these answered that it was no affair of theirs, which pleased the Christians, because they knew that this answer was given to suit their pleasure and secure their support, for they might say that they had full liberty to do what they liked."

Many of the Christians thought the good old times had returned. Alonso de Riquel, writing to his uncle in Jerez in 1545, notes that the colonists had already produced more than four hundred half-bloods, "so that Your Worship may see if we are good Populators, if not Conquerors; and to me, at least, this seems not good." [25] Later, however, he was to compromise with colonial principles, marrying one of the half-Indian daughters of Irala. On her he begat Ruy Díaz de Guzmán, the earliest historian of Argentina, and became an ancestor, if genealogists tell sooth, of Don Miguel Primo de Rivera, recent dictator of Spain.[26]

Again the old game of cruelty was played. Witnesses tell how flocks of natives were driven like sheep, how hosts were killed by ill treatment. The virtuous passion of reformers indeed exaggerated the num-

---

[22] Gandía, "Indios y Conquistadores," 56.
[23] Attested even by Antonio López, pilot, no great friend of Cabeza de Vaca. "Every one went to the Indians' houses to take what they needed, and to trade, which was not allowed before." (Arch. Ind., Justicia, 1131, "Exam. of López.")
[24] Gandía, "Indios y Conquistadores," 82.
[25] Serrano y Sanz, II, 289.
[26] Gandía, "Primeros Italianos," 134.

bers out of all conscience, for in fact the exploiters of the country had no interest in destroying or frightening away their workers. Nevertheless, with all official rigor thrown to the winds, there was nothing to check evil whims and bloody rages. An indignant cleric tells of Irala standing by and watching while a gambler staked a girl on a throw of the dice, the girl holding the candle for the game. The gambler lost the throw, stripped the girl, and delivered her to the winner, saying that he hadn't bet her clothes. There is good reason to suppose that, a little later, Irala sold gangs of Indians to Portuguese slavers from Brazil.[27]

To the Indians the news of their governor's arrest had come with a sound of calamity. Interpreters announced to them that the king had sent word that Cabeza de Vaca, a wicked man, should be imprisoned. Incredulous, they protested that this was a good man, not a bad man. The great distant king must have been mistaken. Several witnesses testify to the Indians' grief; all wept at the good man's imprisonment and wished to rescue him; whereas, by contrast, throughout the Indies the natives hated their masters.[28]

The wondering wild men, bewildered that their august friend could be housed in prison even like their lowly selves, found themselves sharers in his misfortune. They could escape in but two ways. Many, pushed too close by misery, hung themselves or ate dirt until they died. Many more assembled the remains of their goods and quietly disappeared into distant woodlands, where their enemies at least fought with no supernatural arms. Thus the colony soon found itself at a loss for the tractable servants necessary for its ease.

Indian tribes living beyond the Guaranís profited by the dissensions in the city to renounce their allegiance. In an effort to placate the natives, Irala and his officials gave them permission to kill and eat their enemies. Nay more, Gonzalo de Mendoza is said to have given them a fat and tender slave, who was eaten with great festivity, in return for the clearing and sowing of a patch of land.

Mighty lust again became honorable in Paraguay. Irala set the

[27] Gandía, "Indios y Conquistadores," 79–84; "Cartas de Indias," 598–609.
[28] Serrano y Sanz, II, 133, 146, 240.

example; he established a harem two leagues from the city, and there he would retire for his delight, even on Corpus Christi and other high feasts.

Who could be happier under the new rule than the two jolly friars, Armenta and Lebrón? They had immediately allied themselves with the communists, and had preached moving sermons justifying the coup d'état, and daily intoned Ave Marias for the safety of the government. Soon the officials intrusted to them an important mission. They were to journey to Brazil, along the way they knew, carrying letters and despatches to His Majesty. These contained the justification of all the communists' deeds, and in addition a request that the virtuous and pious Bernardo de Armenta be appointed to the bishopric of the province. They set off with five Christians and forty or fifty young and pretty Indian girls, "to whom they were teaching Christian doctrine," says Hernández, with his sour irony. The fair novices in religion were manacled together on the march to prevent their escape to their homes, and by night they were staked to the ground. Pero Vaca stole one of the girls and hid her; the monks excommunicated him and got the girl back; "i no era fea," and she was not ugly.[29]

The sturdy monks arrived safely at Santa Catalina Island, and from there addressed a letter of self-praise and calumny of the governor to their king.[30] But apparently they found no means, or no temptation, to proceed to prudish Spain.

So the days dragged on. The governor would not die, nor would his partizans cease their activity in his behalf. The strength of the opposing parties was such that neither side could annihilate the other. It was a stalemate pernicious to all; though Black held the White King in perpetual check, all his forces were occupied in giving check. Meanwhile the Christians could not rule their country, and with the hostile Indians growing bolder, none knew what doom was preparing in the swamps of the Chaco.

Irala and his cabinet concluded that there was no hope of civil peace and an effective organization of the colony so long as Cabeza

[29] Serrano y Sanz, I, 353; II, 79, 80, 147, 347; Buckingham Smith mss., 257.
[30] Dated Oct. 10, 1544. Arch. Ind., Justicia, 1131.

de Vaca remained in prison. Once get him out of the way, and his followers, lacking a rallying cry and a potential leader, would come round, accept the *fait accompli,* and, in their own interest, support the working government. The important thing was to make the malcontents forget, and this they could not do when daily they walked by the prison of their loved master.

Some, recognizing the soundness of the argument, voted the immediate death of the trouble-maker. But the politically-minded carried the day. They must unite the province, and they had best mollify, not embitter, their opponents. It was wisdom, therefore, to fulfil a promise once given, and make a show of sending Cabeza de Vaca to Spain for trial.

Was there, then, no danger of the anger of the Council of the Indies and His Catholic Majesty himself, if Cabeza de Vaca should come before them to plead his own cause?

Ha! Not much danger! In the first place, he would have to cross the ocean in a clumsy lugger, built in the colony for the navigation of the upper river. There was more than half a chance that she would never weather a good *pampero,* or that, being too square to tack, she would be driven on the rocky lee shore of Brazil. And supposing that she rode through the storms, would not the captain be their man, in charge of the feeding of his prisoner? And supposing even that Cabeza de Vaca should arrive alive in the king's court, he could present nothing but his own unsupported word against the united testimony of the province. For no one was such a fool as to suppose that the attestations of his friends would ever be seen in Spain. The ocean was wide and deep, and the captain would search his ship from end to end for concealed documents.

The temporizers gained the day. The announcement was published that the governor should be sent to Spain, for honest trial before his superiors. And the gentlemen officers requested of the founders and conquerors of Paraguay depositions as to the state of the colony, with whatever complaints any man might be moved to make. Nothing, surely, could be more fair and honorable.

Nothing, however, could be more disingenuous than the means adopted by the men in power.

The officials began to speak to the communists informing them what they had to depose against me, and with gifts and promises they suborned many other persons, in which they spent a large part of my property, and they took that of the Indians, and they took their wives and daughters, permitting those to whom they gave them to sell them and profit by them as if they were slaves, and before Pedro Díaz, alcalde of the commune, they began to take depositions, and the said Pedro Díaz, being one of those implicated in my imprisonment, by indirect ways persuaded the witnesses to perjure themselves, so that when they said something in my favor they said there was no need of writing it, but only what was against me. They deposed many things falsely, both by force and for gifts and promises.

Pedro Hernández specifically mentions one Damiano de Onís of Seville, who confessed that he wrote many falsities for a pair of cotton trousers. Torture was employed as a matter of course to encourage reluctant witnesses. In the insurgents' own voluminous minutes the note: *"question y tormento"* recurs frequently, as a proper agent in the quest for truth. The witness was sentenced to be filled with a fixed number of gallons of water, and at the second or third gallon the verities would be revealed to him. Or he was set naked on a wooden horse, and his arms and legs, being bound, were twisted. One witness disavowed the statements made under torture, saying that in fear of death or permanent disability he had confessed falsely. So again he was put on the *"burro de palo,"* and as the cords tightened the desired testimony emerged.[31]

Most of the accusations dealt with the crime which would most prejudice the Council of the Indies, to wit, overweening presumption. "He called himself king!" was the common cry, repeated until soon a dozen men were ready to swear they had heard with their own ears the words on the governor's lips. The notary, Martín de Orue, would spur the witnesses: "Do you think it just that any one of you should wish to be king in this land? For I want you to know that there is no other king, nor should there be, nor any other lord but His Majesty and I in his name. But Cabeza de Vaca has said that he is king here!"[32]

[31] Arch. Ind., Justicia, 1131, 4A, examination of Juan del Ondono. True, Cabeza de Vaca also employed torture as a judicial process. (Gandía, "Conquista," 138, n. 107; Arch. Ind., Justicia 1131, examination of Cabeza de Vaca, Question 30.)

[32] Serrano y Sanz, II, 346.

Perhaps there was a pinch of truth in this accusation, enough truth to flavor a tubful of falsity. A witness swore to hearing Cabeza de Vaca say: "that he knew how to understand the provisions of His Majesty better than the Councillors of the Indies, because they did not understand them as he did, because they did not know what went on out there, and indeed they knew nothing but how to get drunk and sleep, and if God should disclose any gold in the land no one would say a word, and with it he would stop the mouths of those Councillors." [33] This is at least a credible saying of a man in anger, presented though it was to the councillors to stimulate their venom.

One document in particular was drawn up to insure the governor's damnation. Partly by persuasion, partly by intimidation, the signatures of a hundred and thirty-two colonists were obtained.[34] But the articles to which the signatures were to be attached were not written down at all, nor were they composed until the vessel was well on its way to Spain. It is alleged that Irala's advocates spent a good part of their sea trip inventing calumnious statements which were presented to the Council of the Indies as the assertions of the founders and conquerors of Paraguay. Now this may well be true, for the insurgents' notary, Martín de Orue, crossed with Cabeza de Vaca, and had both opportunity and motive.

Meanwhile all the accusations, testimonies, and documents made in favor of Cabeza de Vaca disappeared.

No, not all. The friends of the governor, well recognizing that legality meant little to their opponents, drew up in secret certain testimonies. These they wrapped closely in a waxed cloth, and secreted the packet cunningly in a piece of timber as thick as a man's thigh and three handspans long. With the connivance of a carpenter, this timber was inveigled into the shipyard, and used as a strut to strengthen the ship's poop, being fastened with six nails above and six below. A sympathetic sailor was let into the secret, and was adjured to reveal it to justice if ever he should arrive safe in Spain.

In March, 1545, a year after the retreat from Los Reyes, the ship

---

[33] Gandía, "Conquista," 190, n. 18.
[34] Arch. Ind., Justicia, 1131, last document.

was ready and stocked with food. On the seventh of the month, at midnight, the embarkation of Cabeza de Vaca took place. I cannot do better, nor half so well, as to reproduce the stirring eye-witness account of Pedro Hernández.[35]

Alonso Cabrera, the Supervisor, and Pedro Dorantes, his quartermaster, accompanied by a large number of arquebusiers, presented themselves at the prison; and each arquebusier carried three lighted fuses in his hand, so as to make the number appear greater than it was. Then Alonso Cabrera and Pedro Dorantes [36] entered the room in which he lay; they seized him by the arm and lifted him out of the bed with the chains round his feet; he was very ill, almost to death.

They carried him in this state to the gate leading into the street, and when he saw the sky, which he had not seen till then, he entreated them to let him render thanks to God.

When he rose from his knees, two soldiers took him under the arms and carried him on board the lugger, for he was extremely weak and crippled. When he saw himself in the midst of these people, he said to them: "Sirs, be my witnesses that I appoint, as my deputy, Juan de Salazar de Espinosa, that he may govern this province instead of me, and in the name of His Majesty, maintaining order and justice till the king may be pleased to make other dispositions." Hardly had he finished speaking when García Venegas, deputy treasurer, rushed upon him, dagger in hand, saying: "I do not recognize what you say; retract, or I will tear your soul from your body!" The governor had, however, been advised not to say what he did, because they were determined to kill him, and these words might have caused a great disturbance among them, and the party of the king might have snatched him from the hands of the others, everybody being then in the street. García Venegas having withdrawn a little, the governor repeated the same words; then García Venegas sprang with great fury on the governor, and placed a dagger to his temple, saying as before: "Withdraw what you have said, or I will tear your soul from your body!" At the same moment he inflicted a slight wound on his temple, and pushed the people who were carrying the governor with so much violence that they fell with him, and one of them dropped his cap. After this they quickly raised him again, and carried him precipitately on board the lugger. They closed the poop of the vessel with planks, put two chains on him which prevented him from moving; then they unmoored and descended the river.

[35] Domínguez, 256.
[36] Cabeza de Vaca himself says Cabrera and Venegas. (Serrano y Sanz, II, 84.)

And so, just four years after landing on the coast of the southern continent, Cabeza de Vaca set forth on his return journey. He had come as governor of half the western world south of the Equator; he was returning in chains, a prisoner awaiting trial. He had come to lead his Spanish gentlemen in a splendid pacification of strange countries, for the glory of Spain and his sovereign; he was returning sick and penniless, with the shameful marks of a rebel's dagger on his brow. He had come in pursuance of a noble purpose, to fulfil a sacred mission toward the humble and the oppressed; and he had failed. The simple wild men whom he loved, and who answered his love with their own, had learned only, from his stay among them, to suffer the more.

In the misery of failure the fetters that bound him lay less heavy than the irons upon his heart. In the long nights he suffered not so much from man's injustice as from God's justice. Examining forever the past and the errors of his spirit, he knew that he was enduring God's terrible punishment for Pride.

CHAPTER VI

THE END IN SPAIN

THE vessel that was destined to carry Cabeza de Vaca to judgment, by his king or by his God, accommodated hardly more than a score of men. There were eleven pairs of rowers' seats along its sides, for auxiliary power on the river or in calms at sea.[1] His prison was a tiny cell with a tiny port-hole. In command were his arch enemies, García Venegas and Alonso Cabrera, with Martín de Orue, the new notary. For fellow prisoners he had his own faithful notary, Pedro Hernández, and a priest, Luis de Miranda, who for protesting the communists' actions had spent eight months in Asunción jail without seeing sun or moon. Why these alone of the partizans of Cabeza de Vaca were shipped to Spain is not clear.

The crew was composed of Basques and Cordovans, hostile to the governor for reasons of local loyalty. The pilots were Gonzalo de Acosta, completing his third round trip to South America, and Antonio López.

Three smaller boats convoyed the governor's prison ship down the river. After long navigation by the cheerless shore, all were amazed to hear a pursuing shout, and to see a long-boat, pushed at full speed, overtaking them from the north. It pulled alongside, and the captain hailed and shouted: "Señor García Venegas, would you have room for another prisoner?"

"Aye, that I have, please God, and willingness to take him and twenty more!" answered Venegas.[2]

---

[1] Groussac (ed. of Guzmán, "La Argentina") and Gandía ("Conquista," 203, n. 52) assert that the ship was named "Comuneros." This is simply incredible. The insurgents could not have challenged the opinion of authority with such a name, for "Comuneros," with its connotation of the rebellion of the Communes against the King in 1520, had no better sound to royalty than has its translation to-day. Gandía's citation: *"la caravela comuneros,"* is certainly a scribal slip for *"la caravela de los comuneros."* The ship was sometimes referred to as a *"caravela,"* sometimes as a *"bergantín,"* or lugger.

[2] Ruy Díaz de Guzmán, in Angelis, I, 59.

So two men were transferred in their chains from ship to ship: Captain Juan de Salazar de Espinosa, and Pedro Estopiñán Cabeza de Vaca.

Captain Salazar soon explained how he had come to join the distinguished repatriates. A few days after the departure of the governor from Asunción he ventured to organize a counter-revolution, on the strength of the appointment as lieutenant governor which Cabeza de Vaca had secretly sent from his prison. Irala, whatever his faults, was no temporizer. He and his men attacked Salazar, and had not Francisco de Mendoza intervened, would have killed him. As it was, Salazar and his ally, briefly known as Pero Vaca, were sent down river to take their place in the prison ship.

The communists were very secure or very thoughtless, thus to augment the numbers of those who could give personal testimony against them in hearings before the Council of the Indies.

Perhaps the communists had made comprehensive plans. One day Cabeza de Vaca noticed in his stew two curious reddish lumps the size of a pea. He identified them as realgar, an arsenical mineral. Though deathly sick for four days from morsels of the meat, he recovered, and for a time his exceeding diffidence about his food proved baffling to his ill-wishers. The lumps of poison he jealously preserved, promising to lay them before the very eyes of His Majesty.

Twice, afterwards, arsenic was fed him, but by the best of fortune he had a sure antidote with him: a bottle of oil and a piece of the horn of a unicorn. This specific was much prized in his time; Torquemada the inquisitor kept a unicorn's horn on his table as a ready counterpoison. Cabeza de Vaca proved the animal's virtues, for, though mightily sick, it pleased God that he should recover by this means. When he protested to Venegas and Cabrera against the malevolent Basque who prepared his food, "they replied that he would have to take his food from whomsoever they chose; if he did not take it from the persons commissioned to give it to him, he might die of hunger, it mattered little to them. He abstained from food for several days, but hunger at last compelled him to take what they gave him." [3]

[3] Domínguez, 259.

By the 20th of April, 1545,[4] the convoy reached the Islands of San Gabriel, where the gulf of the Río de la Plata takes on the aspect of open sea. Here the three accompanying boats were to turn back toward Paraguay.

The night before they left a strange thing happened. As the governor lay, drowsing or waking, enveloped in his grief, a stone shot through his little window, blundered against the cell walls, and lay on the floor. It was a weighted letter, telling him of the precious documents in his interest, hidden in the timber of the poop.

This message, flung by an unknown hand, brought with it a renewal of courage. There were still friends who loved him and who were working in his interest. The hope of salvation came to color and adorn his bleak fortitude. Now he could see in the future a lightening of misery, a recovery at least of honor.

He heard on the deck the sound of farewells and the orders to weigh anchor and set the sails for the open sea. The little lugger, with twenty-seven men aboard, caught the winds that blow to Spain.

Something troubled the mind of Venegas. Treachery and counter-treachery talked too much in this small group of enforced companions, of whom every third man cherished some secret grudge. Venegas made a thorough search of the vessel, discovering various compromising letters. These he confiscated, tearing them to bits and scattering them on the South Atlantic. He tried to explore the persons of his sailors, to seize even innocent letters to wives and kin. The meanest Spaniard has his ticklish honor, affronted by any liberty with his inviolable body. The sailors' ire was roused; they stood to arms, with harpoons in their hands, in defense of their humble rights. Venegas and Cabrera gave up the hunt; the treasure they sought was secure beneath their feet, in its nest in the poop's timber.

If Venegas was pursued by concern, Cabrera, with his rages, suspicions, and violence seemed on the edge of insanity. There were some very strange doings on this crazy ship, doings long explained as inventions of Cabeza de Vaca and his secretary, and only recently proved truth by ample supporting testimonies.[5] Out in mid-ocean, a great

---

[4] Arch. Ind., Justicia, 1131, 6A, fol. 114.
[5] Gandía, "Conquista," 214, n. 84.

storm arose, and the lugger took much water over her sides, which sat so low that men could sit in her waist and pull an oar. All the provisions were spoilt except the flour, lard, fish, and water. As the storm did not relent, Cabrera, in a frenzy, recognized the reproof of God. With Venegas, he entered the prison-cell; he filed the governor's irons, while Venegas, weeping, kissed his feet. The storm, cried Cabrera, was the effect of God's justice. Gladly he acknowledged his misdeeds and errors, and he asked nothing better than to make his precious captive his commander, and serve him duly. "As soon as they had taken the chains off the governor the sea and wind subsided, and the tempest, which had lasted four days, calmed down."

Cabrera and Venegas had not lost all their wits. Their frenzy dying with the storm, they proposed a complete erasure of old scores. They would destroy all the accusations and damning documents they carried, and Cabeza de Vaca should, in manifest of good faith, destroy or cause to be destroyed any secret messages of which he might have knowledge. On arriving in Spain, the three would unite to ask His Majesty only for aid for the distressed colony, and not a single word should be said of all the past. And Cabrera fell on his knees before Cabeza de Vaca, clasping his knees and praying for pardon; he summoned Pedro Hernández and cried: "Witness as notary how I require our lord governor to put me in chains and proceed against me, as governor, and wreak justice upon me, and how I obey him as governor and master in the name of His Majesty!"

Cabeza de Vaca did not fall into the trap. It was too late, he repeated; all this was too late. He knew of no secret letters. He was content now to put the past in the hands of His Majesty and the Council of the Indies, to whom the past belonged. From them, with divine guidance, justice would proceed.

The steady wind of that season blew out of the south, carrying the lugger speedily toward home. Had they fallen into a calm or met persistent head winds it would have gone hard with them. They had no food but flour-cake fried in lard, and a little salt fish. They burned the very planks of their vessel to cook their food. And one black night, as they drew near the Azores, Cabeza de Vaca, with an auger and chisel, extracted the precious packet of testimonies from its hiding

273

place, and found some concealment for it on his own lean body.[6]

After two and a half months of navigation, in sight only of water and sky, they were greeted by the dolphins of the Azores, the playful collies of the sea. On July 16, 1545, they cast anchor under the high green shelter of Terceira Island.

Just seven years before Cabeza de Vaca had passed this way. He had spent two weeks in the mid-ocean harbor of Angra, on his return from Mexico to Spain. The sight of the lovely island now recalled the specter of a different self. Then he was bringing home a message of triumphant valor, the story of one of the most magnificent journeys in man's history. His tale was all of incredible successes, of divine favor, of honors paid him by the Spaniards and the natives of the western world. The dream of his long peaceful eastward-plunging days had been of a happy kingdom in the west, to be governed by Cabeza de Vaca, administered by honorable, kindly Spanish gentlemen, and peopled by grateful races who had gladly left their demon-gods to be Christian freemen.

And now he was again returning to Spain, under indictment for misconduct in office, the prisoner of mean and evil-natured men. Not only had he failed and all his dreams come to nothing, but justice and mercy had failed as well.

In this port of Terceira Island the governor went ashore with his two captors. They wished to persuade him to make a mutual deposition before local notaries, which they might turn to their advantage. Not only did Cabeza de Vaca resolutely refuse, but he cast himself on the island authorities, agents of Portugal, for protection.[7] Probably they remembered him and the adulation which had been his, seven years gone. At any rate, they heard his plea, and took soberly his fear that if he were returned to the lugger he would not be allowed to reach Spain alive. It was arranged, to the extreme displeasure of Cabrera and Venegas, that he and Captain Salazar should be sent to Lisbon in a Portuguese vessel.

Cabrera and Venegas returned to their lugger and sped in hot haste

---

[6] The inventory of what is evidently this packet is contained in Arch. Ind., 1131.

[7] Martín de Orue and his other enemies alleged that he went ashore on the plea of illness, pledging his honor to return, and this pledge he broke. Oviedo, "Historia general," II, 207.

to Seville, arriving in the latter end of August, 1545.[8] Immediately they began telling their calumnious story to all officials, high and low. They announced, among other falsehoods, that Cabeza de Vaca had chosen to go from the Azores to Lisbon, in order to play the traitor to the king of Portugal. When Cabeza de Vaca arrived in Cadiz, a week later, the mischievous first impressions had already been made. He promptly sent an express to the king's officers in Seville, ordering the arrest of Cabrera and Venegas; "but we did not think it proper," said those officers in a report to headquarters.[9]

There was something wild, something fantastic, in the deeds of Cabrera. Now that everything lay clear before him, with the road open to success, he suddenly took fright. It would seem that his fears worked upon Venegas, and the two attempted to flee with their vessel to Portugal or France. Cabrera's fit passed, however, and the two dropped their crazy project and posted to the court, then sitting in Madrid. They laid before the Council of the Indies their great bundle of damning testimonies, with the long tails of signatures.[10] And when his work was accomplished, Cabrera went unmistakably mad. He was prevented by his "melancholy" and by the purgative treatment prescribed by his physician from testifying in Cabeza de Vaca's trial or in his own.[11] This physician reported that he was forever visited by the imaginations which had seized upon him on his homeward voyage.

Cabeza de Vaca filed with the Council of the Indies his counter-accusations, notably the narrative of his fortunes and misfortunes (dated Dec. 7, 1545) from which I have quoted so freely, his "General Relation which I, Alvar Núñez Cabeza de Vaca, make to inform the King and the Gentlemen of His Royal Council of the Occurrences in the Province of Río de la Plata."

The gentlemen of the Council of the Indies, weighing the bulk of papers *pro* against those *contra,* determined to seek the truth by putting the governor on trial. Marcelo de Villalobos, fiscal of the council, was instructed to draw up the formal indictment.

---

[8] The crew of the ship were examined on Aug. 27, 1545. (Arch. Ind., Justicia, 1131.)
[9] Report from Contratación of Seville, Sept. 2, 1545. Contained in Buckingham Smith mss.
[10] "Accusation of Villalobos," Arch. Ind., Justicia, 1130, 1A.
[11] Gandía, "Conquista," 220, n. 96.

The case lay in good hands. Marcelo de Villalobos was a model prosecutor, stern, hard, vigorous, and honest. Possibly, in this case, he was something more. It is of interest, and perhaps of serious importance, that he was born in Jerez de la Frontera about 1490, and was thus an exact contemporary of Cabeza de Vaca.[12] After a judicial career in Santo Domingo and Mexico, he became inquisitor in Seville, and soon was appointed to the Royal Council of the Indies.

Prosecutor and accused had been boys together in the old town of Jerez. Did a family feud make one Guelph, the other Ghibelline? Had some boyish rivalry, some ridiculous, inconsiderable wound left in them a rancor which waited forty years for its resolution? Or did Villalobos's outward sternness mask an inward sympathy, biding its time until it could find a means of effective service? There is no answer to the dilemma, for in 1550, before the five-year trial was finished, Villalobos was dead. At least, he is not to be accused of corruption, for he died so poor that the council granted his widow a year's salary to pay his debts.[13]

Villalobos, then, consulted the great bundle of documents put in his hands by Cabrera and Venegas. From them he compiled a set of thirty-four charges, the mere reading of which would constitute, to an impressionable mind, a presumption of villainy. His charge is dated Jan. 20, 1546.[14]

He accused Cabeza de Vaca of robbing the inhabitants of the Canary Islands, on his outward journey, and of sacking two merchant ships in the Cape Verde Islands. He alleged that on the journey from Santa Catalina to Asunción Cabeza de Vaca had forbidden his men to trade with the Indians, thus reducing them to necessitous straits; that he abandoned on this march thirteen Christians, who escaped only by telling the Indians that they were the sons of Payzume, the native name of that virtuous Franciscan friar, Bernardo de Armenta; that he robbed the Indians along the way of their provisions, occasioning tumults in the country; that he delivered twenty-five friendly Indians

[12] He entered the University of Salamanca in 1505.
[13] "Indice general de los papeles del Consejo de Indias," I, 123, 241.
[14] Reproduced in Bol. Est. Hist. And., I, 24, and in Rev. del Ateneo de Jerez, VIII, 147.

to the Guaranís to be killed and eaten; that he caused an Indian chief [Aracaré] to be hung without a hearing. Villalobos charged further that Cabeza de Vaca would send as a summons to the Indians a medal engraved with his device, a cow's head; that he allowed free Indian girls to be sold; that he forbade all to trade with the Guaranís except himself and his servants, thus establishing such a low price-scale that the Guaranís would rather eat their slaves than sell them; and that he performed other specified acts of cruelty, presumption, and greed. And still the charges went on: that only because a near-by tribe [the Guaicurús] was reluctant to pay a tribute of food he destroyed nine villages and more than four thousand souls; that similarly he murdered three thousand Socorinos, and the friendly Indians of Los Reyes; that when six friendly Indians brought him a present of fruit he took them and branded them for slaves; that he sacked sixteen villages near Puerto de Los Reyes; that on his incursion toward Peru he loaded Indians and Spaniards so heavily that they could not carry food and hence the expedition came to grief; that he took every man's property without pay; interfered in private bargains; confiscated the property of the dead; did not bring sufficient supplies to Paraguay, but arrived poor and needy; took down His Majesty's arms from a ship and put up his own; called himself king and said: "I am prince and master in this land!"; engraved his own bearings with those of His Majesty; would not permit the officials to write to His Majesty, but robbed them of their charges, and tried to torture some to find out what they were writing; permitted infractions of the rules he himself published; and interpreted His Majesty's regulations about taxation all to his own advantage.

In view of these heinous deeds the fiscal asked that Cabeza de Vaca be required to indemnify all the wronged, and in addition that he pay a fine of 100,000 ducats into the Royal Treasury.

The gentlemen of the council, on hearing such an act of accusation, may well have shaken with suspicion and alarm. A man against whom such evil could even be alleged would be safer under lock and key. The governor of Río de la Plata was arrested, and thrown into the public jail of Madrid.

This shameful detention did not last long. On April 19 he was permitted to take up residence in a Madrid inn, but was prohibited from passing its doors.[15]

Summoned before the Council of the Indies, he replied, in a two-day examination, to the specific accusations and to the searching questions put by his judge and jury.[16]

Surely there is no need to give in detail his explanations and denials, nor to judge again the appalling mass of papers to which the contest gave birth. Let it suffice that the governor denied outright most of the charges. Pressed for explanation, he related the circumstances to which the charges pointed, to the best of his memory. In the first accusation, for instance, there was no disputing the fact that his soldiers had killed three cows in the Canary Islands. Cabeza de Vaca told the story as it has already been reported in these pages.[17] Villalobos referred to his great portfolio. A dozen witnesses had deposed that the cattle had been taken by the governor's order.

It was one man's word against a dozen. "Guilty," was the verdict, "on the ground of a sufficient number of witnesses."

And so throughout the two hopeless days. He could not prevail against the united front of his enemies. They had done their work cleverly; they had chosen trifling occurrences of those full years, had lit them with lurid colors, had appended the names of a sufficient number of witnesses, and had challenged: "Disprove it if you can!" Readily enough he entered his denial; the sheer weight of numbers defeated him.

Cabeza de Vaca's attorney, Alonso de San Juan, immediately took exception to the decision. The witnesses, he charged, were prejudiced and incompetent. To obtain justice for his client, he must have sufficient time to interview and obtain depositions from witnesses for the defense.

Granted. Defendant should have a stay of three years in which to prepare his reply. This extraordinary delay suggests that Cabeza de

[15] This decree is reproduced in Bol. Est. Hist. And., I, 23.
[16] Feb. 20–21, 1546. Arch. Ind., Justicia, 1131, "Juramento e declaración de Cabeça de Vaca."
[17] *Ante*, p. 192.

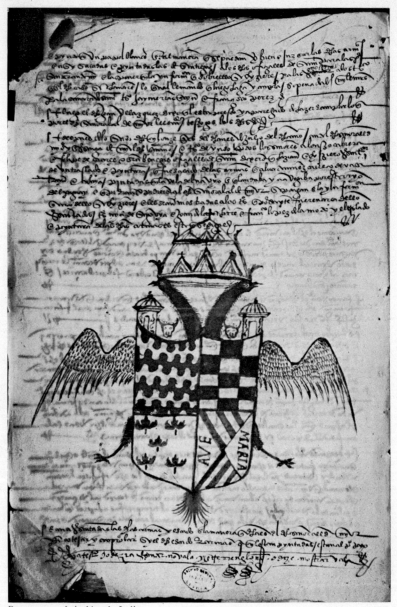

Coat of Arms of Cabeza de Vaca

A page from the accusation drawn up by the colonists against Cabeza de Vaca. He is here accused of hoisting his own arms on a vessel, in place of the King's standard; and the arms are reproduced in attestation. Notice the cows' heads, not a part of Cabeza de Vaca's proper device.

Vaca expected to obtain convincing testimony from his partizans in Paraguay. In this he was disappointed, for no Spaniards succeeded in reaching Asunción till 1552, six years later.

He was restricted, then, to those witnesses at hand in Spain. These were Pedro Hernández, notary, whose fortunes were bound up with those of his master; Pedro Estopiñán Cabeza de Vaca, suspect on grounds of kinship; Captain Juan de Salazar de Espinosa; Fray Alonso de Medina, monk, apparently a passenger on the returning prison ship; three sailors; and certain character witnesses and others who could testify to the habits of South American Indians.[18]

To these witnesses were put seventy-six questions dealing with the events in the course of the expedition. The questions were designed to draw out affirmations and statements on all the matters at issue. The testimonies thus obtained form a thorough substantiation of Cabeza de Vaca's charges, a refutation of his accusers, and a vindication of his policy and character. Had the judgment of the Council of the Indies rested on these depositions, there could have been no question of a verdict of acquittal.

However, these testimonies, together with the slim packet of papers rescued from the lugger's strut, are in bulk far less imposing than the mass of documents submitted by the officials in Paraguay to the prosecution. The chief point at issue was the determination of the value of these accusations as evidence. As we have seen, Cabeza de Vaca and his partizans held that the testimonies were worthless, having been obtained by fraud, collusion, and subornation.

The judges rejected Cabeza de Vaca's contention, and admitted the evidence of Irala and his clique as valid.

My own conviction, and that of the learned Enrique de Gandía, is that Cabeza de Vaca's contention is just and proper.[19] On the other hand, Don José Torre Revello, the incomparable archivist, believes that

[18] What happened to Luis de Miranda, monk, fellow-prisoner on the lugger? He does not reappear; perhaps he died at sea. In one important document, Arch. Ind., Justicia, 1131, 8A, certain parts of the trial are reviewed, with first-hand testimonies to happenings in Paraguay by Francisco Muñoz Alvas, Fray Alonso Bautista, Fray Luis Herrezuela, Luis Hernández, and Alvaro de Colombres. The document is undated. Probably these are transcripts of testimonies taken in Asunción before Cabeza de Vaca's departure.
[19] "Historia de la Conquista del Río de la Plata," *passim.*

the accusations are proper and competent evidence, deserving credence as much as the passionate allegations of the governor.[20]

At any rate, this first engagement was lost by Cabeza de Vaca. No final sentence was pronounced, but a presumption of guilt hung over him. Enemies assembled against him: court gossip, hidden interests, personal animosities. Perhaps the deadliest foe was the three-year stay granted to him. With the passage of years a new working status was presumably established in the colony, and all the past rights and wrongs, deeds and misdeeds, became an old, tiresome, meaningless wrangle. And the figure of the aging governor, forever filled with ancient grievances, lost its tragic grandeur to become the court bore.

Oviedo the historian saw him in 1547, *"pobre e fatigado,"* "very poor and tired, pursuing his case against his rivals, and it is very sad to hear him and learn what he suffered in the Indies." [21] Evidently he had been granted larger liberty than his Madrid inn. Oviedo talked to him at length, for the benefit of his great history, and learned from him many facts that have been put down in the first part of this record.

Meanwhile the legal business grew and grew. The case of Cabeza de Vaca became not one trial but four.

First, the original case, the father of them all, the criminal action of the fiscal Villalobos and the officials of the Río de la Plata against Cabeza de Vaca for misconduct in office.

Second, a case inspired by Cabeza de Vaca, a criminal action brought by Villalobos against Cabrera and Venegas, for their aggressions against the governor and for their attempted flight to France or Portugal with their vessel. The indictment is dated April 12, 1546.[22] Therewith was combined a civil action of Cabeza de Vaca against the various officials of Paraguay for their violent aggressions against his person and property. This trial was hampered by the increasing madness of Cabrera. I have not found the verdict in the case. It was still in active progress, producing document upon document, on Sept. 7, 1547.

[20] Views expressed in conversation.
[21] "Historia general," II, 190, III, 614.
[22] Arch. Ind., Justicia, 1130, 1A.

Third, a suit brought by Martín de Orduña against Cabeza de Vaca. Plaintiff alleged himself to be the heir of Juan de Ayolas, himself heir of Don Pedro de Mendoza. Since Ayolas was dead in the dark Chaco, plaintiff claimed suzerainty and enjoyment of the region of Río de la Plata. This action was brought on Feb. 3, 1546, and was still proliferating vigorously in the spring of 1547.[23]

Fourth, a suit brought by the fiscal of His Majesty and Cabeza de Vaca against Martín de Orue, notary and passenger on the prison-ship, for offenses against His Majesty and Cabeza de Vaca. The suit was filed on Dec. 17, 1549. Orue was imprisoned pending the outcome. Through accusation, counter-accusation, testimony and counter-testimony, the case flourished year by year. Orue asked permission to return to the Plate. Petition granted, Jan. 25, 1553, on condition that he post bonds and confer on his lawyer power to act. Orue left thankfully for the frontier in 1555; the last document in the case is dated Jan. 3, 1556. No doubt the suit was dropped at the death of Cabeza de Vaca.

As one reviews these documents, one recognizes that from the first the opinion of the judges was setting against the deposed governor. To the legal formalists, it was a simple matter of the weight of evidence, and the formidable array of witnesses in the depositions brought from Paraguay easily prevailed against the word of Cabeza de Vaca and the few testimonies he could produce. Further, to those who regarded the letter of the law less strictly than the welfare of the Indies, certain facts were heavy in the balance.

Irala's government was good, insisted the hundred signatories to Paraguayan testimonies, and the crew of the prison-ship corroborated the statement. "Domingo de Irala is so much loved that every one would die for him," said Gonzalo de Acosta.[24] Whereas Cabeza de Vaca had brought with him to Paraguay discord, turmoil, the seeds of rebellion. Villalobos played upon the theme of the welfare of the country and of the Spaniards, harping upon Cabeza de Vaca's unpopularity, favoritism, and present poverty.[25] He pointed eloquently

[23] Arch. Ind., Justicia, 1130.
[24] Arch. Ind., Justicia, 1131, examination of witnesses, Aug. 27, 1545.
[25] Arch. Ind., Justicia, 1130, suit of Orduña, Apr. 14, 1546 and June 7, 1546.

to the many testimonies to the bad order that existed under the brief rule of the reforming governor. He reiterated that the need of the colonists was a ruler strong, tactful, and also rich.

The Council of the Indies was an executive body as well as a judicial one, and was sometimes uncomfortable in fulfilling its double rôle. Now its duty as an active governing committee prevailed. Under the snow of the descending documents, before the decision of the cases, it calmly anticipated the result and appointed a new governor of the Río de la Plata.

A wealthy gentleman, Juan de Sanabria, offered to settle the factious quarrel in a way equally unwelcome to Cabeza de Vaca and Irala. He was a citizen of Medellin, in Estremadura, the natal village of Hernando Cortés. With memories of the great conqueror current in his mind, he proposed to equip an expedition of two hundred soldiers, in return for the title of governor and adelantado.

It seemed a splendid solution. While it would not put an end to the legal broil, it would remove all significance from the decision. More important, it would serve the present needs of the colony, with men and supplies and the stilling of old rancors by a new master. Sanabria was appointed governor and the conditions fixed in a royal decree of July 22, 1547.

Unfortunately for Paraguay, the solution never became effective. For Juan de Sanabria, after many postponements of his journey, died in 1549. In the following year his son Diego, inheriting his father's rights, sent out three vessels. One of these was captained by our old friend Juan de Salazar de Espinosa, officially absolved of blame in the Paraguayan imbroglio, and appointed a Knight of Santiago. His craft carried out fifty women, married and single. The three Spanish ships were attacked by French corsairs off Guinea and lost their goods but saved the women's honor.

The arrival at Santa Catalina was celebrated by wholesale weddings of passengers and crew, led by Captain Salazar and a ripe widow. A few adventurers struggled through the wilderness to Asunción, bringing news but nothing beside; the rest lingered on the coast until 1555, when they too made the overland journey to Paraguay. Captain Salazar made peace with Irala, and ably seconded the enterprises of that stormy chief.[26] Diego de Sanabria, for one reason or another, appears to have resigned his claims.[27]

These were bleak years for Cabeza de Vaca, paroled from prison, unregarded, with the prospect of trial by hostile judges forever in his mind. His best hope was that some day news would come from Paraguay, perhaps of the victory of his partizans, perhaps even a plea that he be returned to them to be again their master. Such a message would render clean his spotted honor before the world. And the Council of the Indies and the courtiers and the king himself would see public reparation done to the attainted escutcheon of the Veras and the Cabeza de Vacas!

Before January, 1549, the news had come, and it was the worst that could be brought.[28] From Peru arrived a troubled message from the king's viceroy, announcing that Domingo de Irala had made a successful communication between Paraguay and his province. Though Irala had performed the feat inadvertently, for his whole purpose was the discovery of El Dorado, the linking of the two colonies seemed to the Council of the Indies a matter of much importance.

Irala, faithful to his promise to his subjects, had prepared his gold-hunting expedition when Cabeza de Vaca was once out of the way. Resolution armed his men as well as greed, and the desire to silence their distant judges with gags of gold. "Though we should have to strip the fittings of our swords to make nails, we are bound to send back a ship with gold." [29]

Two hundred and fifty veterans, twenty-seven of them mounted, left Asunción in July, 1547, and traveled up-stream to San Fernando, about half way to Los Reyes. Here they turned west through the Chaco, and by sheer courage and ferocity cut a way through the barriers set by man and nature. Behind them, in the jungle, all ill-disposed Indians lay dead, while the native women were apprenticed to their

[26] Gandía, "Indios y Conquistadores," 117 *et sqq.*; "Captivity of Hans Stade," 38; "Cartas de Indias," 581, 767, 838.
[27] Charlevoix ("Hist. du Paraguai," I, 197) and others say that he died in the wreck of his ship. According to Padre del Techo, he made another effort in 1554; his pilots, by an amazing feat of navigation, landed him at Cartagena, near Panama. At any rate, he thought no more of his governorship.
[28] Oviedo, "Historia general," II, 208.
[29] Gandía, "Conquista," 234.

trade of populators.[30] When, eventually, they emerged on the edge of Peru, they were met by messengers from the forewarned viceroy, Gasca. He feared the irruption of these hardy bravos, who might well unite with other trouble-makers to unseat him; "we would have chased the governor out of the country," boasts Ulrich Schmidel.[31] Gasca therefore persuaded the expeditionaries to halt, while envoys visited him in Lima. And these envoys brought back some sort of secret gift, pact, or promise to Irala which led him to renounce further conquest, and to return over his perilous course to Paraguay.[32] "We soldiers knew nothing about this compact," says Ulrich Schmidel; "had we known of it we would have tied our commander hand and foot together, and so transported him to Peru." The troops returned with little loss to their base; they reached San Fernando in March 1549, and were in Asunción shortly after.

So the report was laid before the Council of the Indies that Cabeza de Vaca's dream had been fulfilled, and the dream was vain. No golden kingdom had been discovered, and no easy trade route from Peru to Spain. This new entrance to Spain's treasure-land was immeasurably more difficult than the old way across the Isthmus of Panama. But the most damning implication of the report was the fact that Irala had succeeded where Cabeza de Vaca had failed. Irala had shown, with irrefragable proof, that his way with soldiers and Indians worked, while that of the old visionary did not.

This information helped to clear the minds of the judges and point their course. They were not impressed, as were the bystanders, by certain evidences of God's opinion. Villalobos died in great poverty, early in 1551. García Venegas found a sudden and terrible death, his

---

[30] This expedition seemed to Private Ulrich Schmidel quite the right sort. He notes, for instance: "The third day we came suddenly upon the Maijaijs, with their women and children gathered together in a forest with them; these were not the people we sought, but their friends. They did not fear at all our coming to them. Nevertheless, the innocent had to pay for the guilty, for when we lighted upon them we killed many, and took over three thousand prisoners. . . . I, for my part, captured over nineteen persons, men and women, who were not at all old—I have always had more esteem for young than for old people." Domínguez, 65; see also "Cartas de Indias," 594.

[31] Domínguez, 75.

[32] The story casts shafts of light on colonial shrewdness. Irala feared the message from Gasca would not be to his liking; he therefore had some allies ambush and rob the envoys. Thus he reserved to himself liberty of action; "I never got your message!" he could have protested to Gasca.

eyes falling quite out of his head, while Cabrera, his mad accomplice, in a fit of frenzy killed his wife. And "the friars who had taken part in the revolt and troubles also died suddenly, which seemed to show the small blame attaching to the governor in his conduct toward them," avers faithful Pedro Hernández.[33]

The judges of the Council of the Indies felt themselves too close to God to have much fear of him. They pursued the routine of the court, holding the final hearings early in 1551. This judgment was pronounced in Valladolid on March 18, 1551:[34]

In the suit between Licenciado Rabanal, fiscal of His Majesty, on the one hand, and Adelantado Cabeza de Vaca, governor of Río de la Plata, now before this court, on the other hand:

We find that for the guilt which appears in the said suit against the said Alvar Núñez Cabeza de Vaca we must condemn him, and we condemn him to the perpetual deprivation of the said office of governor and adelantado of the provinces of the said Río de la Plata, and of all the right and property which the said Alvar Núñez alleged he held in the said governorship; and likewise we suspend him perpetually from the office of governor, adelantado, or any other judicial office in all the Indies of His Majesty. . . . And further we condemn him to perpetual banishment from all the said Indies under penalty of death, and further we condemn him for the five years next following to serve His Majesty in Oran [in Barbary, now Algeria] with his arms and horse at his own expense, and he must remain in the said service for the said time under penalty of the doubling of the said time of the said five years. And we maintain the rights of the persons injured according to the charges of the said suit, that they may seek compensation for injuries received from the said Alvar Núñez and take action for their payment as and before whom they may see fit. And by this our definitive mark thus and thus do we pronounce and make our condemnation with costs.

Follow the signatures, seals, and attestations.

This judgment can be foreseen by one who follows the progress of the trial, even one who remains convinced of the justice of Cabeza de Vaca's cause. One supposes the judges' deliberations to have run something in this wise:

'All these hard words, these frightful accusations and counter-

[33] Domínguez, 262.
[34] Reproduced in Bol. Est. Hist. And., I, 29.

accusations, are now long past and gone. One witness gives the lie to another, and none of us is so wise as to find the truth under these heaps of contradictions. Suppose we plump for this crazy old fanatic, who deafens us with his cries for justice, suppose we send out to Asunción a writ condemning Irala and summoning him to Spain, to spend a lustrum in one of our dungeons, what then? Why, Irala will laugh at us, and all his friends will laugh too, and he will send back some lawyer-like demurrer, and go on ruling as evidently he knows well how to do. But the old partizans of Cabeza de Vaca will take heart and perhaps revive their plotting, and so the whole colony, now at peace, will be torn again by civil broils. Whereas if we deny Cabeza de Vaca's right to the governorship, the bond and purpose of the dissenters will be broken. And every one will be happy except the old governor, and we can send him to Barbary where he can tell his troubles to the great desert and leave our ears in peace, and where with God's help he will soon die.

'Gentlemen, we must not forget that we are a governing committee as well as a judicial court. We must consider in this matter not only abstract justice, but the king's interest as well. Now all our information shows that Domingo Martínez de Irala is a strong man, who held the colony alive before Cabeza de Vaca came to it, and who, after his departure, has organized it to fulfil the king's purpose. Certainly he has a heavy hand with the Indians, and his habits would not fit a clerk in orders, and he deals justice too readily with the sword, but we all know that the Indies do not brook the milksop and the softling. Of all men who have gone out to that most isolated and precarious of our colonies, only Irala has shown the stuff of the ruler. Therefore, for the welfare of his little band of Spaniards, and for the future prosperity of His Majesty's kingdom, it would be best to lay the blame on Cabeza de Vaca. It would be proper also, out of regard for his misfortunes, to put upon him only a light penalty.'

Whatever the reasoning of the judges, their decision stands in the record of history. Cabeza de Vaca, a prisoner at this time, immediately made an appeal. He also addressed a pitiful petition to the Council, begging his release from custody. "I have no means to buy food nor

APPEAL OF CABEZA DE VACA

The petition, in his autograph, begging release from prison (see pp. 286–287). Notice the formalized, abbreviated signature. The indorsement below records no action on the petition.

to prosecute my case, and I am much in debt for all I spent for my fleet and to bring help to those lands whose officials seized me and sent me back naked." He offered to give bond for his appearance whenever and wherever required. "And I swear by God and by this cross that I know of no one who will lend me anything because my poverty is notorious." [35]

To this the Council replied briefly, on April 11 and May 15, re-affirming his imprisonment.

His appeal from sentence was rejected in a second judgment, pro-nounced on Aug. 23, 1551.[36] Two important alleviations were, how-ever, made in his punishment. His perpetual banishment from the Indies was altered to read "from the Río de la Plata"; and—a matter of great moment to the destitute cavalier—he was relieved of the re-quirement that he serve His Majesty, with his horse, in Oran.

The jail doors opened and Cabeza de Vaca came forth from his last and cruelest imprisonment. He was now a man of about sixty, whose body and spirit had suffered like only those of God's martyrs. He could still endure nakedness, poverty, cold and heat; the agony that bowed his head was the loss of his ancient honor, the sorrow of failure, the proved vanity of his dream. For himself, he could gain comfort, as once in the thorny brakes of the Río Grande, by thinking of the greater pains of Christ, bearing His Cross to Golgotha. But Christ knew that His crucifixion would bring the redemption and satisfaction of the sins of pitiful mankind; while Cabeza de Vaca's passion had eased no whit the sufferings of the brown men he loved, and in vain.

He did not cease to struggle against the judgments of his fellow-men. In response to some new appeal, the Council wearily consented to reopen the case, on Nov. 25, 1551. Cabeza de Vaca assembled a set of testimonies, proving nothing new except the esteem in which he was held in his native city, and the present destitution of himself and his wife. No further judgment appears; doubtless the appeal was dismissed; no cause.

[35] Arch. Ind., Justicia, 1131. Copy in Buckingham Smith mss.
[36] Bol. Est. Hist. And., I, 30.

Still proudly signing himself "Governor and Adelantado of Río de la Plata," he appealed for the right to see the documents in the case, on Jan. 9, 1553, and Aug. 29, 1555.[37] Refused.

In his long leisure he prepared still another set of charges against the officials of the Plate, for their dreary old aggressions, now eleven years past and gone. The last document in the corded bundles is a protest against allowing the officials of Paraguay to see the transcript of an accusation against them. It is dated Nov. 8, 1555.[38]

Now we may thankfully tie again the fading records, to rest undisturbed, perhaps, for another century. The story of Cabeza de Vaca is almost finished.

He busied himself for a time with the publication of the second edition of his account of his North American adventures, which had first appeared in 1542. This new edition, published in Valladolid in 1555, included the narrative of the Paraguayan expedition, written at his direction by Pedro Hernández.[39]

He listened eagerly to the news from Paraguay. Vergara, Irala's nephew, arrived in Spain in 1553 to solicit the governorship for his uncle, and after Sanabria's failure this was at length granted. Indeed, according to all the standards of colonial government, Irala had proved his competence. Returning from his expedition to Peru, he found Asunción in rebellion; in fact, in the course of a second revolt. Francisco de Mendoza had led the first; then a certain Diego de Abreu had risen against Mendoza and had him beheaded. (It was an edifying execution. Mendoza confessed that he had murdered his wife and chaplain in Spain, upon very groundless jealousies. "Thus, giving glory to God, he shew'd there's no avoiding divine vengeance by flying from one country to another." [40] After this public statement he married his mistress on the scaffold to legitimize his four children; and then his head went.) Abreu held the power for only a brief space. Mighty Irala, returning, made short work of him, drove him into the country,

---

[37] Arch. Ind., Justicia, 1131, 1130, 2A.
[38] Arch. Ind., Justicia, 1130.
[39] Serrano y Sanz, I, 148.
[40] Techo, in Churchill's "Voyages," VI, 14.

and had him stabbed as he lay in a hammock, afflicted with eye trouble. Irala made peace in the kingly manner, marrying Vergara and Riquel, Cabeza de Vaca's nephew, to his own daughters. And soon all was again at peace, under the strong hand.

Irala received in 1555 word of his long-sought appointment to the governorship. He lived only a short time to enjoy his eminence. He died in 1557, at the age of forty-five, of a pain in his side, to be diagnosed probably as peritonitis following on appendicitis.[41]

Felipe de Cáceres, Cabeza de Vaca's old enemy, waited long for fate's retribution; at last, in 1573, when he must have reached a considerable age, he was sent to Spain in chains for quarreling with the bishop.[42]

Cabeza de Vaca's cousin and companion on the homeward voyage, Pero Vaca, fell on evil days in his home city of Jerez. He petitioned his king for relief, and in 1565, at the age of seventy-five, was permitted to make the terrible journey to Peru, to join there a brother who had gained riches.[43]

The Paraguayan colony throve, in a certain fashion, enlarging its boundaries, supporting a constantly increasing number of immigrants. Yet few found wealth there, or that magnificence which had tempted them so far. In a petition of 1569, Vergara lists eighteen old conquerors who plead to return to their wives in Spain.[44]

On the development of Paraguay the impress of Cabeza de Vaca's character and purpose weakened year by year and ended in nullity. The colony found the existence it desired, that of the tribute-gatherer, enforcing its ease with the driven labor of the subject race. Irala made of the City of the Assumption of Our Lady a being like his very self— strong, cruel, hard, and possessed of an enormous capacity for living.

But the City of the Assumption of which Cabeza de Vaca had dreamed would have been the wonder of western history! Had he

---

[41] Gandía, "Conquista," 14, 300.
[42] "Cartas de Indias," 728. This bishop was a sorry creature. He spent his time excommunicating his flock for a hundred foolish reasons. He forbade the teaching of Christianity to the natives. He was very vain of his much-bejeweled hands. He would kiss his barrel of wine, but would give none to any man. Gandía, "Conquista," 288.
[43] Torre Revello, in Rev. del Ateneo de Jerez, V, 42.
[44] Buckingham Smith mss.

succeeded, his city of honest Spanish gentlemen, bound by mutual interest to a population of Indian freemen, would have stood, an El Dorado of the spirit, as an example for all colonies to come. His plan was not only the nobler, it was the wiser plan as well. So we wise ones can proclaim, regardless of the triumph of the enemies of wisdom.

Could he have lived another half century, he would have seen God's belated recompense to his Guaraní children. In 1586 two indomitable Jesuits made their way from Bolivia to Paraguay, and began a great missionary work, establishing, in time, a jungle Arcadia organized on the principles of communism. Daily, after their joint mass, Indians and holy fathers would march singing together to the fields. All property was held in common, all labors shared, all profits turned to the glory of God. Music and the dance were fostered, for the Jesuits are lovers of happiness. For a century and a half this idyl persisted, this bright page in the somber record of the white man's dealings with the red and the brown.

But long before this Cabeza de Vaca was dead. Penniless, old, and broken-hearted, he was assailed by illness. He appealed to his king for aid, and the king's ear heard and his mercy responded. On Sept. 15, 1556, he directed his treasurer to pay 12,000 maravedís (perhaps $500 in present meaning) to Alvar Núñez Cabeza de Vaca, that he might be cured of his illness.[45] It is reasonable to suppose that no physician could find and extirpate the cause of that illness. The stubborn body that had endured every most outrageous blow was smitten by a malady that lay too deep for medicine. When hope ceased, his heart might stop too.

Probably in this year 1556 he died, in obscurity, shame, and the conviction of failure.[46]

Perhaps, in the clairvoyant hour of extreme unction, he reviewed

[45] Arch. Ind., Indiferente general, 425, lib. 9, fol. 246. This notation was discovered by Don José Torre Revello, who has kindly permitted me to publish it. There are old traditions that Cabeza de Vaca was awarded an annual pension of 2,000 ducats, was appointed Chief Overseer of the Customs of Seville, and died with much honor and quietude of his person. (Ruy Díaz de Guzmán, in Angelis, I, 60.) It has also been alleged that he entered religion and died as prior of one of the Seville convents. ("Cartas de Indias," 813.) There is no truth in either of these stories.

[46] The records henceforth are mute. He was certainly dead by 1565, for in that year Felipe de Cáceres was in Spain, and the heirs of Cabeza de Vaca brought action against him. ("Cartas de Indias," 729.)

the progress of his soul, from youthful pride to this its last abasement. Perhaps then, as the priest touched with holy oil his eyes, ears, nostrils, lips, and hands, his bruised spirit entered, through the gate of utter humility, into the peace of God.

BIBLIOGRAPHY

This bibliography contains only those works which have been of direct and specific service. I give the editions (not in every case the best) which have been available to me.

Manuscripts

Archives of the Indies, Seville, Justicia, legajos 1130, 1131, 1132; Indiferente general, 425.
Private archives of the Marqués de Campo Real, Jerez de la Frontera.
Buckingham Smith mss., in New York Historical Society.

Books and Periodicals

Juan de Abreu de Galindo, "History of the Canary Islands." London, 1764.
Pedro de Angelis, "Colección de obras y documentos del Río de la Plata." Buenos Aires, 1910.
Enrique Araña, "Ulrich Schmidel." In Boletín del Instituto de Investigaciones Históricas, XII, 193. Buenos Aires, 1931.
Antonio Ardoíno, "Examen apologético de la historia y narración de Cabeza de Vaca." (In González Barcía, "Historiadores primitivos de las Indias." Madrid, 1736.)
Felix de Azara, "Voyages dans l'Amérique méridionale." Paris, 1809.
Antonio Ballesteros y Beretta, "Historia de España." Barcelona, 1927.
Hubert Howe Bancroft, "History of Mexico." San Francisco, 1886.
"The North Mexican States." San Francisco, 1884.
Adolph F. Bandelier, "Contributions to the History of the Southwestern Portion of the United States." (Archæological Institute of America, V.) Boston, 1890.
"The Gilded Man." New York, 1893.
"Investigations among the Indians of the Southwestern United States." (Arch. Inst. of Amer. IV.) Boston, 1892.
Martín del Barco Centenera, "La Argentina," in Angelis, "Col. de Documentos," II.
Roger Barlow, "A Brief Summe of Geographie," (ed. E. G. R. Taylor). London (Hakluyt Society), 1932.

Rafael Barris Muñoz, "En torno a Alvar Núñez Cabeza de Vaca," in Boletín del Real Centro de Estudios Históricos de Andalucía, I, 42.

John R. Bartlett, "Personal Narrative of Explorations and Incidents in Texas, etc." New York, 1856.

William Bartram, "Travels through N. and S. Carolina, Georgia, etc." Philadelphia, 1791.

James N. Baskett, "A Study of the Route of Cabeza de Vaca." In Texas State Historical Quarterly, X.

Hermann Baumgarten, "Geschichte Karls V." Stuttgart, 1892.

Constantino Bayle, "El Dorado Fantasma." Madrid, 1931.

Andrés Bellogin García, "Vida y hazañas de Alvar Núñez Cabeza de Vaca." Madrid, 1928.

A. Bernáldez (Cura de los Palacios), "Historia de los Reyes Católicos." Seville, 1869.

R. Blanco-Fombona, "El Conquistador español del siglo XVI." Madrid, 1922.

Herbert E. Bolton, "Spanish Exploration in the Southwest." New York, 1916.

Daniel G. Brinton, "Notes on the Floridan Peninsula." Philadelphia, 1859.

Richard F. Burton, "Letters from the Battlefields of Paraguay." London, 1870.

William Bradford, "Correspondence of the Emperor Charles V." London, 1850.

Alvar Núñez Cabeza de Vaca, "Relación de los naufragios y Comentarios," ed. M. Serrano y Sanz. (Two volumes; the second consists of valuable supplementary material from the Archives of the Indies. The best edition.) Madrid, 1906.

"The Journey," trans. Fanny Bandelier; ed. Adolph F. Bandelier. New York, 1905.

"The Relation" (same original as preceding entry); trans. and ed. by [Thomas] Buckingham Smith. New York, 1851; 2d. ed. 1871.

"The Narrative" (trans. Buckingham Smith; ed. Frederick W. Hodge). In "Spanish Explorers in the Southern United States." New York, 1907.

"The Commentaries." In Luis L. Domínguez, "The Conquest of the River Plate." London (Hakluyt Soc.), 1891.

"Cartas de Indias," published by the Ministerio de Fomento. Madrid, 1877.

Bartolomé de las Casas, "Apologética Historia de las Indias." Madrid, 1909.

"Historia de las Indias." Madrid, 1874-5.

"Relation des voyages et des découvertes." Amsterdam, 1698.

Pedro Castañeda de Nagera, "The Expedition of Coronado" (ed. Frederick W. Hodge) in "Spanish Explorers in the Southern United States." New York, 1907.

Federico de Castro y Bravo, "Las Naos españoles en la carrera de las Indias." Madrid, 1927.

Pierre F.-X. de Charlevoix, "Histoire du Paraguay." Paris, 1757.

"Journal d'un voyage dans l'Amérique septentrionale." Paris, 1744.

A. and J. Churchill, "Collection of Voyages and Travels." London, 1746.

"Colección de Documentos inéditos relativos a America." (Ed., Joaquín F. Pacheco and others.) Madrid, 1864.

Bethel Coopwood, "The Route of Cabeza de Vaca." In Texas State Hist. Quar., III and IV.

Harbert Davenport, "The Expedition of Pánfilo de Narváez." In Southwestern Historical Quarterly, XXVII–XXVIII. (Oct. 1923–Oct. 1924).

Harbert Davenport and Joseph K. Wells, "The First Europeans in Texas." In Southwestern Historical Quarterly, XXII (Oct. 1918; Jan. 1919).

Ruy Díaz de Guzmán, "La Argentina." In Angelis, "Colección de Documentos," I.

Bernal Díaz del Castillo, "The True History of the Conquest of New Spain" (Trans. A. P. Maudslay). London (Hakluyt Soc.), 1908–16.

Luis L. Domínguez, "The Conquest of the River Plate." London (Hakluyt Soc.), 1891.

Baltasar Dorantes de Carranza, "Sumaria Relación de la Nueva España." Mexico, 1902.

Alonso de Espinosa, "The Guanches of Tenerife." London (Hakluyt Soc.), 1907.

A. María Fabié, ed., "Viajes por España." Madrid, 1879.

A. Featherman, "Chiapo- and Guarano-Maranonians." Boston, 1890.

Martín Ferrador, *pseud.*: see José Rajel.

John Fiske, "The Discovery of America." Boston, 1892.

Richard Ford, "The Spaniards and their Country." New York, 1850.

Georg Friederici, "Der Charakter der Entdeckung und Eroberung Amerikas durch die Europäer." Stuttgart, 1925.

Gregorio Funes, "Ensayo de la historia civil del Paraguay." Buenos Aires, 1816.

Enrique de Gandía, "Historia crítica de los mitos de la conquista americana." Madrid, 1929.

"Historia del Gran Chaco." Madrid, 1929.

"Historia de la conquista del Río de la Plata." Buenos Aires, 1932.

"Indios y conquistadores." Buenos Aires, 1932.

"Los Primeros Italianos en el Río de la Plata." Buenos Aires, 1932.

Joaquín García Icazbalceta, "Colección de documentos." Mexico, 1866.

Garcilaso de la Vega, "La Florida." Madrid, 1723.

Albert S. Gatschet, "The Karankawa Indians" (Archaeological Papers of the Peabody Museum, Vol. I, no. 2). Cambridge, Mass., 1891.

"The Gentleman of Elvas": Narrative of the Expedition of Hernando de Soto (ed. Theodore H. Lewis) in "Spanish Explorers in the Southern United States." New York, 1907.

W. Gleeson, "History of the Catholic Church in California." San Francisco, 1872.

A. González Barcía, "Ensayo cronológico." Madrid, 1723.

R. B. Cunninghame Graham, "The Conquest of the River Plate." New York, 1924.

"Horses of the Conquest." London, 1930.

"A Vanished Arcadia." New York, 1901.

José Guevara, "Historia de la Conquista del Paraguay." Buenos Aires, 1882.

Konrad Häbler, "Die wirtschaftliche Blüte Spaniens im 16. Jahrhundert und ihr Verfall." Berlin, 1888.

Richard Hakluyt, "The Principal Navigations, Voyages, Trafiques & Discoveries." Glasgow, 1904.

Antonio de Herrera y Tordesillas, "Historia de las Indias occidentales." Madrid, 1730.

Frederick W. Hodge, "Handbook of American Indians." Washington, 1910.

Ed., "Spanish Explorers in the Southern United States." New York, 1907.

"Indice general de los papeles del Consejo de Indias." Madrid, 1923.

Alonso de León, "Historia de Nuevo León." Mexico, 1909.

Le Page du Pratz, "Histoire de la Louisiane." Paris, 1758.

Woodbury Lowery, "The Spanish Settlements in North America." New York, 1911.

Bates H. McFarland: see Brownie Ponton.

William C. MacLeod, "The American Indian Frontier." New York, 1928.

P. Margry, "Mémoires et documents pour servir à l'histoire des origines françaises des pays d'outremer." Paris, 1879.

Gerónimo de Mendieta, "Historia eclesiástica indiana." Mexico, 1870.

Roger B. Merriman, "The Spanish Empire." New York, 1918.

Leo E. Miller, "In the Wilds of South America." New York, 1918.

Ministerio de Fomento, "Cartas de Indias." Madrid, 1877.

Matias de la Mota Padilla, "Historia de la conquista de Nueva Galicia." Mexico, 1870.

Marion G. Mulhall, "From Europe to Paraguay and Matto Grosso." London, 1877.

L. Ningler, ed. "Voyages en Virginie et en Floride." Paris, 1927.

Charles L. Norton, "A Handbook of Florida." New York, 1890.

Alvar Núñez Cabeza de Vaca. See Cabeza de Vaca.

Diego Ortiz de Zuñiga, "Anales eclesiásticos y seculares de la ciudad de Sevilla." Madrid, 1677.

G. Fernández de Oviedo y Valdés, "Historia general y natural de las Indias." Madrid, 1852.

"The Expedition of Pánfilo de Narváez." Translation, ed. by Harbert Davenport. Southwestern Hist. Quar., XXVII–XXVIII. Oct. 1923–Oct. 1924.

Thomas J. Page, "La Plata, the Argentine Confederation, and Paraguay." New York, 1859.

Diego Ignacio Parada y Barreto, "Hombres ilustres de Jerez." Jerez de la Frontera, 1875.

Ludwig Pfandl, "Spanische Kultur und Sitte des 16. und 17. Jahrhunderts." Kempten, 1924.

A. H. Phinney, "Narváez and De Soto: Their Landing Places." (Florida Hist. Quar., Jan. 1925.)

Caspar Plautus, "Nova Typis Transacta Navigatio." (No place of publication) 1621.

Brownie Ponton and Bates H. McFarland, "Alvar Núñez Cabeza de Vaca," in Tex. State Hist. Quar., I.

William H. Prescott, "Ferdinand and Isabella." Philadelphia, 1872.

H. del Pulgar, "Crónica de Don Fernando y Doña Isabel." (Bibl. de Autores Españoles, LXX.) Madrid, 1878.

Samuel Purchas, "Hakluytus posthumus, or Purchas his pilgrimes." Glasgow, 1905–07.

Carlyle G. Raht, "The Romance of Davis Mountains and Big Bend Country." El Paso, 1919.

José Rajel (Martín Ferrador, *pseud.*), "El primer Jerezano." In Revista del Ateneo de Jerez de la Frontera, IV, 35 (June, 1927).

J. P. and W. P. Robertson, "Letters on Paraguay." London, 1838–9.

F. Rodríguez Marín, ed. "Rinconete y Cortadillo." Seville, 1905.

Bernard Romans, "History of East and West Florida." New York, 1775.

Ulrich Schmidel (Schmidt), "Voyage to the Rivers La Plata and Paraguay." In Domínguez, "The Conquest of the River Plate." London (Hakluyt Soc.), 1891.

M. Serrano y Sanz, ed. Cabeza de Vaca, "Relación de los Naufragios y Comentarios." Madrid, 1906.

[Thomas] Buckingham Smith, "Narratives of Hernando de Soto." New York, 1866.

Ed. "The Relation of Cabeça de Vaca." New York, 1851, 1871.

Hans Staden (Stade), "The Captivity of Hans Stade," ed. Richard F. Burton. London (Hakluyt Soc.), 1874.

"Hans Staden," ed. Malcolm Letts. New York, 1929.

John R. Swanton, "Early History of the Creek Indians and their Neighbors." Washington, 1922.

"Indian Tribes of the Lower Mississippi Valley." Washington, 1911.

Nicholas del Techo, "The History of Paraguay." In Churchill, "Collection of Voyages," VI. London, 1746.

Antonio Tello, "Historia de Nueva Galicia." In Joaquín García Icazbalceta, Colección de Documentos," II, 343.

José Torre Revello, "A propósito del homenaje a Cabeza de Vaca." In Revista del Ateneo de Jerez de la Frontera, IV, 36, 37, 39. (July, Aug., Oct. 1927.)

"Adición a la relación descriptiva de los mapas, planos, etc. del virreinato de Buenos Aires." Buenos Aires, 1927.

"Notas sobre el gobierno de Cabeza de Vaca en el Río de la Plata." In Boletín del Real Centro de Estudios Históricos de Andalucía, I, 14.

"Papeles viejos del Archivo de Indias." In Revista del Ateneo de Jerez de la Frontera, VIII, 147 (1931, 2d semester).

Joseph K. Wells: see Harbert Davenport.

George P. Winship, "The Coronado Expedition." (Fourteenth Report of Bureau of Ethnology.) Washington, 1896.

Justin Winsor, "Narrative and Critical History of America." Boston, 1886.

Yáñez and Allier, "Jerez en lo pasado y en lo presente." Jerez, 1892.

INDEX

8308 21